Design in
Liberal Learning

Maxwell H. Goldberg

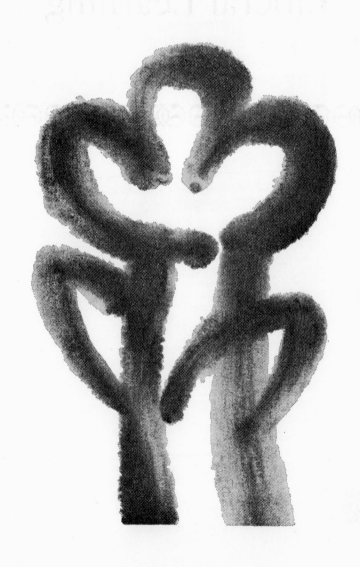

DESIGN IN LIBERAL LEARNING

Jossey-Bass Inc., Publishers
San Francisco • Washington • London • 1971

DESIGN IN LIBERAL LEARNING
Maxwell H. Goldberg

Library of Congress Catalog Card Number 71-110645

International Standard Book Number ISBN 0-87589-102-0

Manufactured in the United States of America
    Composed and printed by York Composition Company, Inc.
    Bound by Chas. H. Bohn & Co., Inc.

JACKET DESIGN BY WILLI BAUM, SAN FRANCISCO

FIRST EDITION

Code 7122

The Jossey-Bass
Series in Higher Education

General Editors

JOSEPH AXELROD
*San Francisco State College
and University of California, Berkeley*

MERVIN B. FREEDMAN
*San Francisco State College
and Wright Institute, Berkeley*

Preface

Design in Liberal Learning is addressed primarily to those in
higher education who are concerned about the future of liberal
learning in the face of the speedup of change and the vehement
demands, on all sides, for activistic or other pragmatic approaches.
It is addressed to the president, dean, professor, and graduate student and to the lay leader who makes policy decisions about higher
education. It is addressed to those who profess the liberal studies and
to those in other sectors of higher education by way of encouragement and of promptings to internal reform and renewal. Both
parties need one another for strengthened liberal learning, and all
stand to benefit. Today, we are all in the same boat, threatened by
the storms blown up by the tragic crisis of cultural survival and
hence by the tragic crisis in liberal learning.

Rejecting the customary segmentation which sets continuing
education apart from the other sectors of education, I devote particular attention to the continuing phases of liberal learning to dramatize the network which should bind together the several phases. The
other sectors once may have regarded continuing liberal education
with condescension as an optional matter. It is now a necessity—for
the good of each and for the good of the whole.

Design in Liberal Learning has a twofold timeliness. It puts
into focus my own harvest of experiences and achievements gleaned
from nearly fifty years in higher education. There is now a revived
concern for the institution of higher education as a teaching-learn-

ix

ing community; and this volume, by long intent, correspondingly focuses upon processes for making it so. There is also a timeliness in the present volume from another perspective. For a number of reasons, continuing liberal learning has been moving from the peripheries toward the center of the stage in higher education. This book not only takes cognizance of this trend, but, especially in Chapter Six, attempts to help solve the problems that mark continuing education in its efforts to move from the sideshow toward the main tent.

Design in Liberal Learning rejects both millennial optimism and Cassandra defeatism. It also rejects both the traditionalist dictum that whatever is is right and the modernist assumption that novelty necessarily marks improvement. Positively, it presents the principle that creative accommodation (not to be confused with passive adjustment) between the enduring and change is both relevant and urgent and that in such creative accommodation—often through strengthened dynamic tensions between opposites—liberal learning may make its most distinctive contributions to education, culture, and the society it should seek critically and constructively to serve.

Furthermore, *Design in Liberal Learning* is positive in its reiterated and varied demonstrations of comprehensive, purposive alternatives to the segmented and specialized proliferations that characterize current higher education, the world of work and social enterprise, and liberal learning itself. It is positive, too, in its propensity toward holism. It does not deny the need for analytical, specialized, and segmented efforts. Rather, it insists, with Alfred North Whitehead, that the great task of liberal learning—in its self-reform and revitalization, in its emphasis on its students, and in its impact on society—is that of creative mediation between the necessary analytic and synthesizing efforts. Indeed, *Design in Liberal Learning* affirms that, in part, concepts and inventions of specialized enterprise, such as the computer and computer-related systems, now provide powerful means for making dominant the integrative, comprehensive way in the whole range of human endeavor, including higher education and liberal learning.

Design in Liberal Learning further affirms that if liberal learning is to make its due contribution to higher education, the individual, and society, it must reject those puristic inversions which have characterized its constituent disciplines—that is, involvements toward cognitive and esthetic purism devoid of explicit ethicosocial concern and commitment; and it must renew explicit ethical involvements. Yet it must do so in a new context—as in the new futuristics courses—through new solutions to current and impending problems, meeting such foremost problems as those created in great measure by the rapid rate of change and the drastic telescoping of the future into the present. It must do so through fresh explorations of the formative nature of man, expressed notably and momentously in telic (end-purpose) models of the admirable man, the admirable life, and the admirable society. These models will replace the robot models of the technocrats, the instant pseudomodels of the cynical apocalyptics, the pathetically idyllic fantasy models of the sentimental apocalyptics, the subjective escapist models of the mystics among the apocalyptics. In place of all of these, what is here urged is a tragic realism.

In its fresh neoethical concern, however, liberal learning must not yield to the power-hungry egoists who parade as altruists, humanitarians, and social idealists or to the hate-filled destroyers who self-righteously appoint themselves ministers of justice and then make a mockery of the very freedom, justice, and love they so adamantly profess. Even when so perversely and destructively defined, liberal learning must accept the implicit moral challenge. It must responsibly and magnanimously renew its own ethical involvement.

Finally, in an epoch characterized, on the one hand, by narrow, technistic, and bureaucratic rationalization and, on the other hand, by various powerful irrationalisms, *Design in Liberal Learning* affirms ethical, imaginative reason, despite all its limitations and with all its psychosomatic adjuncts (perception, feeling, intuition), as the great and continuing main means of higher education. This affirmation is set forth here in the espousal of the architectonic mode in liberal learning.

The discussions in *Design in Liberal Learning* have an internal unity and coherence. The constraints of the audience and the occasion have kept the discussions from extremes of speculation and of mere busy work. I attempt here to test the limits of tension and accommodation between thought and action. My general perspective is interdisciplinary—even multidisciplinary—as well as friendly to the mutual involvement of the academic world and the world of affairs and action. My prime concern is for the humanistic and other liberal studies. Yet, I am also aware of the crucial relationships between these studies and those of the other sectors of higher education (especially the scientific, technological, and professional)— both in themselves and in their responsibilities to the individual and society. I am likewise aware of the impacts on and the implications for liberal learning of the demands for relevance—demands made under the impetus of the phenomenal speedup of technological, industrial, social, and cultural change and under the surge of social and political activism. Hence, chief among the limits of accommodation tested here are those between the past and the present-future.

The laboratories for the inquiries here have been varied: personal interviews, classrooms, conferences, research, to name a few. They have been the workshops for developing new programs in liberal studies and in the relations between students and faculty; between both of these and administration; between the professional humanist and the scientist-technologist; between the academic "disciplines" and "education"; between the theoreticians and the practitioners in the applied fields; between the academic fields and management, labor, government, defense, and journalism and other communications media, as well as the traditional professions (religion, medicine, and law). In this wide range of ventures distinctiveness may be found in *Design in Liberal Learning* as, also, in its attempted eclecticism as to methods.

The discussions here are not linear. They move in mutually intersecting circles toward the objective—to clinch the theme and illuminate the whole. Perhaps the image of the widening upward spiral is better. Concepts, images, motifs recur, yet at varying elevations and with varying comprehensiveness. The intention is not damnable iteration but cumulative and progressive reiteration. Style and method vary with the job at hand. Now their inspiration is Pascal's *esprit de finesse,* with its emphasis on taking in a situation as a whole and quickly yet tactfully applying reason. Again it is his *esprit de géometrie,* with its deliberate, analytical ratiocination toward full conceptualization. At times it is F. C. S. Northrop's theoretic component, seeking what Henry Margenau calls constructs. At other times it is Northrop's esthetic component, seeking concepts by intuition. At times analytic reason asserts itself; again the method is apprehension all at once. When the way leads through the abstruse, the method corresponds—rigorous, rationalistic. When the way leads through sensation and sensibility, the method is intuitive and emotively responsive. The universal joint in all of these methods is, in the words of José Ortega y Gasset, "perhaps one of man's most fruitful potentialities"—metaphor.[1] In short, the method reflects the essential spirit of the work: a spirit which seeks to exploit the creative tensions of paradox and to employ, in the interests of integration, several means that reciprocally augment one another in the mind functioning as a dynamic whole. This variety and versatility of method contributes to the master process in *Design in Liberal Learning*—that is, creative mediation between or among conflicting components. The hope is to achieve, thereby, reformation and re-creation.

Without belittling the past or slighting the present, I have made the orientation decidedly futurist. As Bertrand de Jouvenel[2] points out, it is a futurism that is nondeterministic yet normative and is optimistic within the constraints of the tragic sense and of reason. It stresses the deliberative and heuristic, as distinguished from the speculative or the forensic; and it touches particulars as well as global parameters.

The word *design* in the title has a double meaning. On the one hand, it suggests pattern-making. On the other hand, it suggests a purposive striving to approximate a model which acts both as criterion and as magnetic pull. As for *liberal learning*, after much personal debate I adopted this phrase in preference to other possibilities. For a season, *liberal learning* was a vogue term at conferences on higher education and in the professional literature, and this circumstance alone might set one against it; *liberal studies*, on this score, might be preferred. In the early fifties, liberal studies

---

[1] *The Dehumanization of Art*, trans. Heline Weyl (Princeton, N.J.: Princeton University Press, 1948), p. 33.
[2] *The Art of Conjecture*, trans. Nikita Lary (New York: Basic Books, 1967); and "Personal Freedom and Social Responsibility," in *Values in Conflict* (Toronto: University of Toronto Press, 1963), pp. 21–27.

was introduced to signal a new education for adults. It was favored, too, by those wishing to include the hard sciences, as well as the humanities and the behavioral-social sciences (collectively now called the human sciences), among the disciplines serving liberal education. But the choice here has been *liberal learning* because, among other things, it suggests the body of knowledge gained in the past by the liberal arts and sciences and at least potentially available for new learning today. It also suggests the ever-renewed or ever-renewable process of mastering this vast body of knowledge by passing to succeeding generations what is presently known and by learning what, on the growing fronts of creativity in the liberal studies, is now being born. *Liberal learning* enables treating education as a continuum, and it frees our thinking from the tight grid forced upon us when we accept conventional categorizations, such as liberal arts college, liberal arts curriculum, liberal arts courses. It also frees us from the limitations imposed when the liberal arts are viewed solely in their teaching-learning aspects or solely in their research-scholarship aspects.

Another reason for the choice of *liberal learning* is to stress, in the title, a dominant notion throughout the book—the notion of process. This idea is twofold: the learning process pursued within the academic structure itself and the application of the results of this process to the conduct of life. The second sense is illustrated in the declaration of one of William Shakespeare's characters: "Spirits are not finely touched but to fine issues." It is also represented in John Milton's hauteur as he dismisses a "fugitive and cloistered virtue" and in his praise of that virtue which has "run in the race where the garland is to be won not without dust and heat." Aristotle's observation that the end of life is action, not contemplation, also endorses this latter notion of process.

In American educational thinking, the idea of liberal education as process is not, in itself, particularly noteworthy. It is, indeed, an expression of a dominant emphasis both within and outside the influential Deweyan and Whiteheadian traditions. The process with which we are concerned places strong stress on esthetic and ethical growth and on self-realization in contrast to growth in the ratiocinative virtues. Not that the latter are to be slighted; it is, rather, a matter of emphasis, proportion, and inclusiveness. Ideally, of course, liberal learning should include the several modes of growth in relationship to one another, partly in collaboration and partly, as in our antagonistic muscle systems, in contestation, moving toward integrated and harmonious being and doing.

An overriding question has prompted the varied lines of inquiry pursued in this study: Without sacrificing its essential integrity, how may liberal learning creatively respond to the demands made upon the individual by drastic societal and cultural change? The answer is through the architectonic mode for design in liberal learning. I hope that *Design in Liberal Learning* will show how liberal learning may contribute substantially to successful passage through the shock fronts and intensities of the drastic social and cultural perturbations predicted for the next two decades. I also hope that this book will help those in the continuing sector of liberal learning, as well as those in other sectors, to gain an enhanced sense of profession.

A word of explanation may be in order for my use of new terms taken, often, from different professional areas: *architectonic, apocalyptic, technocratic, holistic, telic, ratiocinative,* and so on. My reasons are twofold: First, I needed distinctive terms for the newly emerged features in our milieu. As has been true all along, those professional and other special areas that are most immediately involved are likely to be the creators or the revivers of the needed terms. Second, in an effort to make ideas of long standing freshly vital and viable, I have sought new terms or old terms in new contexts. Both promptings to these nonconventional or nonstandard usages result from the attempt to make good Thomas Carlyle's dictum that each generation should rewrite history in its own idiom.

Similar explanation may be appropriate for my readiness to draw upon the popular press, the mass circulation periodicals, radio and television, bulletin boards, as well as upon standard works and professional or other publications of limited circulation. In the face of such loud and insistent demands for relevance, resort to the press and media sources dramatizes the often close relationships between so-called abstract academic concepts or principles and concrete activities. Another reason for using the media and the popular press is that often, though at times in simplified (sometimes even distorted) form, these vehicles are likely to communicate to the layman (and each of us nowadays is a layman except in the narrow area of his professional expertise) information about developments in science and technology well before it becomes available in definitive reports and monographs. In *Design in Liberal Learning* I have gone where the action is or is likely to be. I have adopted the traditional humanist attitude: to me nothing pertaining to the human being (or to humanity) is alien. I have likewise recognized the usefulness of wit and humor as instruments of serious inquiry. Also, I have followed David Riesman's prescription for humanistic study: to connect—especially to see interrelationships where such connections are not ordinarily perceived.

To list all to whom I am indebted for the present book would be a happy but hopeless task. I am therefore foregoing the pleasure to be derived from such a listing. Yet some names must be noted. They are Cyril F. Hager, associate dean for continuing education and director of the Center for Continuing Liberal Education, College of the Liberal Arts, The Pennsylvania State University, who has encouraged my studies of liberal learning and technological change; and Joseph Axelrod, of San Francisco State College, who has given crucial editorial counsel.

I dedicate this book to Ethel.

University Park, Pennsylvania   MAXWELL H. GOLDBERG
September 1971

Contents

FREEDOM AND FORM

Design in
Liberal Learning

ONE

Relevance and Revolution

For years an ardent advocate of relevance in liberal learning, I now seriously question the use of this term which has moved to the center of educational as well as other types of discussions. Relevance often hides a thirst for publicity and prestige and frequently represents a sign of servitude to the tyranny of fashion (for example, to avoid the label of square or to achieve the status of mod). Often the cry of relevance[1] is a clamor for the exciting, and the exciting can actually thwart liberal learning. Not that such learning must be dull or that at its climactic phases there should be no excitement, but to use unremitting, strong excitation[2] as a stimulus and a standard for relevance in liberal learning is treacherous. First, it is psychologically unsound. If one tries to be exciting from the outset, he has to keep stepping up the charge of excitation, or the process will sag and he will lose his participants to boredom. José Ortega y Gasset has observed that it is easy to have enthusiasm without faith. Similarly it is easy to have excitement without education. Liberal learn-

---

[1] A whole treatise might be written on the educational, cultural, and sociopolitical implications of the shift from "quest for relevance" [see W. H. Morris (Ed.), *Effective College Teaching: The Quest for Relevance* (Washington, D.C.: American Association for Higher Education, 1970)] to the current "demands for relevance."

[2] See G. B. Leonard, *Education and Ecstasy* (New York: Delacorte, 1968).

1

ing means not just to feel but to think; and to think—especially to
think perceptively and feelingly—is hard.

Liberal learning may also be affected when the uproar about
relevance becomes a naive demand for quick application to the personal or social issues which appear at the moment to be so urgent.
These urgencies are often as varied as the backgrounds, personalities,
interests, and fluctuating moods and desires of the students, the
faculty, the administration, the alumni, or various interest groups.
Moreover, these urgencies are frequently of a fleeting nature. We are
so busy taking care of moment-to-moment urgencies that we badly
neglect the enduringly important. Suppose we were to yield to the
cry of immediate social relevance and set up a course on the plight of
the Biafrans today. By next year, even though the plight may by no
means be alleviated, this concern may be superseded by a dozen
more urgent problems. Thus, such cries of relevance often turn out
to be delusive goals for the college administrators who constantly
attempt to respond to them.

The cry of relevance is often used to embarrass or strike out
at something disliked. For example, it may serve as a means to con-
found the imaginative conservative—however creative—who seeks
to make the past freshly operable. It may further be used as a
means to make tradition a scapegoat of the contemporary antago-
nisms against history (history, it is said, is in mourning); and such
contempt for the past, along with fanaticism of the future, deprives
young people today of the vital education afforded by tradition. On
the other hand, the cry of relevance may be a transfer device
through which the one who complains projects a sense of boredom,
frustration, or guilt about his own intellectual laziness, incapacity,
or atrophy.

With Hamlet, I would have grounds more relative. I cannot
respond to demands that the liberal studies be justified only in terms
of immediate, practical uses, whether for the individual or for
society. Yet I do fully accept the notion that we have a responsibility
to account for the contributions of the liberal studies to the individual and to society—however indirect, implicit, or long-range. We
have a duty to specify how they contribute to the great but ordinary
end—in spite of the Clark Kerrs and the James Perkinses—the still
relevant Newmanian end—of lifting the cultural level of society.

Along with other academic disciplines, the liberal studies should be held accountable, and they must be prepared to render an accounting. Such an accounting may not be in numerical terms or in measurable contributions; rather, it may be in terms of higher usefulness. Let us waive that issue to distinguish among uses and then determine what uses society should expect from the liberal studies and what these studies should, in turn, provide.

In his article "A New Breed of Faculty," Malcolm G. Scully provides specifics whereby one may vividly observe abuse or threatened abuse of the criterion of relevance in higher education and liberal learning. This article reports on a background paper by Martin Trow, prepared for the 1970 annual meeting of the American Council on Education. According to this account, Trow recommends that American higher education adjust to the drives of the new breed. He suggests a shift away from books toward action, a shift away from objectivity toward the "social confirmation of one's moral rightness," a creation of new sets of activities and relationships that are more "rewarding" than ordinary routine and more evocative of "spontaneous energies and motivations," and a formation of small, comprehensive "consent units," each of which is to control its own admission policies, enjoy the highest degree of autonomy, define its own work, and select its own members. Such consent units represent a collectivistic anarchism, self-contradictory though the term may seem.

If Trow not only reported these tendencies, trends, or likelihoods but also recommended that higher education go along with them, then he would be illustrating, from the point of view of liberal learning, an unfortunate type of yielding to what amounts to disintegrative demands for relevance. He would be providing a sophisticated rhetoric for a betrayal of institutional and personal trust and a responsibility for dissolution of the institution of higher education.[3]

[3] M. G. Scully, "A New Breed of Faculty Is Seen Producing 'Marked Discontinuities' on Campus," *The Chronicle of Higher Education*, 1970, 5 (3), 1. A perusal of "Age, Status, and Academic Values: A Comparison of Graduate Students and Faculty," by M. Trow and T. Herschi, indicates that the projections attributed to Trow in the Scully article are not deterministic but are rather tendencies or trends regarded as strong likelihoods (n.b. especially p. 18).

In terms of relevance, liberal learning would be extremely useful in trying to help the student gain the historic perspective (that is, a fresh perspective on the past), the philosophic context, the literary sensibility, the artist's perceptiveness and discipline of form, and the techniques of disciplined and responsible intellectual inquiry. Thus, the student could contain the chaos of the exploding new, shape it to his own constructive purposes, and use it for the enduring good of society. The effort to help the student effect a creative shift from the deeply ingrained traditional work ethic to the new leisure ethic serves as an example of relevance in this context. What binds the old and the new and gives the new its effective form is the perennial value of individual wholeness and human dignity, the dignity of man[4]—a phrase which nowadays, as Lord Kenneth Clark has observed, "dies on our lips."

Liberal learning may further attempt to free the student from the provincialism of time and help him see that limiting his use of reason to contemporary bureaucratic and technistic exploitations of the individual is quite arbitrary. With such help he would realize that there have long been other, more liberal uses of reason—those not only conducive to but necessary for individual self-expression, self-realization, and self-fulfillment, as well as for social well-being, reform, and advancement. In turn the student would appreciate the illuminative power of Socratic reason and the compassion of the Isaiahan "Come, let us reason together." Then, if we are to use the term *relevance* in connection with liberal learning, it is this sort of relevance, obtained through the dynamics of paradox[5] and through creative mediation, accommodation, and integration of the old and the new.

---

[4] See R. N. Iyer, "The Social Structure of the Future," *Looking Forward: The Abundant Society* (Santa Barbara, Calif.: Center for the Study of Democratic Institutions, 1966), pp. 16, 32. See also D. N. Michael, *The Unprepared Society: Planning for a Precarious Future* (New York: Basic Books, 1968). (Hereafter referred to as Michael, *Unprepared Society*.)

[5] See H. A. Slaate, *The Pertinence of the Paradox: A Study of the Dialectics of Reason-in-Existence* (New York: Humanities Press, 1968); S. Hook, *The Paradoxes of Freedom* (Berkeley and Los Angeles: University of California Press, 1964); W. V. Quine, *The Ways of Paradox* (New York: Random House, 1966); S. A. Coblentz, *The Paradox of Man's Greatness* (Washington, D.C.: Public Affairs Press, 1966); and H. S. Broudy, *Paradox and Promise: Essays on American Life and Education* (Englewood Cliffs, N.J.: Prentice-Hall, 1961).

This context of the term points to the positive phase of educative efforts toward liberal learning. Negatively, such relevance would be expressed in what Kingman Brewster has so cogently urged and personally exemplified:[6] unflinching and courageous criticism alike of the established wisdom and our faddist novelties—in terms of long-lasting principles and through intellectual techniques and means, yet refined by modern expertise and tempered by time.

Let relevance be urged in terms of responsibility and accountability; in terms of self-renewal, fresh vividness, and viability; and by competent destructive criticism, dynamic paradox, and devoted synthesis. Then I am for it; and I am ready to use the word, as Howard Lee Nostrand used it in his appreciation of José Ortega y Gasset for his "fiery personality, and his persistent relevance to the burning questions of our own lives!"

"Liberal Learning and the Social Revolution" was the theme of the 1969 annual meeting of the Association of American Colleges. One session dealt with the question, What is the impact of the social revolution on humanistic studies? Instead of responding directly to this question, Marvin Levich dismissed the term *social revolution* as an alarmist hyperbole and set up a different question: What should be the impact of the ideology of relevance on humanistic studies? By the phrase *ideology of relevance* he meant that the humanities should provide justification for themselves in the face of the collectivistic-anarchistic demands that the humanities be radically politicized.

In justifying his rejection of *revolution,* Levich pointed out that people tend to view their time as in far deeper crisis of change than it actually is, whether viewed long range or from the vantage point of the present. By way of support, he cited I. A. Richards' observations of the mid-forties to the effect that those years were a time of drastic upheaval and breakdown. Then he remarked that, actually, in contrast to our own day the mid-forties constituted an era "which we may now remember as one of near dull tranquility." In this characterization, Levich prompts me, without imputing this fault to him, to point out the historic inaccuracy of this impression. Richards' utterances, for many of us at the time, accurately expressed an experience that was all too real: the anxiety caused by the powerful impact of the radical social, technological, and other changes that were already affecting us in the forties. These changes were profoundly disturbing in themselves; they were barometric indications of far greater storms ahead.

Many of us were then anxiously aware of what David Morton described as those ambiguous omens that thronged the angry skies. In 1914, Lord Acton declared: "The lights are going out all over Europe"; in 1939, W. H. Auden saw some points of light flashing where the just communicated with one another. Yet these lights were ironic: in all, how many of the just were there? And how many of the just were exchanging their messages or could exchange them? About the same time, in his "Notations for the Record," Morton was recording that even the few positive lights— those of pity and love and those of learning won with difficulty and precariously maintained—were guttering in an evil wind, and he saw darkness again spreading everywhere, blotting out the works of civilization and making stricken things of men.[7] Hence, even allowing for relative meaning in Levich's "near dull tranquility," I must observe now that the period of the forties was as critically disturbed as its spokesmen of gloom then claimed. If today we do gain the impression that it was a period of "near dull tranquility," we—not they—are the uncritical impressionists, we are the time provincials. The joke is on us, and it is a grim joke at that. It is our blind spot if we fail to see the mid-forties and the early seventies as part of the same tragic circumstances, with the whole of humanity and individual man as the same protagonist.

For us devoted to the life of the mind and the tradition of liberal and urbane intellectuality, the mid-forties were anything but tranquil. We were aware of forces already at work, which made that time in fact, not just in feeling, a period of major—if not mortal— crisis. We were aware that these forces were to contribute heavily to our present sense of crisis, so radical as to be called, with considerable precision, revolutionary. Already, by the mid-forties, we faced the onslaughts of the antagonist—mindless activism—of both the extreme Left and the extreme Right. In these onslaughts, we

[7] D. Morton, *Angle of Earth and Sky* (New York: Macmillan, 1951), pp. 14–15.

experienced the remorseless, disintegrative impetus of today's iconoclasm and nihilism.

By the early fifties, at international student seminars abroad,
nihilist was used to describe a kind of alienated or disaffected student. He might well be regarded as a similar prototype of our
present student alienates. We were working on the reconstitution of
university communities that had suffered the disruptions of war and
social upheaval and on the establishment of such communities in
so-called underdeveloped countries. We felt tremors of the vulner-
ability of the humane intellectual tradition in its resistance to the
resumption of the prewar, mindless, busy activism of Main Street
and free enterprise and in its confrontation with the totalitarian
activisms of radical extremists. We felt these tremors also in the
confrontations of the generous and imaginative rationalism with
the mindless activism of the new technistic impetus. At times we had
difficulty deciding which was the greater menace: what Sidney
Hook has named the explicitly barbarian virtue of the totalitarians,
or the implicitly barbarian virtue of the New Class—the rising
technobureaucratic elite.[8]

By 1949, Walter Mowberly was already writing:

*The active-minded minority have often been in revolt. . . . This
estrangement between the generations has come about largely because students feel themselves to be living in a different world from
their teachers, a world which is grimmer and less secure economi-
cally, politically, and morally. The young are met by teachers whom
they do not understand and who do not understand them. They are
hungering for leadership and there is hardly a man to lead them;
they long for certainty and there is no idea that can grip them. If
they find prophets at all, it is outside the universities; a few years
ago perhaps Shaw and Wells, today more probably a voice from
Moscow. Their teachers' philosophy of life, if any is discernible,
strikes them as academic and unreal.* Out there in the street is

---

[8] See D. Bazalon, *Power in America: The Politics of the New Class*
(New York: New American Library, 1967), especially Chapter 11, "The
New Class," pp. 305–32; and D. Bazalon, "The New Class," *Commentary*,
1966, 42 (2), 48–53. The term is taken over from M. Djilas, *The New Class:
An Analysis of the Communist System* (New York: Praeger, 1957). (N.b.
the parallel term "The New Mandarins.")

something new in the making, which will shatter all the syllogisms
and formulae of the schools.[9]

It could be said that Mowberly's description of the mood of
the later forties reinforces Levich's claims that to each generation its
own crises seem to be ultimate confrontations. I interpret otherwise.
Already in the forties and fifties many in the university world were
aware of dire crisis. Between then and now what we have witnessed
are simply later phases of that agony. In the middle forties Howard
Mumford Jones pictured someone brought up in the tradition of
Western civilization, by a miracle, stepping outside the familiar
patterns of that culture: "Such a person would . . . be over-
whelmed by a single tragic conviction—namely, that the history of
mankind for the last half century has been a history of deepening
horror."[10] This same awareness is suggested in the tragic sense that
pervades George F. Kennan's *Memoirs: 1925–1950*. In these *Memoirs,* the word *tragic* frequently appears, as do other terms contex-
tually associated with tragic uneasiness and disorder, with tragic suffering, exaltation, and emulation: *pity* and *terror, horror, agony,
anguish, catastrophe.*[11]

For those in the academic field the threatened world tragedy
already embraced the university itself. The mood suggested by
Morton and his flickering lights persisted through the fifties and
into the sixties. It was a mood based on an awareness of the precarious nature of the distinctively human enterprise of civilization.
Such a mood is also reflected in the reply of a black father in the
present troubled times to his son who boasts that he could easily
shoot out all the lights of the city block visible from their upper-story

[9] W. H. Mowberly, *The Crisis in the University* (London: Macmillan, 1949), p. 23.

[10] H. M. Jones, *Education and World Tragedy* (Cambridge, Mass.:
Harvard University Press, 1946), p. 3. See also K. D. Benne, *Education for
Tragedy: Essays in Disenchanted Hope for Modern Man* (Lexington, Ky.:
University of Kentucky Press, 1967); A. W. Levi, *Humanism and Politics:
Studies in the Relationships of Power and Value in the Western Tradition*
(Bloomington, Ind.: Indiana University Press, 1969), p. 2; and A. W. Levi,
The Humanities Today (Bloomington, Ind.: Indiana University Press, 1970),
p. 65.

[11] G. F. Kennan, *Memoirs: 1925–1950* (Boston: Little, Brown, 1967),
pp. 110–21. (Hereafter cited as *Memoirs.*) See also pp. 95, 115, 210.

window: "Yes, but could you shoot them back on again?" The idiom, imagery, and context are different, but the signals are alike: a profound disturbance in the spirit of man—as in the forties, fifties, and sixties, so now.

Rather than being concerned with exaggeration of the seriousness of present and impending social change, I am anxious lest too many underestimate its impetus and become victims of inertia and apathy, with the "bland leading the bland." Levich shies away from the term *social revolution* for fear that its very use may magnify conditions resulting from the present and imminent social upheaval. My concern is just the opposite after years of working with labor, business, and professional leaders as well as with academics and after recent visits to more than thirty colleges and universities in all parts of the country. Unless we do dramatically picture how penetrative the social changes may be, we will not be able to rouse people soon enough to an enlightened, realistic, constructive confrontation, to a creative containment and a mastery of these changes. Meanwhile, the very agitators and polemicists about whom Levich has apparently been so deeply concerned are exploiting these gargantuan changes to further their destruction of that humane discourse of reason which both Levich, apparently, and I so deeply cherish. What concerns me is that people whose adrenalin output should be vastly increased may be lulled into apathy, giving such responses as "these things have happened before"; "people got all het up about these things before"; "let's not press the panic button; let's cool it."

Current changes differ significantly from past changes in rate of acceleration, in complexity, in pervasiveness, in ubiquitousness, and above all in totalistic impetus. Consider the computer. As David Sarnoff has put it: "It will leave no life untouched." By such expressions as "exponential rate of speed-up of change" we try to suggest this acute awareness of the uprecedented nature of current and impending change and, hence, of the unprecedented crisis for man. History is now described not as developing steadily but as leapfrogging. Aristotle, Alfred North Whitehead, and Henry Adams have pointed out that, when we get changes of this sort taking place —when the interval between present and future seems to be drastically telescoped and the shadow of the future seems to be falling on the present—we have enough factors adding up, not just to a difference in degree but, rather, to a difference in kind.

If we view history thus, we see that changes are by deliberate invention and are unprecedented, calling for personal and social confrontations and attempted accommodations likewise unprecedented and, hence, in no trite sense, revolutionary. What adds enormously to the impetus of such changes and the radical force of their social impact is that we are daily developing greater and greater efficiency in the engineering of such unprecedented change. Thus, we have already been characterized as the inventing society. A big newspaper ad proudly proclaims, "We can invent anything you want." We have such books as Dennis Gabor's *Inventing the Future* and Donald A. Schon's *Technology and Change: The New Heraclitus.*[12] Michael Crichton tells us that when he first began to look at the Massachusetts General Hospital, he had "the uneasy feeling that there was too much flux, too much instability in the system." Later, however, he realized that "change is a constant feature in the hospital." He then observed: "The true figurehead of modern medicine is not Hippocrates but Heraclitus."[13]

Actually, this figurehead role of Heraclitus goes far beyond medicine and confirms the revolutionary nature of the technological changes which we will be experiencing more and more and which are bound to result in revolutionary social change. Even though scholars maintain that Heraclitus did recognize stability, he has long conventionally been considered the preeminent philosopher of flux; and, along with Proteus as patron divinity, Heraclitus has emerged as patron philosopher of those engineering this change and so often reveling in it.

So we must not allow ourselves to be lulled into apathy or

[12] D. Gabor, *Inventing the Future* (New York: Knopf, 1964); and D. A. Schon, *Technology and Change: The New Heraclitus* (New York: Delacorte, 1967).
[13] Cited by T. O'Toole, review of M. Crichton, *Five Patients,* "Book World," *Washington Post,* June 21, 1970, p. 1. For epigraph to his autobiographic *Scene of Change: A Lifetime in American Science* (New York: Scribner's, 1970), W. Weaver quotes from A. Cowley's "Inconstancy": "The world's a scene of changes; and to be Constant, in Nature were inconstancy." This is to be contrasted with the conventional scientific stress on the orderliness of nature.

self-satisfaction by saying "history tells us" or "statistics tell us" or "in the long run these crises level out." In the long run we all die. Whether we view it historically or circumspectly, the term *social revolution,* as applied to what is going on today, is, then, not banal; it is neither cliché nor hyperbole. It is semantically and existentially accurate; it points to critical reality. We had better accept it as such, use it, and front the full force of its challenge.

In the context of American higher education and liberal learning the use of the term *revolution* is particularly appropriate. Thus, as she studied the students whom *Fortune,* in the early sixties, called "The Forerunners," Elizabeth M. Drews noted: "Gradually the slow simmer of rebellion began to erupt volcanically, sometimes unpredictably, into revolution." Then, basing herself on answers to questionnaires, classroom discussions, in-depth interviews, and "unnumbered conversations," she concluded that "although the situation was so complex as to defy precise statistical analysis, . . . a values revolution was taking place."[14]

[14] E. M. Drews, *Policy Implications of a Hierarchy of Values* (Menlo Park, Calif.: Educational Policy Research Center, Stanford Research Institute, 1970), pp. iii–iv. (Hereafter referred to as Drews, *Policy Implications.*) See also L. B. Mayhew (Ed.), *Higher Education in the Revolutionary Decades* (Berkeley, Calif.: McCutcheon, 1967).

☙ TWO ❧

Quest for Wholeness

The view of liberal education as process rather than as product does not endorse change or development for its own sake. Nor as this term is so often loosely used among educators is liberal education just a matter of growth, regarded as though in itself it were an end.

The view of liberal education as process regards change, development, growth as functioning toward conceptualized and envisioned possibilities which have been projected, as they have been initiated, by the mind of man. They have been projected to fit within the limiting constraints of history and heredity, circumstance, social environment, ecology, and event. Thus, if we take these conditioning yet not determining factors into account, the concept of liberal education as process toward the fulfillment of man-designed possibilities is not fantastic futurism; it does not seek principalities in utopia but rather small bounds within our own environment. It is realistic in its futurism.

In another respect, this concept of liberal education as process is realistic. It is motivated toward the exertions of the liberally educated man as person, as man-at-work or as citizen. Its trajectory takes it through the realm of possibilities. Its target is action. It believes that action converts doubts and merely intellectual conclusions into certitudes. It cannot praise a fugitive and cloistered virtue. It is committed to the enlargement, enrichment, and illumination of the mind. In this respect, it is profoundly traditional. Paradoxically, however, such a conception of liberal learning may successfully handle innovation, too. It can subdue, for instance, the floods of new knowledge. To be specific, let us look at the knowledge explosion and its implications for liberal learning as process.

Let us first consider an analogy, the explosion of a kernel of corn. This explosion may not change the quantity of kernels; it may merely render the given quantity more bulky, more diffusely distributed, as with popcorn. A similar kind of explosion may also occur with knowledge: A diffuse whole replaces a concentrated whole; the basic wholeness remains unimpaired. It is the least difficult type of explosion with which liberal learning has to cope.

Another kind of explosion of a kernel of corn yields an extraordinarily rapid increase of units. This increase may come about through proliferation—through the fractionation of a given whole into two or more parts, each of which may then take on traits according to one or the other of two major types. In one of these, each fraction may become a new and autonomous whole, as happens when a one-celled organism such as a paramecium reproduces itself by division. This sort of wholeness is suggested by the colloquial question: Who is going to pick up the marbles? The marble is here visualized as an entity. The original sack of marbles has been broken up so that each unit emerges as an individual whole. Constructive interrelationships between these new wholes and any remainder of the original whole are not set up; nor are there constructive interrelationships among these new wholes themselves. Atomism thus ensues. This separateness represents a major problem for liberal learning as it faces the explosion of knowledge.

There is, however, another sort of fractionation which takes place when a whole is exploded. It is suggested by the similarly colloquial question: Who is going to pick up the pieces? The fractions that result from this explosion do not become new wholes in their own right. They are and remain fragments. Wholeness has been disrupted in at least three ways: The original whole has had its completeness shattered; the resulting fragments fail to achieve their own new wholeness; these fragments are no longer in a creative interrelationship with what was the original whole or with one another as a possible way for forming a new whole among themselves. For education, this situation represents the ultimate in cognitive anarchy. It creates, for liberal learning, a problem even more serious than that in which the explosion of knowledge yields dilution or proliferation. Whether the results of explosion of knowledge are detached fragments or new autonomous wholes, the consequent problem for liberal learning is indeed grave.

In the threat presented by the current explosion of knowledge, the more segmented, the more specialized, the more immediately practical academic programs—whether from the point of view of the administrator, the professor, or the student—do not begin to have a problem of the magnitude and the complexity of that which confronts liberal learning. By its very definition, liberal learning as general education has the comprehensive scope associated with genus—the scope of generic man—rather than the limited range of species—of men differentiated in terms of specific function. What Ralph Barton Perry has said of the humanities in its highest degree may be said of liberal learning as general education. The humanities, says Perry, have "something to do with man—not man in particular but man in general, the Man in men." Hence, he asserts, humanistic studies, "or studies insofar as they are humane, are good for everybody, and may be said to consist of those studies by which men are made *men,* in advance of being men of any particular kind."[1]

For an individual to achieve wholeness and to keep growing in personal, professional, and social wholeness, his knowledge does not have to show that sort of totality which we associate with the encyclopedia and with its periodic supplements. In liberal learning, wholeness is psychic, resulting in personal, professional, and public self-realization through the total integrity aimed at. For this wholeness and soundness, it is neither necessary nor desirable to force the individual, if that were possible, to encompass, personally, the fast-expanding whole of knowledge.

Let us, then, reject the frenetic pressures to which we needlessly expose ourselves when we wrongly equate the process of educating the whole man with the drive toward encompassing the

[1] R. B. Perry, "When Is Education Liberal?" *Toward the Liberally Educated Executive* (New York: Mentor, 1960), p. 49. This volume of readings contains a number of papers developed by the Humanities Center for Liberal Education in an Industrial Society.

bulging whole of knowledge. Once we have made this rejection, we have taken a giant step toward mastering the explosion of knowledge. What matters most is the mind set with which we approach the problem of liberal learning and the explosion of knowledge. We must have a primary will to wholeness; we must premise man's potentiality, and the imperative of liberal learning, for wholeness. We should recognize this fundamental impelling force toward wholeness as originating internally. It premises a fellowship of educators who share the basic conviction that wholeness is both the driving force and the pervasive value goal of liberal learning. This premise is the opposite of how some propose to proceed in liberal learning. They start as though they were embarking upon an inquiry to see whether there is such a thing as wholeness and whether education can make this wholeness its culminating goal.

In practical terms, then, a liberal learning curriculum is inadequate and may actually be harmful unless, as part of it, there is an ongoing faculty seminar devoted to the progressive clarification and fulfillment of the initial affirmation of wholeness. Such a seminar should devote part of its time to pragmatics, part to theoretics, and part to the interrelationships between the two. The prevailing preoccupation of the seminar should be wholeness and the formation of wholes. The profession needs lively and persistent collective inquiries, on the level of conceptualization related to wholes, wholeness, and the formation of wholes—especially, in the modes of imaginative envisionment and projection. The individual committed to liberal learning needs a parallel ongoing dialogue. He needs to keep himself oriented toward wholeness, disciplined toward it, active on its behalf. So far as wholes and liberal learning are concerned, he must be committed from the start.[2]

Werner Jaeger provides a model for this basic mind set, intention, and exertion toward wholeness. The very word that Jaeger has chosen for the title of his generic work on Hellenic culture is illustrative: *paideia*. Concerning this, Jaeger writes:

It is impossible to avoid bringing in modern expressions like civilization, culture, tradition, literature, *or* education. *But none of them*

[2] See M. H. Goldberg, "The Unity of Knowledge," *The University Today: Its Role and Place in Society* (Geneva, Switzerland: UNESCO and World University Service, 1960), pp. 247–78.

really covers what the Greeks meant by paideia. *Each of these is confined to only one aspect of it: they cannot take in the same field as the Greek concept unless we employ them all together. Yet the very essence of scholarship and scholarly activity is based on the original unity of all three aspects—the unity which is expressed in the Greek word, not in the diversity emphasized and completed by modern developments.*[3]

The same fundamental commitment toward wholeness is seen in his statement that he presents "to the public a work of historical research dealing with a subject hitherto unexplored. It treats *paideia,* the shaping of the Greek character, as a basis for a new study of Hellenism as a whole."[4] The publishers' description of Richard Allen Blessing's *Wallace Stevens' "Whole Harmonium"* reveals a similar holistic motivation in both author and subject. This book, we are told, is "the first study of Stevens' work to treat the body of his work as a single, unified whole, as Stevens himself preferred to consider it"; and "seen thus, each poem takes on a fresh meaning in relation to the whole." Holistic, too, is Harold G. Cassidy's basic intent, in his *Knowledge, Experience, and Action: An Essay on Education,* "to restore wholeness to the curriculum, to bring about the 'one culture,' indivisible in the face of the two, or the seemingly many, 'cultures' "; to bring together "in a connected whole," the humanities, sciences, technologies, and philosophies.[5]

---

[3] G. Highet (Trans.), *Paideia: The Ideals of Greek Culture, 1,* 2d ed. (New York: Oxford University Press, 1945).

[4] *Ibid.,* p. ix. In his review of C. Silberman's *Crisis in the Classroom,* F. G. Jennings harks back to the Greek *paideia.* Indicating the important role that this concept plays in Silberman's study, Jennings cites the following: "The contemporary American is educated by his *paideia* no less than the Athenian was by his. The weakness of American education is not that the *paideia* does not educate but that it educates to the wrong ends." Jennings insists that legislators and the attendant bureaucrats must be told to match Silberman's "most generous and hopeful expression of the yet-to-be-realized American genius for education" with "a more mindful *paideia* than we now possess." ["Asking the Right Questions," review of Silberman's *Crisis in the Classroom, Saturday Review,* 1970, 53 (42), 66, 68.] The stress in *Design in Liberal Learning* is on *paideia* as a pattern and a discipline of wholeness. The telic goal of such wholeness is crucial. The linkage in education between ethics and man as form maker is evident in the title of W. G. Perry, Jr., *Forms of Intellectual and Ethical Development in the College Years* (New York: Holt, 1970), a report "of an investigation of the evolution in students' attitudes and beliefs during four years at Harvard and Radcliffe."

[5] R. A. Blessing, *Wallace Stevens' "Whole Harmonium"* (Syracuse,

For the educator concerned with the explosion of knowledge, this mind set toward wholeness "out there" should be the objective correlative of a corresponding and interrelating wholeness "in here." To experience this mind set, one does not need to aspire to that antique symmetry which Leonardo da Vinci lamented as the one thing "lacking unto" him and of which Jaeger gives the historical shape and process. One experiences this mind set in Wilhelm Max Wundt's summing up of his life's work after thirty years' laboratory experience in his new psychology. In what William James referred to as "the unusually candid confession of the founder of this school," Wundt declared: "From my inquiry into time relations, etc., . . . I attained an insight into the close union of all those psychic functions usually separated by artificial abstractions and names, such as ideation, feeling, will; and I saw the indivisibility and inner homogeneity, in all its phases, of the mental life."[6]

This mind set is, then, a propensity toward wholeness and a similar preoccupation with the conceptualization, envisaging, and dynamic embodiment of the whole. It is, above all, necessary to liberal learning, which seeks to contain the vast explosion of uninhibited knowledge that Faustian man has unleashed in his Promethean quest for power.

By disintegrative proliferation, the specialized expertise that has increasingly marked the several academic disciplines as such is now turning upon its practitioners. This movement toward specialization is working on the very web of the relationships between faculty and administration. It thus tends to force the faculty member into simplicism and affects his stature in the academic collectivity and the educative arts he professes. To fit into this specialized mode, the faculty member becomes a diminished self; the educative arts he practices are reduced correspondingly; and the student too is shrunk. For all, integrity is violated and wholeness impaired.

N.Y.: Syracuse University Press), advertised in *American Scholar,* 1970, *39* (2), 319; and H. G. Cassidy, *Knowledge, Experience and Action: An Essay on Education* (New York: Teachers College Press, 1969), p. 5.

[6] *Philosophische Studien,* 10, 121–24. Cited by W. James, *Talks to Teachers,* P. Woodring (Ed.) (New York: Norton, 1958), pp. 31–32. See also M. H. Goldberg, "The Humanities, Critical Issues and the Quest for Wholeness," *Critical Issues and Decisions* (Washington, D.C.: USDA Graduate School, 1962), pp. 39–67.

Thus, when a national committee on faculty participation in academic government is convened, the simplistic rationale seems to be that academic government involves legalities, policy, administration, management, organization, structure, function, locus of decision making, data, statistics, group behavior, rationalization. In this light the committee should be made up of specialists in the relevant techniques. There is no need for representatives of other academic disciplines—for a philosopher, a historian, a literary humanist, or for that matter an academic citizen-at-large, a "whole academic man."

In the key concepts, too, of such a committee, there is a similar, whole-impairing, simplicism—for example, with regard to the functions of higher education. Here, we are likely to encounter the human resources approach as opposed to the liberal education approach. The former views higher education as a means to improve the economic status of individuals and to promote economic growth for society as a whole; the latter "sees the purpose of higher education as the development of a critical intelligence which is applied to all aspects of individual and social behavior."[7]

In the very dichotomy thus set up, there is a simplistic exclusion of the significant, substantial contribution to human resources that liberal learning may and should make. Moreover, in each of the branches of this dichotomy there is a whole-impairing rejection. Should the human resources approach be limited to the improvement of the economic status of individuals and to the promotion of economic growth for society as a whole? Should utility be the sole measure of human resources? If so, are the compilers of the report not anachronistically or atavistically reviving the reductive myth and stereotype of economic man or of industrial man? The liberal education approach is a similarly atrophied concept. True, the phrase "applied to all aspects of individual and social behavior" suggests a large-visioned inclusiveness. Yet, when one sees that it is only critical intelligence which is to be thus applied, one realizes just how limited is the idea here given of the functions of liberal learning.

What of the nonapplicative functions of liberal learning?

[7] See *Faculty Participation in Academic Governance* (Washington, D.C.: American Association for Higher Education, 1967).

What of the role of liberal education in the cultural refinement and enrichment of the individual in and for himself? What of its role in the growth and refinement of the imagination and the emotions, the nourishment of esthetic and ethical sensibilities, the tempering of ethical stamina so that like seasoned timber it never gives? What of functions which have to do with states of being and qualities of existence—for sheer personal delight; for the individual's self-identification, self-realization, self-fulfillment; for the sense of wholeness?

What of the power of liberal learning to unleash and develop constructively those creative impulses within the individual which both precede and follow the operations of the critical intelligence and for which—as such varied commentators as Matthew Arnold, T. S. Eliot, Sigmund Freud, Max Lerner, and Stanley Burnshaw have emphasized—critical intelligence serves merely as instrument? True, as is often forgotten, critical intelligence is an instrument essential to the full process of creation. Yet it is only one phase—by no means the whole, by no means the big stake.[8] To make it the big stake, as did some apologists for general and liberal education in the 1950s and 1960s, is to confuse means and ends.

There is not a word about any or all the other humanizing functions of liberal learning! Rather, the stress is on the one function closest to the rationalizing drive of the expert in management and administration or in positivistic research. Here, then, is a very illiberal capsuling which runs the gamut of the functions of liberal learning. A managerial-bureaucratic, rational, specialized, simplistic approach to the whole subject projects a truncated image of the academic practitioner and citizen, and a torso image of liberal learning itself—a composite image of diminishment and impaired wholes.

The result, then, is a specific problem of both definition and effective stature and status that confronts those who profess liberal

[8] See review of *The Knowledge Most Worth Having*, W. C. Booth (Ed.) (Chicago: Essays delivered in 1966 at a Liberal Arts Conference): "Northrop Frye's essay is the most lucid of the bunch, but his touchstone is only that education should make us 'critical.'" (*New York Times Book Review*, September 17, 1967, p. 38.) See also S. Prickett, *Coleridge and Wordsworth: The Poetry of Growth* (New York: Cambridge University Press, 1970): "An analysis of creative growth which demonstrates that for both Coleridge and Wordsworth poetic creation and self-analysis were but two aspects of the same process." [Publisher's notice, *The New York Review*, 1970, *15* (9), 7.]

learning—the problem of the role they are to play as phenomenal changes affect American higher education, in academic leadership toward wholeness. Without submitting to arbitrary curtailment or to all forms of change, are they to be with both portfolio and power? This is a critical question which, in all candor and courage, they must confront. At issue is nothing less than the integrity, the wholeness, and hence the effectiveness of liberal learning.

It is often asserted that the quest for wholeness can be pursued through interdisciplinary programs. In such programs many educational planners find the antidote to specialism and the training of high-grade technicians for which our graduate schools are noted.[9] Even with the necessity for interdisciplinary study, there is an important condition: interdisciplinary studies are not *necessarily* contributions to liberal learning. The needed distinction is found in a consideration of the ends set for interdisciplinary studies. The end goal of a given interdisciplinary enterprise determines whether it will contribute to liberal learning.

For example, here from the community-at-large is a problem brought for solution to a university.[10] It is an ecological problem— water pollution and the myriad problems of other sorts that go along with it. Among these are problems involving attitudes of individuals or groups or organizations, hence, calling perhaps for sociologists, social psychologists, as well as industrial psychologists, political scientists, economists, human development experts, metallurgists, geochemists, physicists, marine biologists, public health experts, experts in communication and public relations, engineers, and so on. Let us suppose that we have a utopian budget and that the needed talent can be commanded. All the different specialists from all the indicated areas can be and are procured. Let us further suppose that we have heeded a warning against serious communications gaps

[9] Many of the criticisms offered by O. C. Carmichael in *Graduate Education: A Critique and a Program* (New York: Harper, 1961) still stand, as shown by the current study of graduate education by A. M. Heiss, *Challenges to Graduate Schools* (San Francisco: Jossey-Bass, 1970). See, however, A. S. Nash's interdisciplinary graduate seminar in the humanities and the social sciences at the University of North Carolina.

[10] That an entire college curriculum could be built around such a problem as ecology is illustrated by E. W. Weidner's description of the new curriculum at University of Wisconsin's campus in Green Bay, given in G. K. Smith (Ed.), *Troubled Campus: Current Issues in Higher Education 1970* (San Francisco: Jossey-Bass, 1970).

among the disciplines involved. The experts are brought together; their specialties and their particularized repertoires of expertise are pooled. They constitute one interdisciplinary team, which, if successful, renders important social service.

But now, for the needed distinction comes the crucial question: Do they likewise advance liberal learning, either for the team members or for others outside the team? And accompanying this question is the factor of snobbism. In times past, snobbery has been actively present among some professors and practitioners of liberal learning; and in our more homogenized present it may still persist as a sort of wraith. In raising the question, I do not intend to revive the ancient and invidious distinction, going back at least to Aristotle, between the liberal arts and the servile arts, often expressed, accurately or inaccurately, as a contrast between the useless arts and the useful arts. Rather, in the seventies, the concern involves what liberal learning should try to do—hence, what use it is to be.

As indicated in chapter one, liberal learning does indeed seek to fulfill its perennial responsibility to relevance; and, as will be seen later, it does so as it helps successive generations of students to attain their proper dignity. Dignity involves a sense of worth—of personal worth and of human or generic worth. The achievement of this sense of worth is closely related to a whole cluster of human values —among them is the moral sense, as Eldridge Cleaver is shocked into recognizing in *Soul on Ice*. One may visualize dignity as the nucleus for this whole cluster of living values; or one may regard it as an enveloping, containing, and nourishing matrix for these values. One may have his choice of fictions, or analogical imagery. Each, or either, may prove fruitful. Whichever the choice, one should include such components of socioethical force as integrity, justice, compassion, and rationality (together called, in Biblical terms, the understanding heart). These values are regarded not as static objects or commodities but as vital processes, which, either actually or vicariously through imagination, the liberal learner experiences. In this light, liberal learning becomes the creative conservator of the cultural heritage and the creative mediator between the heritage and emergent learning. It becomes so through encompassing and assimilating present scientific research; scholarly inquiries; efforts of contemporary musicians, painters, poets, multimedia artists, and so on.

Turning back to the multidisciplinary team operation that mobilized a number of specialists to solve a given ecological problem, let us now consider how this team operation contributes as well to liberal learning. It makes such contribution if it fosters the intellectual illumination, enlargement, and refinement of its participants; if it expands their horizons and their awareness of interconnections and interrelationships, of inferences and implications; if it sensitizes them to dignity, engendering and enhancing human values; if it contributes to their sense of personal and human dignity; if it energizes them on behalf of advancing the dignity of nature and of man. This is indeed a large order, but then liberal learning is a magnanimous enterprise; it now plays for mortal stakes.

A common concern among academic disciplines is shown in part through our contemporary preoccupation with the concept of structure. This concern is evident in W. O. Baker's several references to the quest for patterns of order, symmetry, and harmony in the sciences.[11] It is also apparent in the European structuralists who are described as "having instilled fresh life into the humanities," and whose structuralism is described as "neither a method nor a theory but a point of view encompassing such diverse disciplines as anthropology, economics, psychology, and sociology, as well as literature and history." Of them it is said, further, "Though widely diverse, their papers and discussions unite in the attempt to forge a common critical language and redefine the idea of a humanistic research community."[12] Harold L. Burstyn of the Carnegie-Mellon University has observed, "The notion of structure seems the key to our present educational concerns, and one is hard put to think of a really important recent book which does not claim to elucidate the structure

[11] "Scientific Research and Humanistic Learning," lecture at Opening Ceremony and Colloquy, Materials Research Laboratory, The Pennsylvania State University (echoing Conant, Oppenheimer, Hoyle, and other noted scientists), November 13, 1969. Baker (vice-president for research, Bell Telephone Laboratories) at one point referred to "the beautiful consistency of science," later to "the harmony of nature."

[12] From advertisement in *The New York Review of Books,* 1970, *14* (11), 46, for R. Macksey and E. Donato (Eds.), *The Language of Criticism and the Sciences of Man* (Baltimore: Johns Hopkins Press, 1970). See also D. W. Gotshalk, *The Structure of Awareness: Introduction to a Situational Theory of Truth and Knowledge* (Urbana, Ill.: University of Illinois Press, 1969); and T. C. Oden, *The Structure of Awareness* (New York: Abingdon, 1969).

of something." Burstyn thus stresses structure within the disciplines and asserts that "each academic discipline has a structure peculiar to itself—what we call its methodology."[13] This concept is generally accepted among educators. It provides a base for a valuable educative function toward wholeness: the structural concept of model making. In model making we have an activity common to the liberal arts and the formally designated scientific, technological, and applied fields and hence useful for their collaboration in liberal learning.

There are two major types of model making. One is conducive toward the ends already designated for liberal learning: the factual, empiric, or working model. It deals with things as they are, with processes as they are or as they could be put into practice immediately. It is the sort of model produced when there is a positive response, as regards community development, to the following challenge by a social scientist: Tell us the sort of development you want; we'll make alternative models that show whether you can do it, and, if so, how.

Another kind of model, the telic, or end-purpose, model, is equally important for consideration of community relations, social relations. These are not models of what works immediately; but rather models of what might be, could be, ought to be, or should be. These models incorporate values that may elude the literal efforts of those who shape day-to-day working or operational models. Yet the values may be precisely the goals, often not expressed, let alone envisaged, of the various working models. These models represent the objectives, the end goals, of numerous specific structurings and strivings. As with the development of the community, so may the development of the individual benefit through liberal learning. Effective telic models are necessary for the growth of the individual's sense of personal and human dignity and the assemblage of values with which this sense of dignity is associated. These objective models serve as electromagnetic lifts (exemplified in the hover vehicles, which are held above the ground and transported across distances by a moving electromagnetic system above them); they also serve as target to constrain trajectory; they serve, too, as criteria.

[13] "Tradition and Understanding," *School and Society*, 1969, 97 (2320), 419.

The mechanism and dynamic of liberal learning could be first a telic-model shaping and a projecting; then a process for trying, in one's development, to approximate the telic model chosen for emulation. Whether through continuing systematic liberal studies or not, this process can go on through life. This futurist and developmental view of liberal learning, with its stress on telic models, can be central to liberal learning. It is in marked contrast to the traditional stress on the humanities as dealing with artifacts, that is, with things done.

The developmental view encompasses, too, continual dialectic between telic models and empiric or working models toward the ends both of increased general understanding and of improved practical effectiveness, between models shaped in the past and the demands of the present and the future, and between models of man and models of society. All three of these modes of heuristic dialectic are seen in C. Wright Mills's volume of readings in the classical tradition of sociological thinking.[14] The selections themselves show that "the classic sociologists construct models of society and use them to develop a number of theories and that "neither the correctness nor the inaccuracy of any of these specific theories necessarily confirms or upsets the usefulness or the adequacy of the models." The "models can be used for correcting errors in theories made with their aid. And they are readily open. They can themselves be modified in ways to make them more useful as analytic tools and empirically closer to the run of fact." All in all, Mills declares: "It is the models that are great." And, for him, the greatness of these models is in part historically dialogic—through their "influence on subsequent sociological thinking" and through the many revivals of the thinkers who have formulated them. He goes so far as to maintain that it is the perennial potency of these models that makes the works in which they are shaped classics.

[14] *Images of Man: The Classic Tradition in Sociological Thinking* (New York: Braziller, 1960), pp. 3–4.

❧ THREE ❧

Self-Emergence

Liberal learning is put to its test when we examine its results, for as a *paideia* toward wholeness, it should enrich the individual, enable him to grow toward the maturation of capacities which may have long been overlooked or neglected; that is, it should enable him to grow, in wholeness, toward self-actualization and self-emergence.

True, liberal learning also educates for personal responsibility. We find Hillelian dicta applicable: If I am not for myself, who will be? If I am only for myself, what am I? If not now, when? I cannot really be myself except through continual, creative involvement with others and with society, whether I am sympathetic toward their views or antagonized into confrontation and contestation. If society depends on me for its self-realization and its self-renewal, then I, on the other hand, depend on it for my own self-emergence. Awareness of this vital interrelationship pervades this present treatment of self-emergence, self-identity, and the fulfillment of the basic possession of wholeness through liberal learning.

SELF-EMERGENCE

As many use it today, the term *emergence* is objectionable. It has become banal. For a Pierre Teilhard de Chardin, the term may encapsulate vast knowledge, imaginative thought, and mystical intuition. But when educators, publicists, professional humanitarians, and philanthropists use the term *emergence*, they betray a provin-

25

cialism of both time and spirit, and the term suffers atrophy or perversion.

"Step to Man" by John R. Platt affords an instance. Before it appeared in a volume,[1] the essay had already been published separately more than once—in the *Journal of Psychiatry*, in *Science*, and in a special issue of the *Journal of the American Association of University Women*. In digested form, "Step to Man" had likewise appeared in *The Saturday Review*, in which it was later enthusiastically reviewed by Stuart P. Chase. As with so many others who talk of the emergence of man, Platt seems to imply that, until the biotechnicized millennium, of which he is an enthusiastic herald, there will have been no real man. "Step to Man" would seem to rewrite the Browning poem so as to make it read: "Grow old along with me: the *man* is yet to be." There is Faustian arrogance in this derogation of man—past and present. Have there not been universal men before?

I share the general wonder at our technistic instruments and an awareness of their beneficent promise. But because these technistic agencies have brought us together—as Marshall McLuhan has put it—in a cosmic neotribalism and since we now constitute one global village, it is absurd to claim that a new, superior generic man has emerged or soon will emerge. Much more than physical propinquity, achieved through vast, complex networks of electronic circuitry, is necessary to achieve such a new creation; more than a conceptualized model of oneness and togetherness of all mankind; more than the reports that the Apollo astronauts have given us of their strong sense, in viewing the Earth from the moon, of men as united in an earth brotherhood. Especially misleading is this loose talk about the emergence of man when it is clothed either naively or hypocritically in religious garb; specifically, sometimes, in parodies of the magnificent intellectuality of Teilhard de Chardin.

[1] J. R. Platt, "Step to Man," *The Step to Man* (New York: Wiley, 1966): "A striking collection of visionary essays on the evolving social and intellectual nature of man." For the author's criticism of "Step to Man," see "The Agony, the Ecstasy and . . . the BIG 'If'," *Penn State Alumni News*, January 1967, pp. 8–12; "Cybernation: The Dilemma of Control," *The Spectrum*, 1967, 7 (1), 12–14, 44–47; "The Structure and Problems of Human Values: 2000 A.D.," *Symposium II: Technological Education in the 21st Century*, Center for Technological Education, San Francisco State College, 1967, pp. 69–98. (Hereafter cited as *Symposium II*.)

These criticisms of the current emergence-of-man cult may not seem relevant; the topic is *self*-emergence, but I have been talking *man*-emergence. Actually the two are intertwined. A model for personal self-emergence is made up of the implicit purposes imprinted on the personal genetic code; the desires of personal temperament; the projection of deliberate will; the reasoned train of thought, and so on. But also among these components of the self-emergence model are the social templates of the modular man which family, ethnic group, neighborhood, class, state and region, nation, religion have contributed; and finally the generic idea of man dominant in one's time.

All these derivatives from social ecology enter into the master model entertained for personal self-emergence. Suppose, now, that the social matrix provides, as generic model of man, a technological man. Even if no technological man, as such, has ever existed or ever will exist, the development of a projective image of such a man, the propulsion of such an image into the current cultural stream, gets absorbed into the fashioned model of self-emergence.[2] This image of man can have serious practical consequences because, as Ludwig von Bertalanffy has observed, the future goal is anticipated in its symbolic image and so may exercise an influential, controlling, or determining power as to present or impending action.[3] On these bases I criticize the about-to-emerge modular man widely trumpeted by the technistic millennialists. My strictures are prompted by the strong desire to have such a model dissociated from our consideration of self-emergence. For reasons too complex for presentation here, such a modular figure is problematic in conception and, if embodied, is productive of further serious problems. Once this dissociation has been effected, we are ready to consider the idea of self-emergence as applied to the individual throughout his life. But here, too, distinctions are in order.

[2] Since this book was written, two such models have been provided by V. C. Ferkiss, in his *Technological Man: The Myth and the Reality* (New York: Braziller, 1969), pp. 3–10.
[3] L. von Bertalanffy, *Organismic Psychology and Systems Theory*, *1* (Worcester, Mass.: Clark University Press, Heinz Werner Lecture Series, 1968). (Hereafter cited as Bertalanffy, *Organismic Psychology*.) Revised and republished under the title *Robots, Men and Minds: Psychology in the Modern World* (New York: Braziller, 1967).

Associated with the idea of emergence are such images as a ship appearing out of the fog, a whale surfacing to spout, a submarine likewise surfacing, a Botticelli Venus rising from the sea, a moth extracting itself from its cocoon, a butterfly emerging from its chrysalis. In all these images there is a notion of regular, durative process along a maturation continuum; and there is also a suggestion of gradualism. The very terms *stages, phases, process* suggest something gradual, regular, and systematic; hence to a degree predictable; hence reassuring, comfortable, hopeful. This suggestion is evident in Teilhard de Chardin's statement: "I cannot define the world otherwise than by a gradual awakening of consciousness. Research is precisely the frontier in the spreading of universal consciousness."[4] This statement implies what emerges from obscurity to prominence, and what is likewise superior to what has gone before. There is also an optimism associated with this whole concept of emergence.

Other notions associated with emergence may be melioristic, but they are in contrast to gradualism and due-process notions. According to this second set of associations, we might picture emergence, in terms of creatures rising from the sea, as the surfacing of a school of porpoises accompanying a ship. Here is a general pattern that is discernible but temporary. Its shape is the porpoises' trajectory. Within this progressive pattern, there is tumultuous and seemingly nonpatterned emergence, submergence, reemergence. The porpoises proceed, not in a systematic, rational order, but apparently, in riotous improvisation. Their behavior reminds one of the opinion that some have of evolution itself, that it is opportunistic and singular and therefore follows no law. The porpoises proceed discretely, by fits and starts, by breaks and veerings, discontinuously. Carl Jung has said, "If you follow the story of evolution, you will find that man completes creation."[5] However, man may complete this creation, either through gradualistic and due-process development or through acts of special creation and special happenings.

For a number of decades—indeed for almost a century— education in this country has accepted, on the level of rhetoric at

---

[4] Quoted in N. Braybrooke, "C. G. Jung and Teilhard de Chardin: A Dialogue," *Journal of General Education*, 1969, *20* (4), 280. (Hereafter cited as C. G. Jung and Teilhard de Chardin.)
[5] *Ibid.*, p. 279.

least, a gradualistic philosophy, and in many quarters this hardy perennial still persists. But especially in our time of rapid speed-up of change, when life itself is described as futurized,[6] we must entertain fresh ideas as to emergence. We must give more attention to what happens when powerful agents of incitement to change— whether catalytic, participative, or disruptive—invade the universe of development connected with emergence. We must give more attention to such agents when, as in atomic reactors, they invade and bombard the process of emergence and abruptly change the phases or the direction. We now experience self-emergence, not only through orderly progress but also through discrete jumps.

Such attention is not to dismiss orderly and gradualistic self-emergence. Rather, it is a matter of *both–and*. Yet here, let the stress fall on self-emergence that occurs, often, through emergencies. Such emergencies as moments of critical confrontation and contestation elicit self-emergence, sometimes most abruptly. This idea is dramatized in Robert Browning's monologues, in Walter Savage Landor's imaginary conversations, in Ernest Hemingway's Nick Adams stories, and in Robert Frost's condensed poems of tragic pathos. It is mildly suggested in Abraham Maslow's concept of "peaks of learning," and in Robert J. Havighurst's "the teachable moment." It is signaled in James Joyce's celebration of artistic epiphany. At its most intense, it is the moment of illumination, the moment of truth.[7] It may be in part what Frost meant when he observed that college is a place where a boy hangs around until he catches on, and the moment of catching on may be the moment that makes the breakthrough for immediate or ultimate self-emergence. It may be the momentary flash of real knowing that Wallace Stevens has symbolized in the image of the flamelike tail of the pheasant as the bird disappears over the hedge.[8]

[6] See R. J. Blakely, "The Futurization of Life," *Critical Issues and Decisions* (Washington, D.C.: USDA Graduate School, 1962), pp. 81–103; and R. Heilbroner, *The Future as History* (New York: Grove, 1961).

[7] See Plato's Seventh Letter: ". . . The truths of philosophy are not expressible as those of other subjects, after long study and discussion under the guidance of an experienced teacher. *A spark may suddenly leap*, as it were, from mind to mind, and the light of understanding so kindled, will feed itself." Cited by H. D. F. Lee (Trans.), Plato's *Republic* (Baltimore, Md.: Penguin, 1967).

[8] See J. H. Miller, *Poets of Reality* (Cambridge, Mass.: Harvard University Press, 1965).

Here, then, at the heart of the educative process we have a
paradox expressed by wordplay: often we make our breakthrough
toward self-emergence when we are confronted by emergencies.
Here is a basic dilemma for the teacher and the student. Courses,
curricula, and programs demand order, schedule, and plan; syllabi,
assignments, preliminary diagnostic tests, mid-term tests, and final
examinations. Where the teacher professes to be concerned with
self-emergence, the premise of these courses is that the student
maintains systematic procedures as motivations, channels, and constraints for orderly development. Yet, so often, the actual achievement of self-emergence is not that way: it is, rather, by fits and
starts; it is often wayward; *the wind bloweth where it listeth.* So the
teacher has to be a shrewd observer, ready at a moment's notice,
while he plods along as a horse of instruction, to become airborne,
a Pegasus with his students, an inspiration.

Beneath the given ostensible agenda of course descriptions
and outlines, beneath the analyses of texts, expositions, and recita-
tions, lie the hidden agenda; and to make them surface, to take
advantage of them when they have surfaced, the teacher has to be
a pedagogic opportunist with an epiphanic sense. He carries a
central role in the climactic play of the serious games of classroom
confrontation.

Personal experiences provide instances of this sort of play for
the epiphanic breakthroughs to self-emergence. Some took place
during an experimental course in continuing liberal education for
adults at The Pennsylvania State University. For the most part, the
participants were of limited schooling; but they were successful in
their work and, some of them, in community service. They were
leaders from Pennsylvania locals of the United Steelworkers of
America; and they had been elected, by their fellow members, to
participate in the Summer Steelworkers Institute at The Pennsylvania State University—strongly backed by Emery Bacon, at that
time Education Director of the Union and at present Executive
Director of the Federal Interagency Committee on Education for
the Department of Health, Education and Welfare.

The procedure was to take participants who had already
been through severely practical programs and to have them participate in a program of a different sort. This program, too, would

serve practical ends but in a different sense: It would have a larger utility—long range and indirect. It would meet the individual's needs—perhaps as yet unfelt, or if felt, still inarticulate—for better understanding of other people and social relations; for better self-understanding. The intent of this experimental program was to deal with those qualities, attitudes, and practices which help people to a freer and richer appreciation of self; to lead the participants to a more sensitive treatment of other people, to a more confident confrontation of a fast-changing future.

The immediate goal was to help the participants come to experience human values as part of their own growth in self-awareness and more mature wholeness. The end was to be accomplished through treatment of works of imaginative literature—poems, plays, novels. The people in the program were expected to come with biases and suspicions about the man who made words and books his profession, and who talked of such effeminate things as poetry, art, and culture.

Of all the aids that buttress the professor appearing before a college class, I, the instructor, was to be stripped bare. No captive audience: If I bored or alienated them, these men would vote with their feet. There was no leaning on rank; as with dissident students now, to these men, university degrees, academic titles, publications, teaching abroad, offices held in professional societies meant nothing positive and, possibly, something negative. For support, academic jargon—the special vocabulary of literary criticism and of philosophy—was unavailable. No manuals or guidebooks. At the first meeting I took the plunge and introduced myself. I gave a thumbnail autobiographical sketch, in this way setting a pattern—in effect, an informal telic model—the men could follow when they in turn introduced themselves. I told how I had been born in this country, but of immigrant parents; and how, as a boy, I had learned what it means to try to make out in a new country, with strange customs, a strange language, and no social status, and when one is poor and has a family to support. I related how my parents had come to this country from Czarist Russia to escape, at worst, persecution and the wholesale slaughter of the dreaded pogrom; at best, indignity; how through them I came to hate cruelty, humiliation, indignity, and to pity the victims of such evils; and how through them I had a strong love of freedom, linked with a sense of duty and responsibility toward all that makes for freedom. I told how, from my parents and their Judaic tradition, I had imbibed a deep love of learning, a faith in the power of learning, and a sense of duty to use, in the service of freedom, whatever talents in learning I might have. I told how I became strongly committed to work for the other human values that enrich life and make for a more just and kindly society, as well as for a sense of personal dignity and wholeness.

The group then picked up and carried on. Some sketches were perfunctory—the minimum: name, local number, place, office held. But others followed my example. One said: "Me, I haven't been to school much. Only through eighth grade. But I've done a lot of reading. I keep up with all that comes out on labor legislation. I analyze what I read, and then I pull it together. I like the brainwork. I like to apply it." Another said: "I saw a lot of cruelty and violence when I was young. I want my kids not to have to go through that. I want to help make a more decent world. I want them to have more fair play." A third said: "I want them to know better how to use their time when they're not on the job." Still another said he wanted to learn more in order to help the older—and so often depressed—people in his neighborhood when they got depressed. As they spoke, I jotted down brief notes focusing on the working values implied in what was being said. These notes were not a list of abstractions but rather concrete words and examples. They stood for values to be put into action. In no trite sense, they came straight out of the book of life. With these notes before me, I saw the next steps: first a coffee break, during which I could take stock; then, after reconvening, a brief report on my impressions of the introductory go-round; then a general discussion about some key concepts in the inventory. This discussion was not of cloud shadows or heavenly pillars of fire but of earthly shapes, and it was not just solemn: it included the running fire of wit and frequent bursts of earthy humor.

Then, together, we read Frost's "Death of the Hired Man." In it, Mary (a model of compassion) gently but persistently helps free her husband (a model of strict righteousness) from the entrapment of strict adherence and the bitter feelings quite inappropriate to a changed situation. She also helps prepare him for his emergence into the larger freedom of justice tempered by tact and pity. Later, one of the men applied this notion of entrapment and enfranchisement to himself. He had gotten many of his present hostile reactions toward management from his father, who had fought through the black, union-organizing years of the thirties (and who had served as his model). His father may have been justified in his hate. But conditions were changed; it was no longer appropriate for the son to react as the father had reacted. He now saw that another model was necessary, and he expressed how he felt freed from a long entrapment of his own.

On another occasion, we were taking up one of Hemingway's stories. Since I had been told that these men were not readers, I read aloud, with them, *The Old Man and the Sea,* a selected excerpt each day. They kept calling it "a fish story," saying: "Come on, Max! When does the old man catch the big fish?" When I had finished the account of the catching of the fish, I slammed the book shut and said, "O.K., the story's finished." They protested: "What do you mean, finished?" I countered: "You said it's a fish story. In a fish story, when the fish is caught, that's the end." One of the men said, "You're wrong. There's a fight still going on." "What fight?" Beating his fists against his chest, he protested: "In here." That was the moment of breakthrough. Without using any conventional terms of literary criticism, I was able to move into talk of the tragic awareness faced by an older man in his continued need for self-testing, his need for reassurance that he is still competent, and is respected as such. Here, nothing less than his self-identity is at stake.

After this program had been written up and widely publicized, people wrote in for copies of the syllabus. I was wryly amused; there was just a fragment of a syllabus. In addition to "Death of the Hired Man" and *The Old Man and the Sea,* there were a few short poems, a few short stories. I had not pressed for subjectmatter coverage. The ostensible assignments were just the inciting pretext for the efforts at eliciting wholeness-related self-emergence. Admittedly, this sort of practice can be treacherous. This pedagogic "opportunism" can be an excuse for sloppiness and careless improvisation, for uncritical and sentimental dignifying of amorphous bull sessions as whole bursts of epiphanic moments. Yet the risk is justified.

There are some further reflections on the idea of self-emergence in relation to liberal learning. On the one hand, emergence suggests the manifestation of what has existed all along but of what until now has remained obscure. It involves making explicit what is implicit, bringing up to the surface the buried self that Matthew Arnold, anticipating Sigmund Freud, probed in several of his poems. In this view, the child, as William Wordsworth has put it, is indeed father of the man. On the other hand, there is a line of meaning for *emergence* which denotes innovation, the coming into being of what has not been at all. It is emergence in this context that we get, as recently revived, in Lloyd Morgan's theory of emergent evolution. According to this theory, new properties appear in the course of development that have not been manifest in earlier stages and that contribute to innovation. When life is emergent, there are new forms of rational expression, new syntheses—at deeper levels and carrying their "distinctive marks of the unexpected." Morgan further points out that, if you were to ask the poet, the musician, the artist, the novelist, the man of science (consider Poincaré and his account of his discovery of the Fuchsian Functions), "one and all would reply that, however it may be verbally expressed, however we may seek to explain it, in their best moments *something veritably new does just come* and is accepted as a gift to be greeted with glad surprise." Morgan cites this reply as illustrative of "the emergence of the new."[9]

In his discussion of general systems theory, in which he treats organisms as open systems, Ludwig von Bertalanffy—principal architect of general systems science since its inception about thirty years ago—suggests this innovative concept of self-emergence. Of these living, open systems, he says: "They are maintained in a state of fantastic improbability in spite of innumerable, irreversible processes continually going on. Even more, organisms in individual

[9] C. L. Morgan, *Life, Mind, and Spirit,* The Gifford Lectures, University of St. Andrews 1923, under the general title of *Emergent Evolution* (New York: Holt, 1925), pp. 86, 134; and *ibid., The Emergence of Novelty* (London: Williams A. Norgate, 1933).

ontogeny, as well as phylogenetic evolution, develop toward very improbable states."[10] In various ways, von Bertalanffy thus ascribes to the open organic system, the living system, the spontaneity of functioning which is not available to the mechanical, closed cybernetic system. He feels that whatever our professional or personal fields, here lie important implications for us. So he stresses spontaneous activity as a concomitant of the organism as an open system, able to maintain a state distant from equilibrium and spend existing potentials in spontaneous activity or in releasing stimuli.

There are thus alternative views about emergence: the continual, gradual, due-process notion and the notion of emergence through spurts, breakthroughs, mutations, as well as the notion of spontaneous self-originating improvisation. For the biologist as well as the philosopher, these alternative views provide searching problems that take them, on the one hand, into the frontiers of genetics and, on the other hand, into those of metaphysics. However, for the time being the educator may waive these questions of theoretic and speculative inclinations. From the point of view of pedagogic strategies and tactics, he may treat them both as scientists treat wave theory and corpuscular theory. He may choose to treat them both as "fruitful fictions" and apply them as he finds them pragmatically justified.

Suppose the teacher were to adopt the concept of self-emergence as actualizing what has been all along but what hitherto has remained only a potential. Thus, liberal learning would become a process of peeling away the tough outer coatings which, for the individual, had inhibited the transformation of the potential into actuality. Hence, liberal learning is a process of reactivating what has suffered partial atrophy. (If there is total atrophy, then there can, of course, be no reactivation.) It is to clear the paths along which the process from potentiality to actualization is to move. It is to help establish more and more complexly and vitally nutritive networks of interconnection among these paths, helpful to the emergence of the self.

The teacher of liberal learning who adopts this sort of con-

[10] Bertalanffy, *Organismic Psychology*, pp. 44, 47, 53. See also his *General Systems Theory: Foundations, Development, Applications* (New York: Braziller, 1969).

ceptualization prefers the organismic imaging of the process of self-emergence. This imaging is of the sort that Jules Romains uses in describing the creation of his novels, which he has likened to planting a seed that germinates, sprouts, and grows until it fully unfolds as a mature plant, with stem, twigs, and leaves; and, finally, the crowning phases—inflorescence and fruiting. If such organismic imaging is adopted, then, to make the analogy fit, we must allow for the constraints, needs, emergencies, and unexpected factors, which must be seen as bending and twisting—sometimes warping, certainly modifying—the developmental drive of the liberal learning process toward self-emergence.

But suppose, whether as a literally propounded theory or as fiction, we adopt the concept of emergence that is associated with Morgan's emergent evolution and apply it to liberal learning and self-emergence. When we talk about the appearance of the utterly innovative, what are the implications for teaching rationales, programs, and practices? This concept of emergence suggests that self-emergence leaves much to chance, that at certain critical stages or levels the orderly processes of liberal learning somehow cause the self to emerge as though by mutation, like wrestlers who play for an opening.

When he is dealing with adult students, the college or university professor operating under either of these conceptualizations of self-emergence will, in all likelihood, feel at a disadvantage. For example, suppose in continuing education he takes his stand right at the point where, for liberal learning, the adult student and he, as teacher, come together. Then the view he has of the student's self-emergence is likely to be either retrospective or circumspective. In either case, the chances are against this view's being futurist, for in terms of life career the adult student may regard himself—and be regarded—as having arrived, as being set.

However, this tendency toward a static view on the part of the instructor in continuing education is not justified. For one thing, such a view contradicts the often demonstrated capacity of adults—even those beyond what are regarded as the prime years—to experience psychic growth. For another, it ignores a basic truth about self-emergence which Alfred Tennyson described as rising on stepping-stones of our dead selves and which other poets, John Donne and John Milton, for example, saw symbolized in the Phoenix myth—the new Phoenix rising out of the ashes of its former self. John W. Gardner has discussed the same theme.[11] From the practical, pedagogic point of view, the tendency on the part of many teachers to picture the adult—even the college-age young adult—as already having achieved, or been conditioned into, a self of sorts, must leave them, as teachers, feeling incapable of serious impact.

A philosophy that regards liberal learning largely as a future-oriented situation should alleviate such a feeling. True, there is a need to go back into the past and to take due cognizance of the present. Yet, liberal learning is most importantly a dynamic process of attempted actualization of telic models. Donald Michael suggests in part what I have in mind: In his discussion reminiscent of Lester Frank Ward's treatment of telic in reference to the future direction of his sociocracy, Michael recommends an overall plan for shaping the future, which is flexible enough to have self-correcting feedback and which would thus allow for alternative futures.[12]

Telic models—end purposes or end goals—are projected into the plastic future and then serve as electromagnetic pulls on the individual. These pulls are directed toward the individual's self-fulfillment and serve as stimuli for his self-actualization. According to this view the student gains effective will to project an ideal model of the ever-renewed self, and the projection is almost as though by an Indian rope trick. Moreover, through liberal learning the individual moves toward the actualization of this telic model. The movement is along the path from where the student is now, to where, in the realm of the potential, the model—continuously renewed, often

---

[11] J. W. Gardner, *Self-Renewal* (New York: Harper & Row, 1964). See also L. Margolis, "For Renewal, Societies and Individuals Need Future Orientation, Gardner Says," *The Futurist*, 1968, 2 (6), 127. This article follows a piece by Gardner: "How 20th-Century Man Let His Institutions Go to Pieces: A View of the 23d Century," pp. 126–27.

[12] D. N. Michael, *The Unprepared Society: Planning for a Precarious Future* (New York: Basic Books, 1968), p. 68. See C. J. Karier's review of this volume in *Journal of Aesthetic Education*, 1970, 4 (1), 142; and L. F. Ward, *Dynamic Sociology* or *Applied Social Science*, as based upon statical [sic] sociology and the less complex sciences (New York: D. Appleton, 1924).

with revisions—is sustained. This movement, too, is within the context and the constraints that form the ecological field of that path.

IDENTITY, MYTH, AND TELIC MODELS

The capacity to form and project such telic models of the worthy self and to strive toward their actualization helps to distinguish man from many of the other animals. Brought to its maturity, the telic model is one's excellence, his integrity, his wholeness. When it is dynamically present before the individual's inner vision, such a telic model of man is potentially his emergent self.

Through at least partial actualization and at best perhaps only an approximation, the telic-model image of the potential good man or admirable man becomes the self that emerges at a particular time and place, by an unforeseen occurrence or accident. Indeed, the emergence of self consists largely of the determined striving toward actualization of the telic self, of the potential self, through contestation in and with flux. What is the identity crisis that so many talk about? It is often the setting in of entropy, prohibiting the creative energy necessary to transform telic image into actualized or emerged self. It is the failure to hold on to a meaningful and moving telic image of the self as this image actually emerges, or the atrophy of such an image once it has emerged.

Consider the advertisement that appeared in *Business Today*:[13] "Do you have to give up your identity to make it in a big corporation?" And the answer: "Not at General Telephone and Electronics. We are looking for more people . . . who aren't afraid to stand up and try themselves out"—like those who "developed the high-energy liquid laser, who came up with the sharpest color TV picture, who pioneered instant electronic stock market quotations." So, "All you need to make it with us is to have a good head on your shoulders." This advertisement implies that, to maintain his identity, one needs to use his brains and produce new inventions, especially those inventions that turn out to be profitable to the corporation.

Such notions of identity send the sensitive students away from the corporate cybernetic complexes toward the world of the senses and inner streams of consciousness. From empty extroversion they react to solipsistic introversion. The television series *The*

13 *Business Today*, 1969 (1).

Prisoner presents melodramatic episodes depicting one person's brutally dogged, incredibly ingenious efforts to maintain his personhood—his autonomous wholeness—in the face of the equally ingenious and fantastically sophisticated efforts of malevolent wizards whose methods vary from subtle time manipulation and thought control to primitive bludgeonings. These wizards rule over a people who live unquestioning for contrived and programmed fun but who have no thoughts, no feelings of their own, no enterprise or action of their own. They live in a perpetual picnic-carnival atmosphere, obedient to each directive of their invisible controllers. If the Prisoner maintains an almost desperate grip on his identity, the lotus-eaters in the euphoric utopia-prison exhibit the total dissolution of identity. Here is a surrealist counterstatement to B. F. Skinner's *Walden II* and a brutal caricature of it. It means total dissolution of the telic self and telic images. It is the reverse of self-emergence into one's wholeness.

Myron B. Bloy, Jr., on the other hand, cogently illustrates the positive functions of telic models in self-identity and the search for wholeness in one's life and personality. Drawing upon his own reading of the Gospels, he seeks to give a straightforward, experientially verified characterological description of Jesus Christ—a master telic-image of man, in this case, since the life and personality of Jesus were themselves the actualization of the ideal. Stressing Jesus' own achievement of self-identity, Bloy depicts its manifestation in "the unique, dynamic, and shaping presence of the historical Jesus," in all the "dynamic richness of his life, its centeredness, its wholeness."[14] Hence, Bloy's attempt to envision Jesus thus, to imitate creatively his modular example, to internalize this image and make it operative in one's own life, contributes in turn to the resolution of one's own personal issues of self-identity and wholeness—of one's own self-emergence.

Clinical psychology provides numerous case histories showing what happens to the telic-model image of the personal self or the generic self when something goes askew either in envisioning a

[14] M. B. Bloy, Jr., *The Crisis of Cultural Change: A Christian Viewpoint* (New York: Seabury Press, 1965), pp. 25–26. (Hereafter cited Bloy, *Crisis of Cultural Change.*)

telic model of man or in establishing and maintaining the right relations to it. A modern poet has been referred to as suffering from
a wounded imagination. The phrase is applicable to three illustrative case histories from a study by Milton Rokeach at the state
hospital in Ypsilanti, Michigan. Rokeach[15] tells of a farmer, a clerk,
and an electrician, each of whom believes that he is Jesus Christ.
The study asks: What impelled them to renounce their real identities? What led them to adopt the name that symbolizes the greatest
and best in man (that is, the name that evokes perhaps the most
potent telic image of man and his ideal wholeness in Western culture, if not in all the world)? Rokeach set out to discover what impelled each of these men to break contact with his actual self and to
do, pathologically, what the normal person knows he cannot do yet
what is encouraged by the current sociopsychological jargon term
identify with (perhaps stemming from the belief of traditional
Christians "that the meaning and purpose of life is to be discovered
by identifying with Jesus").[16] Each man was acting as if he had
totally approximated the telic image self. Here we have three imaginations so traumatized as to have suffered pathological distortion in
the image of the telic self—misinterpretations, misapplications,
abuses. In his play *Openended Moonsong*, John Orbach presents the
three Christs of Ypsilanti as characters; and he uses excerpts from
the patients' recorded talks.[17] Orbach takes great liberties with the
original subjects of the case studies. He transmutes them into free-
floating participants in a time-and-space annihilating, surrealist
drama of the absurd. Yet the words and actions—often abortive,
dissolving into nonsense—pathetically, grotesquely portray the vagaries of the person whose relations with his telic self have been fouled
up. As with many true believers, their claims collapse into treacherous non sequiturs or erupt into brutal action. While one of the
three Christs in the play fills the role of a life-fostering obstetrician
and consoling concomitant of death, the other two—one with a
whip, the other with tongs—become torturers and remorseless in-

[15] M. Rokeach, *The Three Christs of Ypsilanti* (New York: Knopf,
1964). See also M. Rokeach, *Beliefs, Attitudes and Values* (San Francisco:
Jossey-Bass, 1968).
[16] Bloy, *Crisis of Cultural Change*, p. 39.
[17] An unpublished play submitted in partial fulfillment of require-
ments for the degree of Master of Fine Arts, The Pennsylvania State University; produced locally at the Pavillion Theatre, May 28–30, 1970.

flictors of death. Thus, in both the Ypsilanti reports and the play, we have oblique, inverted, or perverse testimony to the human hunger for telic-model imagery, relationship, and realization.

In contrast is Malcolm Muggeridge, former editor of *Punch* and a columnist in *Esquire,* described by his publisher as a "maverick," a "veteran agnostic and iconoclast," "at one time an ardent atheist," "a man who never belonged to a church." Yet he is one who has rediscovered Jesus Christ as the only fitting actualized telic model for him—"the Man who backed up his teaching with his life." "All I can say is, as one aging and singularly unimportant fellow man, that I have conscientiously looked far and wide, inside and outside my own head and heart, and I have found nothing other than this Man and His words which offer any answer to the dilemmas of this tragic, troubled time."[18]

A far more positive and poignant illustration of a telic image of man effectively realizing his humanity under most dehumanizing pressures is found in *That Day Alone,* Pierre van Paassen's moving book from the tragic forties. Van Paassen relates how, as a fitting sequel to beating to death a lad who has refused to make statements betraying others and as a fitting climax to revolting physical indignities inflicted upon a rabbi, Nazi torturers order the rabbi to deliver the sermon he has prepared for the coming Sabbath. Elaborating upon his text, the rabbi gravely says, "When we consider that in creating man God poured out His own spirit into him, our bodies are the temples of His holy spirit." Here the rabbi is interrupted by the jeers of the Nazis, who point to him, naked and with half his beard shorn away, and laugh, "God's image and likeness!" "Yes, and look at that fine temple on the barrel over there!" one of them shouts, as all of them glance at the dead boy. Then one of the boy's killers asks the rabbi, "I am not a temple of God, am I?" The rabbi nods his shorn head and replies, "*Doch!* Yes, you are indeed!"[19]

Here is an individual whose telic image of man is an immediate presence. Yet not for a moment does he make the mistake of assuming he has approximated it, that his actual self has coalesced

[18] Cited by C. M. Bunch in *St. Louis Post-Dispatch,* September 14, 1969, p. 3B. See also the publisher's advertisement for *Jesus Rediscovered* (Garden City, N. Y.: Doubleday, 1969) in the *New York Times Book Review,* September 14, 1969, p. 31.

[19] P. van Paassen, "The Prepared Sermon," *That Day Alone* (New York: Dial Press, 1941), pp. 310–12.

with it. Holding it at its due distance, he nevertheless has its telic energy work on him and through him. In spite of his pain, he keeps his vision of it unconfused, vivid, and vivifying. Despite the Nazi bestialities he does not fail to recognize and acknowledge in his torturers their universally human telic images. They may strip him of his clothes and shear away half his beard. They may seek to shear him of his personal and human dignity. Nevertheless, in them too he sees the same telic image of man—the replicated although reduced image of God, as he envisions it within and for himself.

Germans in this period of genocidal horror and holocaust recognized the need of a health-bringing, integrity-maintaining image of man. As George Kennan points out, and contrary to Franklin Roosevelt's view of them, the older Prussian aristocracy yielded "some of the most enlightened and courageous of all the internal opposition Hitler was ever to face." Among them was the grandnephew of the famous nineteenth-century military leader, Count Helmuth von Moltke. Kennan was "particularly impressed by the extent to which Moltke [the grandnephew] had risen, in his agony, above the pettiness and primitivism of latter-day nationalism." The anticipated loss of his personal estates in Silesia, after the war, was, for him, sad but not important. "For us," he declared, "Europe is less a problem of frontiers and soldiers, of top-heavy organizations and grand plans. Europe after the war is a question of how the picture of man can be reestablished in the breasts of our fellow citizens." Already, Moltke had turned to the task of reestablishing this picture of man. Kennan found this Prussian aristocrat, employed by the German general staff in the midst of a great world war, "hiding himself away and turning, in all humility," to a serious study "for ideas as to how Germany might be led out of its existing corruption." Yet, while through private study, Moltke sought to envision and shape a new telic model for his people, in public, on behalf of his ideals, he acted with exemplary courage. A Protestant, he defied the regime by giving refuge in his own home in Silesia to the local Catholic school, and, after its own premises had been closed by the Gestapo, he permitted the school to carry on there. Such defiance was lethal. In 1945, Moltke was tried by a People's Court and was later hanged. For Kennan, Moltke became an exemplary model in the tragic mode: "With his death, to which he went

bravely and movingly, the future Germany lost a great moral force."
Yet, for Kennan, "the image of this lonely, struggling man, one of
the few genuine Protestant-Christian martyrs of our time," remained
"over the intervening years a pillar of moral conscience and an un-
failing source of political and intellectual inspiration."[20]

Telic models, however, need not be limited to a lofty tragic
stage. They function everywhere and at all levels, and they can be
expressed in low-keyed as well as in exalted terms. Samuel Taylor
Coleridge observed that a symbol participates in the reality of that
which it represents. Might not the distich in the song lyric by Rod
McKuen be a simple rendition of the idea of telic models, self-
identity, and the image of man; that is, is not each of us, made by
God, beautiful in His mind's eye? In her keynote address at the
1969 national conference of the National Council of Teachers of
English, Adele Stern quoted the ghetto youngster who said: "I gotta
be me."[21] The "me" is the telic me. In fulfilling its responsibility to
relevance, in inducting the oncoming generations into their proper
dignity, liberal learning must help such young people become their
telic "me."

There are numerous other illustrations of the crucial need
for effective telic models of the good society, the good life, the good
man to achieve self-emergence. Many Afro-Americans are reaching
back through time and across space in search of their own African
genesis quite different from that which Robert Ardrey has found so
fascinating. Indeed, what they are doing is not so much searching
scientifically for what was, as rather shaping mythopoetically an
image of what they might have been and hence of what they might
yet become. The term *black* American, intended to function linguis-
tically like the word *white,* is revealing for reasons having much to
do precisely with telic models as central means toward self-identity
and self-emergence.

During the February 1969 conference on the Humanities in
the Middle East and in African Studies, sponsored by the Humanities Center at Baldwin-Wallace College, two relevant points were

[20] Kennan, *Memoirs,* pp. 119–23. The von Moltke citation is from
*A German of the Resistance: The Last Letters of Count Helmuth James von
Moltke* (London: Oxford University Press, 1948).
[21] A. H. Stern, "Hello, Socrates," *The Humanities Journal,* 1970, *3*
(3), 13.

made. The first was that African novelists have been moving from earlier stereotypic, externalized, and simplistic telic models of the admirable new African as national liberator to individualized, internalized telic models of the meaningful person in the developing endogenous African culture. The same conference brought out that, ironically, many young black Americans are energetically and efficiently working to actualize for themselves the very success model of the affluent American which is held by so many of the black bourgeoisie, and which so many of their own white contemporaries—often in the name of the counterculture—are rejecting. In working toward this success model, these black students seemed to ignore James Baldwin's observation, which Eldridge Cleaver uses as a chapter epigraph in *Soul on Ice*. Baldwin asserts that "the white man is in sore need of new standards, which will release him from his confusion and place him once again in fruitful communion with the depth of his own being." Hence, he declares, "white people cannot, in the generality, be taken as models of how to live."[22]

As Baldwin and Richard Avedon have put it: ". . . we live by lies . . . Nothing more sinister can happen, in any society, to any people. And when it happens, it means that the people are caught in a kind of vacuum between their present and their past—the romanticized . . . past and the denied and dishonored present."[23] They declare this conflict to be a crisis of identity. It is also a crisis in the telic realm, for with a romanticized past and a dishonored present what chance is there for envisioning a motivating future—that is, of shaping, projecting, and striving toward exemplary telic models?

Telic models are thus often incarnated in myth, whether they are thrown backward against the screen of the past (actual or fantasized) or projected forward against the screen of the future. According to Lewis Mumford, such utopias as Plato's *Republic* show an interesting paradox. On the one hand, they may be demon-

---

[22] E. Cleaver, *Soul on Ice* (New York: Dell, 1968), p. 65. J. Baldwin, *The Fire Next Time* (New York: Dell, 1969), p. 130. See also the following: ". . . the American Negro can have no future anywhere . . . as long as he is unwilling to accept his past. . . . An invented past can never be used; it cracks and crumbles under the pressures of life like clay in a season of drought" (p. 111).

[23] J. Baldwin and R. Avedon, *Nothing Personal* (Baltimore: Penguin, 1964), p. 28.

strated as retrospective models generalized from specifics out of the past. On the other hand, they may be used, prospectively, as emulative models for the future. Hence, we may witness the dead hand of the pluperfect resting heavily upon the heart of the future perfect. Since, in the realm of the potential—as in the realm of Buck Rogers[24] —present, past, and future are meaningless, both these modes of telic imaging may turn out to yield the same or similar results for psychic health and self-emergence.

What is needed, then, is creative mediation of telic models achieved through retrospection and telic models achieved through projection (one is tempted to say "pro-spection"). A result of this mythopoetic process of creative mediation might be a telic model that is innovative, magnanimous, stimulating, moving—one's personalized image of man. As Richard Arrowsmith has reminded us, such model making is the central process in the works that constitute the body of both the traditional humanities and the new humanities. Such formation of telic models as well as the study and criticism of models already made, both positive and negative models (as those in satire), are essential to self-identification and the continuing process of self-emergence through liberal learning.[25]

In his *Do It*, Jerry Rubin shows his awareness of the role of myth in providing telic models. "Myths," he states, "offer kids a

[24] See J. Seelye, review of *The Collected Works of Buck Rogers in the 25th Century* in *New Republic*, 1970, *162* (8), 25: ". . . as any sci-fi fan can tell you, man in space moves backwards and forwards [in time] with equal ease."

[25] For a much more detailed treatment of the role of telic models—both positive and negative—see M. H. Goldberg, "The Humanities and Mankind Teaching," to appear in a forthcoming volume, Gerhard Hirschfeld (Ed.), the Council for the Study of Mankind (1971). (Condensed versions in the Council's *Views and Ideas of Mankind*, Bulletin No. 25, December 1969, pp. 11–13; and in *School and Society*, 1971, *94* (2331), 176–178.) See also M. H. Goldberg, "Human Values for Human Beings: The Role of Telic Models for the Self-Renewing Community," *Adult Leadership*, 1967, *15* (8), 270; and his "Models, Values and Research," *Blindness Research: The Expanding Frontiers: A Liberal Studies Perspective* (University Park, Pa.: Pennsylvania State University Press, 1969), pp. 498–521. In "The Search for Alternative Models in Education" [*American Scholar*, 1969, *38* (3) 377–88], D. Riesman illustrates a fairly cautious, probabilistic approach toward the use of telic models. G. K. Smith (Ed.), *The Troubled Campus: Current Issues in Higher Education* (San Francisco: Jossey-Bass, 1970) treats new educational models. See also J. R. Seeley, "Mankind as Fact by Faith," *Education and the Idea of Mankind*, R. Ulich (Ed.) (New York: Wiley, 1968).

model to identify with." Asserting that America's "myths—from George Washington to Tarzan to John Wayne—are dead," Rubin maintains that American "youth must create their own myths." He pictures such a myth, which, he maintains, is not imaging as yet unactualized potentialities but is rather combining already existing fragments into modular image—in this case the image of the Yippie. "The reality was there," declares Rubin, but a "myth was needed to coalesce the energy." Once the "Yippies forged the myth," it in turn served as an activating telic model: it "inspired potential Yippies in every small town and city throughout the country." However, for Rubin such a myth and such a telic model do not merely combine segments of actualities. The myth "builds a stage" and the models provide the characters "for people to play out their own dreams and fantasies." Hence, "the myth is always bigger than the man." "The myth of Che Guevara is even more powerful than Che. The myth of SDS is stronger than SDS. . . . Marx is a myth. Mao is a myth. Dylan is a myth. The Black Panthers are a myth. People try to fulfill the myth." The myth, then, indeed, provides the potent telic model: "it brings out the best in them."[26]

The claim that this myth and model bring out the best in those who embrace them is certainly open to challenge. The blunt and unqualified appeals of both the myth and the model to the uninhibited playing out of one's dreams and fantasies are socially dangerous and personally self-destructive. Even so, the account given of the formation and propagation of a new myth with its effective model—partly empiric, partly telic, pervasively emotional-imaginative—is pedagogically useful. It provides material for analysis and criticism in liberal learning that deals with self-identity and self-emergence. On all sides, either directly or through the media, often spectacular dramatizations of this myth and action pictures of this model fill our imaginations. Any efforts at liberal learning that involve human values, personal and human dignity, self-actualization must vigorously confront the challenge of one of the most potent combinations of dramatic myth and activistic model that the

[26] J. Rubin, *Do It: Scenarios of the Revolution* (New York: Simon and Schuster, 1970), p. 83. Also, note the paradoxic title and subtitle of J. H. Griffin's *A Hidden Wholeness: The Visual World of Thomas Merton* (Boston: Houghton Mifflin, 1970). The book deals with seeming externals—photographs by Merton and Griffin.

Jerry Rubins have been projecting and acting out in pursuit of their counterculture.[27]

Soul on Ice is a case in point. A literary work, it provides opportunity for study of the complex but vital interrelationships between telic model, self-emergence, self-identity, self-respect, one's sense of personal dignity. In a chapter significantly entitled "On Becoming," Cleaver, who has contributed the Introduction to *Do It,* tells how, in prison for raping white girls as revenge against the white race, he took a long look at himself and, for the first time in his life, admitted that he was wrong. In so judging himself, he referred, as criterion, to a telic model transcending ethnic limits. He had "gone astray—not so much from white man's law as from being human, civilized," for he "did not feel justified"; he "could not approve the act of rape." As a result, in his own words, "I lost my self-respect." His whole "fragile moral structure seemed to collapse, completely shattered." His "pride as a man dissolved."

How can he regain his pride as a man, his self-respect? He explains: "I realized that no one could save me but myself. . . . That is why I started to write. To save myself." Writing was his way of carrying on this vital search for self-identity. He "had to seek out the truth and unravel the snarled web" of his motivations. He had to find out what he is at present and his telic model: what he wants to be, what type of man he should be. He also had to find out how he could actualize this model: what he could do to become the best of which he was capable. He realized that at stake was more than his personal salvation, that if successful he could provide an effective generic telic model for "countless other blacks."[28]

Soul on Ice read thus is a major document for liberal learning in the study of self-emergence, self-identity, telic models, and the collection of enduring values that make up personal and human dignity. It is no small wonder that this book has appeared on the best sellers' list of a large number of college and university bookstores.[29] Such models are especially attractive to young people whose world, as the director of Runaway House in Washington has de-

---

[27] See T. Roszak, *The Making of a Counter Culture* (Garden City, N.Y.: Doubleday, 1968), especially p. xiii.

[28] Cleaver, *Soul on Ice,* pp. 14–15.

[29] *Change,* 1970, 2 (2), 14.

clared, "is running away from under them." Stripped of all cultural heritage, they are the "first generation of natives," and their major problem is that they lack models.[30]

Margaret Mead provides several modes of telic modeling as related to self-identity and self-emergence.[31] In her postfigurative culture, the telic model is derived from the past, and it exerts its influence on a youngster who internalizes it unconsciously. It is very close to a working model—embodied in living examples—the grandparents and parents. In her cofigurative culture, too, virtual working models are available, but they are found among the youngsters' peers and tend to be far more pluralistic, varied, and impermanent. Their internalization is neither so deep nor so enduring as in the first type. In Mead's prefigurative culture, the tables are turned: the youngsters, for whom the future is now and who are hence frontiersmen along the growing edges of the culture, become the models that the parents, more or less successfully, should seek to emulate. In effect, this third case represents a relocation of the future: a folding back or a telescoping of future time into the present. This telescoping of future time should provide most vivid, immediate, and pervasive telic models in the mind.

Taking her cue from the young, who "seem to want instant utopias," Mead invites us to relocate the future and reshape our thinking: "We must place the future, like the unborn child in the womb of a woman, within a community of men, women, and children, among us, already here, already to be nourished and succored and protected, already in need of things for which, if they are not prepared before it is born, it will be too late." The prefigurative models must now be located in the womb of the present. If we are to use them exemplarily, we must know them now, hidden though they may be in the womb. But how? by palpation? by X-ray? by infrared photography? by physicochemical extrapolation? Suppose, through one or more of these means, we contrive to formulate a

[30] Television interview, May 26, 1970.
[31] M. Mead, *Culture and Commitment: A Study of the Generation Gap* (Garden City, N.Y.: published for The American Museum of National History by National History Press and Doubleday, 1970), pp. 1, 96–97. See too H. L. Hodgkinson, M. B. Bloy, Jr. (Eds.), *Identity Crisis in Higher Education* (San Francisco: Jossey-Bass, 1970).

model. What then? Through the remainder of the period of gestation the model will develop—and such growth means change. So, at birth—when that will be Mead does not tell us—the model will be quite different from the one inferred or extrapolated during its period of gestation. In short, appealing though her metaphors may be, Mead leaves us with a tantalizingly obscure notion of just what the telic models may be for people—young or old—for whom the future is now. If this notion is what the now-generation has to go on as it tries to envision those telic models that are essential to psychic economy and vital to self-identity—small wonder that, for all Mead's bland and buoyant reassurances, the now-generation sets up the universal wail: Who am I?

Then the bitter thought occurs: for all her soothing metaphors and her engaging style, does Mead provide anything better than the paper-tiger pseudomodel which Jerry Rubin boastfully announces the Yippie telic image to be? Far from providing possible solutions to the problem of gaining exemplary telic models when the future is being telescoped into the present, Mead, in last analysis, sentimentally restates the dilemma of the liberated. The warm, reassuring metaphor of the womb, far from clarifying, is a mask concealing we know not what. It provides an opaque envelope for a big question mark. Far from contributing an answer, the question, like the serpent that swallows its own tail, consumes itself and vanishes. The sought-after telic model turns out to be a Cheshire cat.

William Horosz provides a useful corrective to the notion encouraged by some cultural anthropologists and other social scientists that telic models which express man's formative nature are merely those of goal-directed activity "out there." He postulates four levels of human purpose: ontological, phenomenal, analytic, and artifactual. Of these, he assigns all but the first to the operational realm of the "out there." He locates the first of these, the ontological, in the "in here," and regards this function as "the deepest sense of purpose that man can experience—namely, through "seasoned thought and seasoned passion," the sense of "self-direction in existence." Hence, for him, the most fitting model for embodying the ontological dimension of human purpose is summed up in the dictum: contribute to thyself. This statement "does not merely mean that man is decisive only in his actions, that he is only an achiever. It also means that man contributes to his becoming by his purposive being."

The Horosz corrective is implied in my earlier elucidation of the linkages between self-emergence, self-identity, and telic models. As Horosz himself points out, stress on this subjective, dynamic dimension of purpose has relevance to two major current preoccupations: immediacy and authenticity, both of which in turn have to do with self-identity and self-emergence. He prescribes this dimension of purpose as an antidote to the "malaise which grips us in the modern age"—"that we expect contributions to our life from practically every walk of life other than the ontological factor of purposeness," that tragically "we are passive toward our purposive being and think of purpose merely as an external image"; and he accounts for this passivity as "merely the demand of the organization man in the cybernetic age." As an antidote, he recommends the implicit ontological generator of purpose as "the source of model making and myth making." Without drawing heavily on this source, "we are impotent to make correlatives with existence."

Horosz thus tends strongly to downgrade the objective, operational factors of purpose, which he links with "mindless living and mindless inquiry"—namely, models of existence that offer "pre- and post-purposive designs for living"—"goal-directed designs for living." He labels these designs for living "substitute forms of directionality" that "get in our way and dissipate our substance with riotous models." Indeed, he declares his whole volume to be concerned with "the battle of the models for an understanding of existence."

I suggest, rather, that a dialectic effort to reconcile the objective operational factor in human purpose with the subjective ontological process factor is far more fruitful, especially if the reconcilement is expressed through shaping and seeking to actualize the telic models of the good man, the good life, the good society. Even Horosz does not entirely shut the door to such creative mediation. He does not altogether insist upon a radical disjunction between the ontological and the other levels, as he calls them, of purpose. While he does speak of the latter as yielding "forms of substitute directionality," he does not altogether reject them. He simply dismisses them as "never entirely satisfactory models of directive agency."[32] He thus leaves the door open for the sort of telic imaging of man to which we would direct the central efforts of liberal learning—an imaging that embodies a creative reconcilement of the factors of operational end purposes visualized as "out there" with those connected with internally initiated organismic voluntarism. The setting and means for this creative reconcilement is man's form-making impulse—his propensity toward wholeness.

In her *Policy Implications of a Hierarchy of Values,* Elizabeth Monroe Drews is also concerned with images of man, a characteristic of whom is "to develop pictures of himself." At the outset she depicts five such generic images, each of which has recurred from century to century: *Homo Homini Lupus* (man is a bad animal), the Hobbesian picture also attributed to Freud and exemplified in our century by the Hitlers and Stalins; *Tabula Rasa* (man is a blank sheet, determined by external impressions), the Lockean, Watsonian picture; *Steppenwolf* (man is a "schizoethic" mixture of good and evil), the dualist-humanist, the Goethean, Hessean view; Noble Savage or Nature Boy (my terms: man is naturally good and perfectible), the picture presented by Rousseau, Condorcet, and so on (an image to which Drews seems quite partial); *The Transcending Self,* the Blakean-mystical, the Maslovian-humanistic picture (an image to which Drews likewise seems quite partial).

These typologies illustrate processes of modular imaging, and the last three models especially seem to intersect with our concept of telic imaging. Yet they are not quite identical conceptualizations, for they are offered as allegedly factual models, the key word being *is;* whereas telic models are frankly mainly fictive models, the key words being *could be, might be, should be, ought to be,* and other optatives. Telic imaging brings together and makes central to liberal learning the vital interrelationships between telic models and awareness of potential within, and the "unfolding and often conscious perception of that which was perceived but 'already within us.' " Drews' declaration in her "Research Memorandum"

[32] W. Horosz, *The Promise and Peril of Human Purpose: The New Relevance of Purpose to Existence* (St. Louis, Mo.: Warren H. Green, 1969), pp. ix–x.

presents one of her closest approaches to telic imaging: young people "need to find themselves to become their best selves." The "best selves" are the telic selves.[33]

Recent publications augment the classics in providing opportunities for the imaginative and critical study of telic models as a central function of liberal learning. V. C. Ferkiss,[34] observing that the future is already here, presents the American astronaut, the "hero of technological civilization," as one type of the "everyman of the future" and such a bland yet mordant nonentity as Adolf Eichmann as another. He then considers the question: Which is myth and which actuality?

In addition to Ferkiss's technological man let us consider Robert J. Lifton's protean man, a working model for the age of Heraclitus or the age of Aquarius, an image suggesting fluid, shifting change. Irving Kristol has described Lifton as "brilliantly naming" this new psychological type, "constantly and casually inventing new identities for himself—'putting on' these identities—as he flies from the smell of death that emanates from hollow institutions and decaying values." Kristol acknowledges that this idea of protean man "is one of those insights that have only to be expressed to carry conviction." He asks if this is a "viable psychological type" or "a pathological mutation," if it is "creative response or nihilistic desperation." He states that Lifton is optimistic about this type and thus implies that Lifton's answer would be twofold: Protean man is a viable psychological type and a creative response. But Kristol thinks otherwise: "Some thousands of years of human history stand ready to wager he is not."[35] What do we think? What do our students think? Here is the opening gambit, set up for what could prove to be a valuable exercise in liberal learning and head toward apprehending and actualizing our own telic imagery.

Taking its cue from such humanists as Erik Erikson, a critical task of liberal learning is, then, negatively, to provide, by educational means, appropriate therapy for identity crises or blocks to

[33] Drews, *Policy Implications*, pp. iv, 1–9, 46, 122–23.
[34] *Technological Man*, pp. 3–10.
[35] I. Kristol, "A New Psychological Type Emerging, 'Protean Man'," review of R. J. Lifton, *History and Human Survival: Essays on the Young and Old, Survivors and the Dead, Peace and War, and in Contemporary Psychohistory* (*New York Times Book Review*, August 2, 1970, p. 2).

self-emergence. Its task, positively, is to encourage and guide the student in the process of self-emergence, which in turn is an on-going process toward the apprehension and actualization of one's telic image of himself in relation to the good life and the good society, to his sense of personal and human dignity and wholeness.[36]

[36] In what *Life* has called its "worldwide success" (within seven months of its first release as a recording) the "wrenching and reverent" rock opera *Jesus Superstar* by two young Englishmen, Andrew Lloyd Webber and Tim Rice, illustrates the process of attempted creative adaptation of telic models—in this instance, a traditional image of man. *Life* observes that because it portrays Jesus as a modern man, it has bridged the generation gap, and because it is both secular and reverent, "it has been embraced by many of the clergy as a way to rock youth." As often happens with such efforts at creative adaptation of telic models, this image of Jesus Christ evokes, at the extremes, opposite reactions. On the one hand, it has been played on Radio Vatican. On the other hand, the strongly traditional have protested *Jesus Superstar* in order "to defend God because he is being publicly blasphemed" (*Life,* May 28, 1971, pp. 21–26).

❧ FOUR ❧

The Technetronic
Age

In a report on science and contemporary social problems from the
Oak Ridge Institute of Nuclear Studies, *science* is sometimes intended to include technology and sometimes to exclude it. One
scientist there flatly asserts: "The search for order in nature cannot
be separated from the instruments and machines employed; in turn
the concepts derived from that search cannot stand isolated from
the means by which they were obtained."[1] A second scientist, however, points out that, while machines and instruments are essential
tools used by the scientists, they are contributions of technology, not
science.[2] For some types of inquiry and application, then, it is significant to distinguish between science and technology. As James
Bryant Conant points out, along one of its lines of development,
technology derives from the empiricism of the craftsman and from
the practical inventions of unlettered men—untouched by scientific

[1] *Report on Science and Contemporary Social Problems* (Oak
Ridge, Tenn.: Associated Universities of Oak Ridge, 1964), p. 5. See also
W. Weaver, *Science and Imagination* (New York: Basic Books, 1967); D. J.
Price, *Science Since Babylon* (New Haven, Conn.: Yale University Press,
1961); *Little Science, Big Science* (New York: Columbia University Press,
1963); and A. M. Weinberg, *Reflections on Big Science* (Cambridge, Mass.:
MIT Press, 1967).
[2] *Report on Science and Contemporary Social Problems, ibid.*, p. 5.

theory and training.[3] For some purposes, Marcel Mauss's claim stands that "even science, especially the magnificent science of our day, has become an element of technique, a mere means," and likewise Jacques Ellul's comment upon this statement: "There we have the final word: science has become an instrument of technique."[4] Side by side with such statements, we need to place the following, by Stanley M. Garn: "Now I agree with those who find the bright advances of science too often converted into mere technology and technology too soon converted to ultimate ugly ends."[5] Were we to become involved in the particulars of curriculum building or of disciplinary jurisdictions, we would, at times, be wise to draw a distinction between science and technology. But, for the present discussion, these distinctions need not be made.[6] Stanley L. Jaki treats science and technology as having a composite cultural significance warranting the use of unitary terms to suggest both taken together. Habitually, Jaki thinks in terms of a scientific-technological composite.[7]

[3] J. B. Conant, *Modern Science and Modern Man* (Garden City, N.Y.: Doubleday, 1952). See also B. Barber, *Science and the Social Order* (New York: Collier, 1962, rev. ed.), pp. 86–87, 104.

[4] M. Mauss, *Sociologie et anthropologie* (Paris: Presses Universitaires de France, 1950). Cited by J. Ellul, *The Technological Society*, J. M. Wilkinson (Trans.) (New York: Knopf, 1964), p. 10. (Hereafter referred to as Ellul, *Technological Society*.)

[5] "The Sciences Are Humanities," *Antioch Notes*, 1964, 42 (3), 3–4. H. G. Cassidy indicates that the title of Chapter 8 in his *Knowledge, Experience and Action* was suggested by this piece, which he entitles "The Sciences and Humanities" (p. xii).

[6] This position is in keeping with E. Ashby's treatment of the title and subtitle of his *Technology and the Academics: An Essay on Universities and the Scientific Revolution* (New York: St. Martin's, 1963).

[7] S. L. Jaki, *Brain, Mind, and Computers* (New York: Herder and Herder, 1969), pp. 11, 14–73. In the publisher's description of R. K. Merton's *Science, Technology and Society in Seventeenth Century England* (New York: Fertig, 1970), the word *science* appears five times; the word *technology* not once. In adopting, from M. Eliade, the phrase *technicians of the sacred* for his anthology of "primitive poetry," J. Rothenberg suggests that shamanism was the science-technology of the day and that in our day words with the *techne* root carry prestige. [*Technicians of the Sacred: A Range of Poetries from Africa, America, Asia and Oceania* (Garden City, N.Y.: Doubleday, 1969).] In his "Nixon Reorganizing Vast Science Complex," R. D. Lyons shows that the "Science" of the headline is used to cover science and technology viewed as a composite or complex: "The Nixon Administration is moving to make the hydra-headed Federal science and technology apparatus

To avoid awkward repetition of the compound *scientific-technological* and, at the same time, to signal what seems most characteristic and critical in current and impending developments along the scientific-technological front, let us adopt Zbigniew Brzezinski's term *technetronic.*[8] This adoption counteracts legitimate objections to using verbal barbarisms or hybrids. Yet for the novel features of the age into which we have been so precipitously pushed or which has rushed so precipitously to engulf us, this new coinage, in which lopped-off limbs of two words are combined to produce a third, is powerfully suggestive. It combines the *techne* (structure) from *technology* with the *tronic* from *electronic* to yield a network image in which complex, kaleidoscope patterns are swiftly made and broken by mazes of electronic circuitry. And whether or not cybernetic-electronic instruments and processes that achieve these simultaneous, intricate, and multidimensional networks are all derived, genetically, from science, certainly science at present is inextricably bound up with them, in mutual cause and effect relationships.

Certainly, too, the term *technetronic* helps dramatize the radical discontinuity between the Scientific Age, which, by the time of Thomas Henry Huxley, in the nineteenth century, was already beginning to make its strong bid for dominance, and the new age in which we so abruptly find ourselves. Huxley found the great cementing agency for human solidarity in biological science—in the protoplasmic chain of being. For Marshall McLuhan and his disciples, the electric technology—the cosmic network of electronic circuitry—sets up intimate, empathetic relations fostering human solidarity among men the world over and, so they claim, makes us man—at least the neotribal, global-village man.[9]

---

more responsive to the nation's needs" (*New York Times,* November 1, 1970), pp. 1, 81.
   [8] See Z. Brzezinski, *Between Two Ages: America's Role in the Technetronic Era* (New York: Viking, 1970). See also *U.S. News and World Report,* April 20, 1970, pp. 71–72. H. Cox justifies a new coinage for identifying a distinctive feature of our times: "For purposes of comparison we shall make use of a somewhat contrived word, *technopolis.* It will be used here to signify the fusion of technological and political components into the base on which a new cultural style has appeared" [*The Secular City: A Celebration of Its Liberties and an Invitation to Its Discipline* (New York: Macmillan, 1966), p. 5].
   [9] See M. McLuhan and Q. Fiore, *War and Peace in the Global Village* (New York: Bantam, 1968).

The phrase *human competence* suggests ability and skill, as well as finesse. As used here competence covers everything from the contemplative to the applied in liberal learning, from the most specialized skills to the most generalized. This twofold notion of education and competence has been enlarged by Peter E. Siegle, who states the need for education toward both external and internal, or psychic, competence.[10] He sees this latter type of competence as necessary, in a prophylactic sense, for facing a world of geometric increase in the rate of speed-up of change. The achievement of such competence is necessary for a healthy man—that is, a whole man, one who can understand the impacts to which this fast-changing world subjects him, who can achieve and maintain wholeness, and who can establish stability in the eye of a hurricane.

Liberal learning can lead to human competence by assisting a man to accustom himself to rapid technetronic change and to its impacts. In his Preface to the *Lyrical Ballads,* William Wordsworth assigns this function to poetry; and a reassertion of this view is made by the contemporary poet May Swenson, both in her article "The Poet as Anti-Specialist" and in her poem "Landing on the Moon."[11] In this poem, written before any moon landing, she employs the substance and imagery of space technology, by imaginative projection, to satisfy what she calls the craving of the psyche for a "complete and firm comprehension of the whole." In her prose commentary on this holistic poem, she demonstrates how the technetronic age fires the creative imagination, and she makes the point that, thus inspired, the poet can enable the individual, in advance of an aerospace age, to absorb vicariously into a wholeness the emotional and psychic implications of it.

In the prize-winning poem of a high school senior, we find a similar contribution to our emotive-imaginative accommodation to unprecedented technetronic discoveries, inventions, changes. The poem ostensibly reports on "The Egyptian Pharaohs Speaking about a Moonwalk."[12] Glancing from Amenhotep I to Apollo XI, this

[10] P. E. Siegle, "Education, Automation, and Humanistic Competence," *School and Society,* 1969, 92 (2248), 309–10; and W. W. Brickman and S. Lehrer (Eds.), *Automation, Education and Human Values* (New York: School and Society Books, 1966).
[11] *Saturday Review,* 1965, 48 (5), 16–17; and *To Mix with Time* (New York: Scribner's, 1963), p. 10.
[12] This poem was one of three simultaneously judged first-award

poem has imaginative grandeur and a sense of irony. It traverses vast expanses of time, space, and cultural terrain, juxtaposing the paradoxic extremes. Reading it illustrates what liberal learning may do for competence in the technetronic age. As it describes the wooden lips of the pharaohs moving in terrible hymns of joy and fear for the astronauts, it helps us, by drawing on the traditional, to achieve psychic competence in creatively uniting past, present, and future and in perceptively, emotively, imaginatively becoming acclimated to the radically altered or even utterly new modes of holistic sensibility called for by such an age of drastic change.

Education for human competence in the technetronic age also calls for understanding the dislocations that disturb wholeness and are created deep in man's psyche by technological feats such as those which caused the holocaust at Hiroshima. For such education, we need the combined insights of the whole range of the arts and sciences, as well as of explicitly technological studies. Before we can begin to formulate viable alternatives for attitudes and action, we need to understand the problem intuitively and emotionally as well as rationally—that is, we must grasp it holistically. In an example of such holistic effort, Robert Lifton presents the total psychic impact of massive death on the individual from data gathered through behavioral-social science techniques.[13] Lifton describes the reactions of the people of Hiroshima not only in medical terms but, in his treatment of the symbolism they adopt, as a semanticist and almost as a poet—certainly as a humanist and humanitarian. In his case, at least, the new term for the combined behavioral-social sciences and the conventionally designated humanities seems fitting: the human sciences. Certainly Lifton's study—now expanded into a volume—is a contribution to the fast-growing interdisciplinary literature pertinent to education for competence in a technetronic age.

This education, then, is markedly holistic (from the Greek root meaning whole). Holism is not pictured here as a total systematic philosophy. It does not refer to a doctrinal credo or a

---

winning poems by E. Lane published by Scholastic Magazines, New York, 1970.

[13] "Death and Death Symbolism: The Hiroshima Disaster," *American Scholar, 35* (2), 257–72. See also Lifton's full treatment of this subject in *Death in Life: Survivors of Hiroshima* (New York: Random House, 1967).

dogma. It is used to suggest a general attitude—a way of visualizing problems and approaching their solution, a general intellectual style or habit of mind.

To make clear the use of holistic here, René Dubos' concept of a humanistic biology is useful.[14] In discussing creativity and genius, Dubos states: "Whether it manifests itself by revealing heretofore unrecognized aspects of reality or by making new patterns out of facts already known, creativity often involves the ability to contemplate the world with a holistic and unconditioned attitude." He observes that "the oscillations of physical and mental processes affect all activities of the organism and even the efficacy of therapeutic procedures." He points out that the "orthodox reductionist approach is not suitable for the study of these observances because biological clocks, like the mind, disappear when the organism is dissected into its lifeless component parts." He then affirms: "In fact, the most important problems of life can be recognized only when the organism responds actively to its environment as an integrated unit"—that is, when it responds holistically. In his *So Human an Animal* (which Caryl Haskins has bracketed with Theodosius Dobshansky's 1961 Silliman Lectures at Yale as both carrying "perhaps the most important message of our times")' Dubos provides an extended exposition of the holistic way. A leading laboratory investigator, he sets the holistic approach against the typical, highly fragmented attacks by science on the predicaments of man. Reminding one of Goethe's similar strictures, he scores the belief that increasingly detailed comprehension of special, isolated aspects of the great problems of society, in all their magnitude and complexity, will in itself necessarily lead to wide and deep understanding. He points to the poor judgment in thinking that such infinitely complex and sensitively interacting systems as human societies and cultures can be represented as merely and only the sum of their parts.[15]

Already, people associated with liberal learning are drawing

[14] R. Dubos, "Toward a Humanistic Biology," *American Scholar,* 1965, *34* (2), 188–89, 191–92. (Hereafter referred to as Dubos, "Humanistic Biology.") See also R. Dubos, *So Human an Animal* (New York: Scribner's, 1968).

[15] Summarized by C. D. Haskins, "A Message for Our Times," review of R. Dubos, *So Human an Animal, Virginia Quarterly Review,* 1969, *45* (1), 128–35.

support and sustenance from Dubos' organismic holism. Thus Stanley Burnshaw acknowledges his indebtedness to Dubos for reading the manuscript of the first chapter of his latest volume; the chapter title, taken from John Donne, suggests this holism: "The Body Makes the Minde." In the text, Burnshaw cites Dubos in support of the assertion that "the relationship between somatic and mental processes is recognized as being exactly the same as that among all somatic processes in their single indivisible totality." He reports Dubos as affirming that such words as *mood* and *emotion* "as commonly used cannot possibly refer to attributes located in fragments isolated from the body or associated with special chemical reactions"; "they denote activities of the integrated organism responding as a whole to external or internal stimuli." This view, declares Burnshaw, is "not lofty philosophic humanism but clinical plain talk." By way of reinforcement, Burnshaw cites what Abraham Maslow has called "one of the greatest classics of the century, not only in psychology but also philosophy and biology"—Kurt Goldstein's *The Organism:* "We are always dealing with the activity of the whole organism the effect of which we refer at one time to something called mind, at another to something called body."[16]

When Karl Deutsch proposed studying the comprehensive idea of growth of civilization to bring the sciences and the humanities together,[17] he provided a ruling principle usable in holistic education. When, in the same discussion, the term *accumulation* was defined by one commentator to mean not merely more and more knowledge but specific criteria as to how knowledge fitted together —"a kind of connectivity, as in a knitting pattern"—holistic education was being marked. The following excerpt, from John J. Compton's paper entitled "The Human Meaning of Science" (p. 15), has holistic implications for liberal education.

Recent physical theory, the uses of mathematics in the social sciences, and certain epistemologies of science have led many inter-

[16] S. Burnshaw, *The Seamless Web: Language, Thinking, Creative Knowledge, Art-Experience* (New York: Braziller, 1970), pp. xii, 10–12 (hereafter referred to as Burnshaw, *Seamless Web*); Dubos, "Humanistic Biology," p. 65; and K. Goldstein, *The Organism* (Boston: Beacon, 1963).

[17] This and the following citations are from papers presented at the 1964 conference at the Oak Ridge Institute of Nuclear Studies (now Associated Universities of Oak Ridge), cited in the first footnote of this chapter.

*preters to consider theoretical constructs in science as void of
existential import, functioning largely for prediction or control. . . .
I suggest that it may yet be necessary to construe the aim of science
as an intellectual or philosophical one, namely as the formulation,
however abstract, of the order and dependencies of events in nature.
Continued analysis of the logic of scientific explanations and continued attempts to express the substance of scientific findings in
relation to the world of common experience will be needed in order
to help restore integrity to man's understanding of nature.*

This holistic emphasis (integrity means wholeness as does
health) calls for continuity in the individual's educational process. It
calls for liberal education that is vital—changing, developing, growing, that consists in progressive mastery of the heuristic art of learning how to learn and that, like a sturdy plant, bears fresh fruit, year
after year, through adulthood as well as in youth; that maintains
integrity even while it allows for discontinuities; that exfoliates
through time, so that what was earlier potential, inward, and im-
manent becomes manifest, palpable, and effective in the individual's
personal world.

This holistic vision of liberal learning renders it perpetually
relevant, for, whatever man's ethics or social system, it has to do
with his enduring humanity. It was relevant to the ancient Greeks,
to the Duke of Urbino's universal man of the Renaissance, to the
religious humanism of Desiderius Erasmus and of John Milton, to
the Olympian humanism of Johann von Goethe, to the homespun
Yankee yet universal humanism of Ralph Waldo Emerson or Henry
David Thoreau. It is relevant also to cybernetic man—as is demonstrated by the doctrines of Ludwig von Bertalanffy, Buckminster
Fuller, René Dubos, Lewis Mumford, Lancelot L. Whyte, Geoffrey
Vickers, Edward F. Haskell, Peter Drucker, John R. Platt, and so
many others. Indeed, the holistic habit of thought and imagination
encouraged in those who work in the field of general systems should
make holistic liberal learning particularly compatible in the cybernetic, or technetronic, epoch.

One may ask: What curriculum should be set up to get such
holistic competence through liberal learning? The first requisite is
very practical. The central administration must be committed to

such a program and must be prepared to put its money where its mouth is. The necessary feeling of mutual respect, of freedom and equality, among the members of the faculty is much more likely when it is backed up with this endorsement. The second requisite is to set up an ongoing faculty seminar in which the interplay of minds and sharing of ideas provide a nourishing and constraining matrix within which the teaching program can develop. For the teaching and curriculum I picture it is a practical way to build communication among a faculty. It also provides a base on which to build additional opportunities for faculty education—for example, summer institutes. It is a way to develop group spirit and group competence through tough-minded, substantial study together, as well as through the fellowship of shared commitment.[18]

The curriculum itself should contain at least one basic course dedicated to synthesizing humanistic and other liberalizing studies through a holistic approach. Ideally, there should be one such course for the freshman and another for the senior. Beyond that, there should be intensive, particularized courses handled by men with holistic commitment. The student should not only get the picture of disciplined effort but, as Fred Hechinger has so strongly urged, also be encouraged to push his fist through the specialistic wall, to break through and get a glimpse of the interrelationships, with other fields, that must be recognized on the other side and make for a sense of wholeness.

What is sought here is a general intellectual habit rather than a specific capability. Following this concept requires an inter-disciplinary fellowship of faculty members united in their commitment to stimulate in the student the habit of interdisciplinary transaction and the set toward wholeness. Disciplines are coming together to provide a growing collection of anthologies stressing humanities-science-technology interrelationships. This development points to heightened awareness of the need. To habituate a student to integrative liberal learning for human competence, a college need not wait for the creation of multidisciplinary courses. The main objective is motivating the student toward the habit of wholes. If an instructor has this intellectual bent, his course, no matter what he teaches,

18 See J. Randall, Jr., "The University Seminar as a Source of Spiritual Power," *American Scholar*, 1965, *34* (3), 452–57.

will be directed accordingly, and his students will be correspondingly drawn in the same direction.

Admitted, few—if any—men are trained in all fields. Therefore, how can one teach holistically when he lacks a command of all knowledge? Granted, the model of the universal man of the Renaissance is not a realistic one today; therefore, I postulate an analog of the Renaissance man. He is an individual who, as Norbert Wiener and Deutsch, as Drucker and Bernard Muller-Thym picture him, takes advantage of cybernetic instruments for integrating and visualizing, as a whole, critical selections from large masses of complicated data on complex and wide-ranging phenomena. As William James and Robert Oppenheimer picture him, he quests inductively, upward and outward toward making concrete more and more inclusive configurations of knowledge—operational, not speculative, configurations. Such a comprehensivist, to use Fuller's term, is not that sort of intellectual giant whom Pierre Laplace envisaged as achieving, in one moment, a unified view of universal knowledge; not even Fuller himself is such, and he has been hailed as the reincarnation of the universal man of the Renaissance—a twentieth century Leonardo da Vinci. Not even McLuhan would thus qualify.

It may be suggested that, in liberal learning, the humanities serve not only as a mediator but as a reminder to scientists of what they want to forget, this reminder opening up vistas to the ocean of the whole. The validity of this suggestion is doubtful. The humanistic branches of liberal learning hold no monopoly on sensitivity to the extrascientific dimensions and values of experience; some scientists have demonstrated far greater awareness of these dimensions than some of those who profess the humanistic disciplines. Apparently an increasing number of scientists—among them Harold Cassidy—not only are demonstrating social consciousness and sensitivity but also are saying that science itself can develop, for liberal learning, adequate ethical and esthetic norms and sanctions. They are no longer content with the limited concept of the function of science as ethically disinterested. This new attitude provides an opportunity for science teachers and other teachers to unite. Not long ago, most of the gatherings dedicated to such cooperation seemed to be attended mostly by nonscientists. In recent years, the seminars and institutes in the interarea of science, technology, and the humanities have sometimes had more generous responses from distinguished scientists than from their counterparts in the humanities.

Literary texts contain an increasing amount of social science material, and some maintain that such interdisciplinary mixture inhibits the presentation of literature as an art. This is not necessarily so. A holistic habit of mind—such as May Swenson's—in teaching poetry, for example, helps the student to experience the poem, above all, as an esthetic whole rather than merely to learn its inert contents. This approach enables the student to sense, in literary works, what Alfred North Whitehead calls an architecture of purposes—that is, telic models of wholeness.

❦ FIVE ❦

Ethic-Centered Curricula

The suggested curricular reforms demand—in Sidney French's phrase—the redirection of all undergraduate education. But it is clear from the upheavals on our campuses and in the world-at-large that this redirection will not wait for the deliberate pace of normal institutional administrations. It must take some leaps, which include changes in attitude, and it is this matter of attitude to which I now turn.

As we have been told by Marshall McLuhan, Walter Ong, August Heckscher, Daniel Bell, Robert Theobald, John Kenneth Galbraith, and many others, we have changed so much, we have moved so far, we have already been projected so deep as to seek a new name for the post-industrial age. We have witnessed the invention of the laser, the phenomenal development of the computer and computer systems, and the equally breathtaking development of highly sophisticated machines of production, distribution, communication, and transportation; as well as the instruments of medical, biological, psychological, social, and bureaucratic engineering. The rate of speed-up of this multiple, interrelated change is suggested by a high NASA official's remark that he reads no books more than three years old and nothing on space written more than six months previously. This phenomenal speed-up of change is seen in numeric control—harnessing sophisticated machines to the controlling computer. A new symbiosis and increased efficiency are thus achieved. As we hear of many of the resulting marvels, we wonder what the computer and the laser will do as grown-ups if, as infants, they produce such marvels.

The post-industrial age may come, finally, to be characterized as the nuclear age, the space age, the bionic age; with Donald Michael, Alice Mary Hilton, and others, as the cybernetic age; with Marshall McLuhan, the age of neotribal man; or with Zbigniew Brzezinski, the technetronic age. However characterized, one essential is already clear: For the relevance that might rightfully be demanded of it, liberal learning in this age will have to center on ethical concerns. This essential idea was the theme of a paper I presented at one of the Oak Ridge conferences on science and society. My discussion stemmed from an address by Hyman Rickover, entitled "Toward a Humanistic Technology,"[1] presented at the Georgetown University Anniversary Symposium on the Cybernetic Revolution. Essentially, what Rickover advocated was that the liberal arts provide the future engineer decision makers with the moral education that would help humanize their decisions, technical yet fraught with political and social implications. Currently, Rickover maintained, these decisions showed a barbarous indifference to human values.[2]

I hoped to get a lively response but was not prepared for the explosive reactions that came or for the quarters from which they came. Some seemed directed against me personally for having even mentioned the name of Rickover. According to this reaction, Rickover was no educator and, worse, he was a most irritating person. It did not seem to matter that Rickover had forestalled this criticism

[1] *The American Behavioral Scientist*, 1965, *8* (5), 3–8.
[2] *The New York Times*, October 28, 1965, and the *Des Moines Register*, October 29, 1965, carried stories on Rickover's public speeches. The *Times* summarized his latest complaints against the misuse of science and technology for ends violating human values. (It quoted from a paper he had presented in London, before the British Association for the Advancement of Science.) The article from the *Des Moines Register* summarized Rickover's testimony before a House Appropriations Committee. In this testimony, Rickover showed his customary concern for what he regards as the moral and social shortsightedness and irresponsibility of those of our scientists and technologists who rush too soon from invention and discovery to application.

in what he was reported to have said at Washington hearings. Told by committee members that some of his remarks might not sit well with his colleagues, he said: "I am not engaged in a popularity contest, Sir." It did not seem to matter that the present reactions dodged the question of the intrinsic merits in Rickover's proposal. Further responses revealed where the shoe really pinched: the Admiral's assumption that the responsibility of liberal learning was to deal with character development, especially with the moral training of the future engineer decision makers.

Nor were the scientists and technologists present the detractors of Rickover's thesis, even though professional pride and jurisdictional or disciplinary jealousy might have been expected to draw such objections from such sources. Rather, they were several of the professional humanists. Taking an extreme position, they maintained that to teach the student cognitive and esthetic standards would be acceptable but that to regard the ethical education of the student—his character education—as a responsibility of liberal education was ridiculous.

Liberal learning, as they saw it, was to be effected largely through a process best described in terms of what the participants had been witnessing at the nearby nuclear reactors. What was proposed, in a time of great social and cultural turbulence, was liberal learning by perturbation. According to this pedagogy, the chief function of the instructor is to throw the student off balance by bombarding him with fast-accelerated intellectual particles. These particles are to be shot at him from outside his own customary life field and cultural field. They are psychic particles such as might be emitted from James Joyce's *Ulysses,* Samuel Beckett's *Waiting for Godot,* or Eugene Ionesco's *Bald Soprano.* One might call this the perturbation rationale for liberal learning. It had the merit, at least, of being couched in the idiom and the imagery of the nuclear age. The procedure was to throw the student off balance and then, as he sought to right himself, to continue bombarding him so as to throw him, again and again, off balance. The positive phases of such an educational process consist in the growing stamina and skill the student would gain through these successive attempts at recovering intellectual and esthetic balance. Why this liberal learning by perturbation should stop at the cognitive-intellectual and the esthetic, why it should not concern itself also with the ethical (including the character of wholeness and balance, was not clarified. But the very insistence on ruling out the ethical helped explain the overreaction against Rickover's proposition.

I did not intend then, nor do I now, to hold a brief for Rickover's particular thesis. It is too limited in the range, complexity, and intricacy of modern ethical problems and, hence, too reductionist in the contents and methods of an ethical education suited to preparation for grappling with these problems. In calling for a direct return to the conventional moralities in the heritage, the thesis seems too sentimental and oversimplified. Certain strictures in Rickover's own observations at Washington Committee hearings partially support these strong reservations: "Pious platitudes about honor and leadership constantly emanate from the service academies. . . . They [the academy authorities] impose standards on the youth in their charge which probably they themselves have never met and which are not realistically practicable in the services." Is not Rickover here applying, to the service academies' approach to the moral problems of their students, the criticism to be applied to his own nostalgic approach to the ethical education of his future engineer decision makers? Too reductionist, too naive—too unrealistic. What he proposes, in effect, is advance implanting of moralistic hormone pellets into the psyche of the future engineer-bureaucrat. These pellets are to function at future moments of critical decisions having to do with the welfare of entire populations.

Yet none of these grounds for resistance to Rickover's particular thesis warrant belittlement of the basic issue that he thus brings to the fore: In American colleges and universities at a time of accelerating technological change and powerful drives by technology toward the hegemony of social change, does liberal learning have a particular and explicit responsibility for ethical education?

The Oak Ridge rejectors of Rickover's thesis likewise dismissed the claims to an ethical responsibility in liberal learning made by fellow practitioners—present and absent—of the humanities. They rejected the eulogies of the humanities as ethicizing agents[3]— the praise found, for example, in the Humanities Commission Re-

---

[3] For example, see I. Dilliard's Report on the humanities, in the *American Scholar*, 1965, *34* (2), 274, 290.

port of 1964, in the bills for the establishment of a National Foundation for the Arts and the Humanities, in the statements on behalf of these bills, and in articles commenting on these bills. They rejected the claims for ethical responsibility in liberal learning made by a scholar of such accomplishment and integrity as Douglas Bush, and by so balanced and urbane a scholar-teacher-administrator as William Clyde DeVane. Nor, in this rejection, were they just a few eccentrics.

These rejectors of Rickover's thesis drove home the idea that those in liberal learning should—as they say—either put up or shut up. Once and for all, either they remove from their apologias all claims to ethical responsibilities and functions or they work to discover just what, for the technetronic age, is the nature and the method of the ethical component in liberal learning for which they claim a responsibility. They should also investigate and decide just what should be the relationships between the ethicizing function and the other functions of liberal learning and how they may appropriately bring about these relationships. Some may say that there is nothing new in this stress on the issue of ethical responsibility in liberal learning. Was not Marcus Quintilian's model for the liberally educated person a good man, effectively speaking? And did not this model prevail through the intervening centuries into our own? Yet even if the neoethical education were essentially the same sort as liberal learning has traditionally professed, there would still be the need to consider it anew. In the words of John Stuart Mill: "However unwillingly a person who has a strong opinion may admit the possibility that his opinion may be false, he ought to be moved by the consideration that however true it may be, if it is not fully, frequently, and fearlessly discussed, it will be held as a dead dogma, not a living truth."[4] There is, also, Thomas Carlyle's observation that each generation has to rewrite history in its own idiom.

The New Humanists, under the leadership of Irving Babbitt and Paul Elmer More, afford a case in point. In the late twenties and early thirties, they staged a vigorous campaign to ethicize liberal education, and they received a fair amount of public recognition. They got into the comic strips with a Skippy sequence devoted in a

[4] J. S. Mill, *Utilitarianism, Liberty, and Representative Government* (New York: E. P. Dutton, 1951), p. 26.

genial way to poking fun at their advocacy of the great classics of the East and the West. They got into the national limelight with a public debate, at the Madison Square Garden, on their manifesto. Yet, all in all, they failed to connect. There were several reasons for this failure. As that major interpreter of More and Babbitt, Norman Foerster, acknowledged, one was a failure in idiom; hence a failure of communication; hence lack of persuasion and decisive stimulus to action. As Eric Ashby has observed of classical humanism in our time: if it no longer reaches the bloodstream of society, it is impotent,[5] and no amount of intrinsic validity will make up for this impotence.

Each generation of professors of liberal learning has to clarify and identify its own feeling tone, its own appropriate style, and should become adept in the exercise of this style. This need for continual renewal of style applies to scientists with regard to the advancement of their professional efforts, as well as to artists, musicians, poets, playwrights, and other traditionally labeled practitioners of liberal learning. Conceptualizations, modes of attacking problems, ways of phrasing them, types of procedure, modes of envisioning fruitful fictions, types of analogic formulations vary from decade to decade. The result is that often a given scientific presentation does not get its appropriate hearing because it is stylistically askew. If this matter of renewal of style holds for such allegedly depersonalized and cognitive matters as scientific hypotheses and theories, it applies much more to matters of feeling, emotion, motivation, attitude—which are caught through style as well as by denotative statement.

This updating of the idiom of the ethicizing component of liberal learning is particularly important for this age of advanced technological and social change. For a creative intermeshing (interdigitating is a recent vogue term) we must prevent lack of contact or locking of the gears. Casuistry in the favorable sense, Talmudic

---

[5] See E. Ashby, "Technological Humanism," *Journal of the Institute of Metals,* 1957, Part II; and *Technology and the Academics: An Essay on the Universities and the Scientific Revolution* (New York: St. Martin's, 1963), especially pp. 81–89. For an interesting commentary, see "Technology and the Academies," by D. R. O. Thomas, chief education officer, United Steel Companies, Ltd., in *Technical Education,* March 1959, pp. 30–33. For detailed treatment, see M. H. Goldberg, "The Impact of Technological Change on the Humanities," *The Educational Record,* 1965, *46,* 388–99.

pilpul, Socratic dialogue and dialectic are among the means for fashioning and employing such an idiom of relevance and interrelation.

Changing circumstances call for fresh intermeshings between the heritage and the education we are now called upon to provide through liberal learning. In the past, the sheer abstractness of such concepts as the brotherhood of man, universal social sympathy, universal social responsibility (I am my brother's keeper) made it so hard to turn comprehensive humanitarianism from romanticism to realism, from sentimental and idealistic aspiration to operation. Now, because of the astounding advances of technology, we have cosmic immediacy and cosmic simultaneity of specific experience. In some ways the world has become, physically and neurologically, a neotribal unity, a global village. The immediate image of starving Biafran babies with their swollen bellies and bulging eyes and the image of Vietnamese villagers eating their pitiful dole of rice or dying of wounds come right into our own homes. These people are closely juxtaposed to us, seated at our affluent American tables. Even as we eat, we hear the shots ring out, the moans of the wounded and dying, and the wails of the bereaved. The appeal is direct—to gut reactions.

This immediacy, simultaneity, multisensory appeal and cosmic sweep of emotionally charged sense experience call for a whole rethinking of how we teach for liberal learning and, in particular, of how we teach those aspects which do have a strong socioethical component. While they have the educational virtue of concreteness, both the immediacy and the simultaneity have drawbacks—even dangers. The gut responses carry the threat of overreaction or wrong reaction. Such dramatic vividness may in fact prevent the disinterestedness which, at some stages in liberal learning, is just as important as, at other stages, are empathy and engagement. The immediacy and simultaneity also have the drawback of eventually rendering us callous, through overfrequency of impact, to world hunger, pain, and grief; through triteness, they may cease to provoke any response—except irritation and boredom. This reaction occurs because, while the starving, suffering, grieving, human images have closeness and immediacy, the faces and voices in the crowd remain nameless. There is plenty of liberally educative intermeshing to do here between professed altruistic ideals and aspirations of world brotherhood and the actual functioning of such sentiments within the individual.

The need for awareness of the interrelated functions of liberal education in its ethicizing aspects has other recent and almost daily illustrations. On the *Today* show, Hugh Downs interviewed Norman Vincent Peale, who forthrightly reported how students justified the new sexual morality on the grounds that they were furthering—in depth—their philosophic studies of the Buberian I–Thou relationship or their sociopsychological studies in interpersonal relations. Peale likewise gave the following datum: A student at one of the famous women's colleges in the Northeast had informed an interviewer that a fellow student caught pilfering the refrigerator would be much more liable to censure by her peers than one found fornicating on the divan of their dormitory lounge. Peale then gave recommendations to our morally troubled or disturbed youth. For triteness these bits of wisdom seemed to come right out of Samuel Smiles.

How could Peale's prescription help a teen-ager or a young adult—whether in college or out—trying to come to personal terms not only with the fast-shifting sexual mores of his own subculture but also with such issues as drugs, the hydrogen bomb, Vietnam and Cambodia, civil rights, the cult of absurdity, solipsism, anarchy, and nihilism? One may not favor Gore Vidal's life style, yet his scathing review of David Reuben's best seller *Everything You Always Wanted to Know about Sex But Were Afraid to Ask*[6] would seem to be far more useful than the Pealean truisms. One may not subscribe to the new sex code proposed by the United Presbyterian Church;[7] yet certainly its attempts at realistic grappling with the

---

[6] "Number One," *The New York Review of Books,* 1970, *14* (11), 8, 10, 12–14.

[7] "Sexuality and the Human Community," produced under the direction of J. C. Wynn, Presbyterian pastor and professor at the Colgate-Rochester Divinity School, and proposed as the new sex code for the United Presbyterian Church. (W. Oursler, "Religious Storm Center: the New Sex Code)" *Parade,* May 17, 1970, pp. 10, 23.) See also L. Kinsolving, "Church Battles over Sex," *Pennsylvania Mirror,* July 25, 1970, p. 2; J. Star, "The Presbyterian Debate over Sex," *Look,* August 11, 1970, p. 54; R. Ald, *Sex Off Campus* (New York: Grosset & Dunlap, 1970). Characterizing this issue as "imminently explosive," Ald declares that "off-campus cohabitation has

current problems and issues of sex are likewise far more useful than these same truisms.

What one news story has called "the agony at Berkeley" provides a twofold warning: Liberal learning has not done its due share in the ethicizing job, and it had better smarten up and try to do this job—or else. In part, the Berkeley, Columbia, Harvard, Cornell upheavals and those at scores of other colleges and universities have been warnings of cyclones moving into an ethical vacuum in American higher education. I do not mean that old-fashioned preaching-teaching can fill this vacuum with outright moralistic didactics or pious homiletics. At the college level, especially, liberal learning should sharply discriminate between moralism and ethicism. It should induce fresh ethical dialogue and ethical dialectic. The socratic dialogue is the main instrument of liberal learning. Programs in liberal learning should be developed as cumulative experience in the arts of vicarious ethical probings through sustained and empathetic dialogue.[8]

One of the first tasks here is to clarify the convictions of liberal learning and to discover the best ways of reestablishing and maintaining the dialogue. Furthermore, in this ethicizing phase of liberal learning, we should not neglect the importance of emulation—that is, the emulative teaching that we do as faculty members and administrative officers. Witness the many replications that George Lyman Kittredge engendered in colleges the length and breadth of the land, the myriad Reinhold Niebuhr replications, and those of Stephen Wise. Students soak up the implicit and contextual ethicism, as well as the total reality field of the teacher. If teachers

---

been rendered all the more so by the conspicuous avoidance of a confrontation on the issue by all concerned parties." Observing that ours is a nation whose academic institutions have been founded upon the Puritan ethic, he declares, "The perpetuation of the illusion that the same guiding principles can be imposed upon the present college student generation is a shaky premise. . . ." Hence, the author "reasoned that a book on the subject, with a balanced representation of the forces inherent in the college students' rapid accommodation, would serve a timely and exceedingly valuable purpose." He hoped that it "would siphon off the shock value and preclude a precipitous action" (pp. 8–9).

[8] See V. Comerchero, *Values in Conflict: Christianity, Marxism, Psychoanalysis, Existentialism* (New York: Appleton-Century-Crofts, 1970), especially p. xii. Comerchero's *Values in Conflict* is not to be confused with the earlier *Values in Conflict*, 32d Couchiching Conference.

are ethically indifferent, cynical, skeptical, iconoclastic, so will students be. As Archibald MacLeish noted with chagrin in the forties, if the teachers eat of bitter fruit, their students' teeth will be on edge. (Witness, for example, MacLeish's appeals against the "irresponsibles.")

There is a reluctance on the part of many people inside the system and out, to admit they are working at this ethical liberal learning. In part the reluctance results from a fear of being labeled stuffy—or worse, a prisoner of the protestant ethic. In part it results from a wariness of the harm that good men do, because of the dangers of moralistic fanaticism. We shudder at the risk of becoming Savonarolas. In part it occurs because of a distaste for the stiff-necked or unctuously self-righteous—the *unco guid* of Robert Burns —or because of a recollection that the somberness of Puritan moralism banished joy from Merrie England. In part it stems from a sympathy with the antiphilistine defiance of a Toby Belch retorting to the puritan Malvolio: "Because thou art virtuous, thinkest thou there shall be no more cakes and ale?" Finally, reluctance to confess to making the ethical an explicit factor in one's practice of liberal education results in part from disillusionment, revulsion from the high-sounding moralisms that have preceded, accompanied, and followed the wars—declared and undeclared—of this century—the most violent wars in recorded history.

There is almost a horror reaction to moralism—so high sounding, so naively, irresponsibly, or hypocritically mouthed. This reaction explains why many of the most conscientious and devoted teachers in liberal learning would rather be caught dead than be heard speaking from the heart of ethical matters, let alone make them an explicit function of their teaching. They keep their lips zipped and allow ethicism to appear, if at all, through cryptic asides. Where residual inhibitions from the Joseph McCarthy inquisitions do not still hold, two dominant features of contemporary academic style aid them in avoiding emotion-charged ethical matters in the classroom: The first is the now stereotypic and discredited scientific stance of objectivity. The second, most prevalent in literature departments, is the triumph of the new criticism that in the thirties began to gain ground in academia and eventually won out over those who espoused the conservative ethicism of the new humanists or the social moralism of the liberal or radical Left.

Tact and a tactical sense should mark the teacher who, despite all these deterrents, does explicit ethical teaching. All else in liberal learning should not be rudely twisted so as to fit within a narrow, rigid moral frame. Ethical liberal learning should not guarantee to lead the student, by the time he gets his bachelor's degree, to a full ethical clarification and consolidation. Further, even the best-intentioned practitioners of liberal learning should not impose on their students a definitive, ethical model for judgment and emulation without examination or analysis.

Not long ago, I was with eight or nine other educators, on our way to a meeting. The group discussed such matters as student demonstrations for Vietnam or for the Viet Cong; students' selling stamps for the Viet Cong relief; students' selling blood—for I'm not sure which relief. They also discussed students' tearing up draft cards or burning them and student draft deferments. They expressed personal feelings, sentiments, prejudices, fears, and resentments; resentment, for instance, against those who become perennial students or left the country to dodge the draft.

Why, it was asked, should there be student deferments, anyway? Trained brain workers were in great demand and relatively short supply. So were trained brawn workers; and even if the latter were not in such great demand and short supply, why favor some young American apprentices (for example, graduate students) over other young Americans (for example, plumbers' apprentices)? This favoritism was not democratic. Besides, a year of service in the armed forces was good for any young American. But why waste time and money training new batches of raw recruits? Why not call the veterans back into service? At this idea, there were sharp objections from the veterans present. They'd been through it once. They'd had it.

One of the impromptu symposiasts admitted that, while sound in principle, this concept of parity in drafting—this concept of nondiscrimination—should not apply in certain cases—namely, the speaker's since his son was involved in this very issue and he happened to have a long deferment. He explained that his son's deferment was justified since in his immediate family several members had already been war casualties. So in the son's deferment there was a sort of balancing of accounts. At which point the group observed that this view was not exactly dispassionate, disinterested. They expressed regret that personal feelings had been permitted to intrude. The end result was that this group, anyway, would not come to a definitive conclusion that evening.

This unstructured colloquium is quite pertinent. Here were academics—bound for a national conference on liberal learning— presently involved in teaching the liberal studies. They were discussing some of the very issues about which students the world over are deeply disturbed. Yet they could not discuss these issues altogether in the dry light of reason conventionally associated with the academic mind and its aims. Rather, they discussed these issues activistically—through the iris web of human emotions and passions —and finally they admitted that they would have to leave the discussion open-ended. This admission was far from disappointing. The participants proved to be questing toward appropriate relations among the dictates of reason, the demands of feeling, the pressures of circumstance. As their hidden agenda, they seemed to be searching for some general principles of equity. They proved to be tuned to the ethical function central to liberal learning. They did not press for the one definitive answer to any of the problems. Yet they did try to discuss ethical issues in relation to some general principles which, even at the end, never did quite get articulated. Such ethical concerns (at once old and new) provide the appropriate thrust and direction to liberal learning, and these concerns should have their expressions as integral to the courses themselves.

During the post–Cambodia-Kent weeks of tension in May 1970, and in accordance with newly adopted academic guidelines, the planned units in a Penn State course entitled Technological Change and Personal Dignity were replaced by units on Urgent Issues. Invited to designate what, in their opinion, these issues were, the seventeen students consulted named—impromptu and within a ten-minute period—the following: the U. S. in S. E. Asia (brief history of the war), new Indo-China War (how and why), Campus Problems (politics on campus, role of the university), Race Issues (root causes, history, urbanization), Drugs (why drugs? harmful

versus harmless—how determined? present laws), Environment
(present level of pollution, balance between nature and man, solutions), Religion (the effect of change on its function(s), its organization, its effectiveness; the functions it should perform; its relation
to science), Sex and Revolution (changing sex roles, women's
liberation, *Playboy* philosophy, textbook love, the swingers), Putting
It All Together. The last item under each unit was projections/res-
olutions. One of the first rules adopted was no bull sessioning (the
actual word was much blunter). Another was no monopoly by
either extreme along the spectrum of polarization of opinion. There
was also a decision for genuine dialogue, and voluntary informed
working papers. Immediately, there were four volunteers for such
papers. In the sessions that followed, the volunteers made good.
Most gratifyingly, they spontaneously linked the immediate urgencies they discussed with the more permanently relevant, general
principles that developed during the preceding weeks of the course.
The success of the course suggests what the faculty should bear in
mind as they now seek to have liberal learning contribute to education for competence in a technetronic age.

In class and through ongoing faculty seminars figured into
service load, more educators should contribute to the development of
techniques in liberal learning at least a portion of the ingenuity,
inventiveness, and drive they have displayed for the pursuit of
knowledge as an end in itself or of art for art's sake, to make friends
and to interact with people, to gain wealth and power, or as a more
or less refined intellectual game or pastime.

Elizabeth Monroe Drews' *Policy Implications of a Hierarchy
of Values* presents the heightened neoethical concern in higher education and hence in liberal learning. This concern is a telic, holistic,
universal ethicism. True, the severe critic of this study might find
that Drews tends to dismiss arbitrarily value norms (such as the
relativistic ones) which she considers undesirable or repellent, and
she correspondingly tends to affirm tautologically her preferred sentimental humanitarianism blended with neomysticism and psyche-
delics (a sort of afterglow of the enlightenment and romantic
revival). But, even if it were warranted, such critical reaction would
be beside the point. Here the mind set is important: "This is an
inquiry into values, into their sources and meanings and their rele-

vance to Man. In the deepest sense, the inquiry is about Man himself. What is Man? That is the perennial question which every generation has asked anew. The answer we are suggesting is this: 'Man is what he values. By his values, thoughts, you shall know him.' " (Compare this view with John Ruskin's: "Tell me what a man likes, and I will tell you what he is.") Yet while both the key question and the answer constantly recur, they are immersed in the churning present-future with which we are forced to cope. For collaborative support, we often resort not only to the greats of the heritage but, very often, to present thinkers and writers—more or less authoritative—who demonstrate in their own work such a creative ability to cope with an increasingly futurized present. In short, Drews' ethically charged efforts are her response to the crucial questions put to her by the forerunners—perhaps half of the intellectually superior young people in the 1960s, those who at the beginning of the decade "were already muttering about the meaninglessness of much that was being taught in the schools."[9]

The opening issue of the *CEA Forum* provides an indication of the revived ethicism—a tragic ethicism—in liberal learning. In this issue Princeton Chaplain John H. Snow is approvingly cited when he observes that perhaps "our greatest failure is our failure to communicate to the young the most important value of western Judeo-Christian society: the tragic sense of life," which consists in "the knowledge that the best-intentioned, most dedicated and loving people can make the most dreadful mistakes and suffer the most terrible consequences." The gravity of this failure, which is extended to include the humanities themselves, is further emphasized by Snow: Out of this "sense of the tragic come all compassion, all agreement to negotiate, compromise, communicate, and accept a pluralistic society."[10]

A *Program Description and Course List: 1970–1971* for the Cornell Program in Science, Technology, and Society has come to my desk. This program is interdisciplinary and draws its students,

[9] Drews, *Policy Implications*, p. iii.
[10] D. A. Sears, "The Failure of the Humanities," *CEA Forum,* 1970, *1* (1), 13, citing *Today's Youth and Moral Values* (Preliminary Conferences for the 1970 White House Conference on Children and Youth, April 22–24, 1969), Academy of Religion and Mental Health, 1970, p. 59.

faculty, and research workers from all areas of the university. It includes the physical and biological sciences, the social sciences, and the humanities, as well as engineering, business and public administration. A joint fellowship has been arranged between the program and the Study for Humanities, which will bring a visiting scholar to Cornell to work on some aspect of the relation between science and technology and humanistic concerns (pp. 1, 3).

Several years ago, I received, from the Division of Engineering at San Jose State College, a brochure for a new course called Cybernation and Man. The course claimed to be the first of its kind in the country. It sought to encourage engineering faculty to project more forcefully the concept that engineering curricula should be liberalizing and not confined or restricted to nuts-and-bolts courses; hence, that engineering should provide a valid foundation for specialization in other disciplines. Granted U. S. Office of Education support, this course, under the direction of Ralph Parkman, has become an institutionwide elective in general education and has served as a model for similar courses set up in Hawaii and elsewhere. Moreover, its developers have been running intercollegiate summer institutes where the philosophy and method of their course may be studied and tried out and where alternative models may be developed. Parkman has received support for a sabbatical leave to complete a book, making widely available the fruits of his own experiences in developing the course Cybernation and Man. Thus, as in ecological programs, people outside the disciplines traditionally associated with liberal learning are moving increasingly into this area of socioethical emphasis in college courses. A chemist, Harold G. Cassidy, has written an essay on liberal education, *Knowledge, Experience and Action,* which points to "the interacting consequences and responsibilities of scientists and humanists" and which "reminds us of the ethical principles that emerge when the Humanities, Sciences, Technologies, and Philosophies are brought together in a connected whole."[11]

In both the Cornell and the San Jose programs, as well as in the Cassidy treatise, there are lessons for those in liberal learning.

[11] Cited from publisher's (Teachers' College Press) description of this book in *School and Society,* 1969, *97* (2321), 469.

If educators in liberal learning do not freshly ethicize their own teaching, others in other branches of higher education will do so and with emphases and outcomes—unlike those of the San Jose experiment or the Cassidy book—quite at variance from what we might choose.

◈ SIX ◈

Liberal Learning for Life

George Bernard Shaw once observed that "education is not confined to children; in fact liberal education is mostly adult education and goes on all through life in people who have active minds instead of second-hand habits."[1] Shaw thus anticipated a pervasive theme of this book. Thus far, we have purposely maintained the inclusive view of liberal learning as life long. Let us now sharpen our focus to concentrate upon the conventionally designated "adult" students. We come immediately face to face with the problem of assuring equal opportunity in continuing liberal learning for adults.

LOGISTICS AND DYNAMICS

In the United States, the phrase *equality of opportunity* brings to mind one of two pictures. The first is entirely in the economic realm. It depicts someone deprived of an opportunity to continue his education because he lacks money to pay fees or is not able to find a replacement for his job position while he takes the course. This inequality results from immediate economic lack.

The second picture—the one usually depicted by champions of democratization of higher education—shows a chronic and

[1] G. B. Shaw, *Everybody's Political What's What?* (New York: Dodd, Mead, 1944), pp. 69–70.

81

cumulative condition to which the individual has been subjected all his life in the culture of poverty. It may have been the persistent condition, too, of his parents before him and of their parents, for several generations back. In this case, the economic factor turns out to be merely one cause of pervasive inequality. It is the symptom of total social and cultural inequality. The term *cultural deprivation* is given to this composite, complex situation.

Those in the developing sectors of higher education are being called, more and more insistently, to the vast problem of inequality through cultural deprivation. Confronting this problem is like trying to wrestle with an octopus. Swelling tides of public funds for meeting this responsibility have made it all the harder. To apply these funds constructively, we have needed rationales worked out and policies defined; nontraditional—even antitraditional—programs contrived; and, above all, adequate, devoted, technically competent staff provided. We have needed instant programs and instant personnel.

In light of highly publicized demands for correcting inequalities of economic, social, and cultural deprivation within the affluent United States and among the poor who exist (we cannot say *live*) in Michael Harrington's *Other America,* those charged with responsibility for higher education often feel hard pressed. They face numerous restraints which limit the fulfillment of the imperative for equal opportunity. There is the scarcity of devoted and expert personnel. For the purposes of higher education, particularly for programs in liberal learning for the culturally deprived, just any teacher will not do. Although the criteria for quality in courses in liberal learning are often not so technically exacting as those which train for specific professional tasks, there are, nonetheless, numerous restrictions imposed in the name of academic standards.

In addition there is the matter of strategic conservation of personnel and professional energies. At the moment, especially because exhortations to equalize opportunities for the culturally deprived are so pressing, we are in danger of having our resources dissipated by allowing them to flow outward too fast, to spread too thin, from the academic sector to the community-at-large. Trying to be all things to all people, we are likely to become nothing to anyone. Moreover, to the degree we successfully mobilize, for the "other Americans," our limited resources of energy and vitality, personnel and profession, we are likely to neglect other responsibilities toward higher education.

Scanning our educational situation will show types of cultural deprivation other than the socioeconomic. An example is found in the individual who, from childhood, instead of being liberally educated as a whole individual, has been shaped on the machine of modern specialism. Such a person may be chronologically an adult; he may have achieved success as a specialist. Yet so far as full adulthood is concerned, he may be a poor fragment of a self. When, bitterly or sadly, he begins to feel that he is so diminished and so deformed, he is likely to turn to higher education to help him make up the years of cultural and psychic deprivation. He, too, needs our enthusiasm and energies to help him become a whole person.

Continuing education has a duty to such deprived persons. To fulfill this duty, we must at times resist the importunate demands to throw ourselves unstintingly into the battle waged for equal opportunity for the dwellers in slums and ghettos. Consider, for example, the engineer who has a fifteen-year professional lifetime. Unless he continuously refurbishes his knowledge with the new and fast-changing data in his field, he will soon find himself obsolete and jobless. The same holds true for the civically deprived—those laymen who suddenly, as adults, find themselves charged with social responsibilities that demand the best-informed thinking they can muster and who turn to continuing liberal learning to help make up their cumulative deficiencies.

Here, then, we have a master dilemma which confronts continuing liberal learning in the United States. If we yield to the strident demands to pour our resources—inadequate at best—into direct education for the multitude of poor, we run the risk of neglecting other types of deprived adults, among them scores of professional people and laymen facing the task of civic leadership. If we insist on paying appropriate attention to the latter types of culturally deprived, then we are likely to appear self-centered, antidemocratic, snobbish—and in a bad sense, élitist. The acuteness of this dilemma is seen precisely in the flow of noncredit programs in liberal learning from formal institutions of higher education to other institutions: churches, corporations, profit-making enterprises (such as the *Encyclopedia Britannica*), clubs (the Book-of-the-Month Club), cultural establishments (the Metropolitan Museum of Fine Arts), and so on.[2]

What should be done about this dilemma? I am in basic agreement with the demands of both types of deprived adults, and in sympathy for both I offer one suggestion called the spectrum concept. According to this concept, one seeks to provide, through college- or university-related liberal learning, a basic set of educating experiences which are meaningful in different ways to different groups. One sees in how many different ways he can exploit the potentials of a given program in liberal learning. From a unifying center he seeks the maximum number of multipliers.

A good composite illustration may be drawn from our experience in a project of the Center for Continuing Liberal Education (CCLE) in the College of Liberal Arts at Penn State. This is the CCLE–IBM Humanities Project on Technological Change and Human Values. The project has produced at least four different informal, nondegree programs of liberal learning: 1. A three-day consultation in which participants (academic leaders or leaders in the world of business and public affairs) educated one another and helped lay the basis of future liberal learning for many others (a kind of self-fueling process of adult higher education), with the theme the impact, in terms of human values, of institutional and organizational bigness on the individual. 2. A three-day conference on technological change and human values, in which about two hundred participants (again, drawn from leadership levels within and outside Pennsylvania) developed motifs uncovered in the first consultation, clarified terms and problems, and dramatized issues. 3. A three-day seminar (six months later), much more intensive than the conference, devoted to the theme work, leisure, and education in a changing industrialized democracy, with some participants from the preceding conference and with newcomers, chiefly professional experts. 4. A number of programs, not conducted at University Park but in other parts of Pennsylvania, designed not so much to explore new ground as to apply, to different circumstances and

    [2] See M. H. Goldberg, "Continuing Education for the Professions," to appear in *Convergence, An International Journal of Adult Education,* J. R. Kidd (Ed.), Toronto, Canada.

for different groups, what had already been brought out in the preceding sessions.

This last set of programs varied from converted bridge-club gatherings to large groups involving lay and professional leaders drawn from entire regions. There were the three-day discussion programs sponsored in Sharon, Pennsylvania (for the Shenango Valley Area), communitywide forums drawing several hundred participants, and the four-day conference on the broad theme Can Man Survive? which was held in Pittsburgh and co-sponsored by the Public Affairs Committee of the Greater Pittsburgh YWCA. This conference involved three hundred lay and professional community leaders in a three-state, five-county area, and was keynoted by August Hecksher, with John Coleman as chairman of the opening session. Other gatherings that added increments of liberal learning to the CCLE–IBM Humanities Project involved professional groups: the faculty of a large high school; the faculty of an entire school district; several hundred members of the Department of Supervision and Curriculum Development of the Pennsylvania Education Association; members of another professional society, the Pennsylvania Library Association, gathered for their annual conference; members of still another, the Pennsylvania College English Association; and alumni of Annual Summer Penn State Steelworkers' Institutes.

In each of these instances, general ideas gleaned from the opening consultation, the first conference, and the intensive seminar were brought to bear, in cumulative continuity, on the particular concerns of the communal or professional group, as is illustrated by themes of the gatherings: Technological Change and Community Values (Shenango Valley Annual Forum); In the Name of Man: The Implications of Technological Change and Human Values (Pittsburgh); Technological and Social Change, Human Values and the Library (Pennsylvania Library Association); Technological Change, Human Values, and Educational Change (Pennsylvania Education Association, Department of Supervision and Curriculum Development); Automation, Human Values, and the Steelworkers (United Steelworkers Alumni Institutes); Technological Change, Human Values, and the Profession of English (Pennsylvania College English Association).

Such projects were interrelated ventures in liberal learning.

Not only was the chain effect a result of a continuous flow of energy and experience from program to program, but also the papers were put into permanent form—for example, into symposia (one appeared in *School and Society*) and then into a volume (*Automation, Education and Human Values*). Later, the wheel of development turned full cycle. A twelve-session adult study-discussion program called Technological Change and Human Dignity[3] was produced. Through mass media, the educational reach of the CCLE–IBM Humanities Project was extended from top leadership levels to the housewife and the man on the street. The work of such projects is one way of resolving the master dilemma, serving both those disadvantaged by cultural deprivation and those by specialistic deprivation. The approach includes the housewife who wants to be lifted out of the rat race of children, kitchen, and church (to which Dr. Spock has recently been recalling her but from which Women's Lib has stridently been seeking to free her) and who wants to be given a second chance at higher education in self-maturation.

The second method of attenuating the acuteness of the master dilemma is likewise exemplified by the Center for Continuing Liberal Education. In the face of fast-increasing demands, the Center has adopted the policy of restraint through selectivity—that is, of concentrative unification. Because of limited resources, this action has required the courage to say no, and the stamina to stand by the refusal. For those in the public sectors of American higher education, the systematic application of such a principle of restraint, selectivity, and concentration is difficult. Historically, and especially since the Land Grant College Act, public institutions of higher education have responded quickly and directly to community requests for immediate educational and technical services. These responses have been prompted partly by altruism, partly by enlightened institutional self-interest. In recent years, among the already powerful pressures exerted by the community, there has been a new factor,

---

[3] "Automation's Challenge to Education and Human Values," *School and Society*, 1969, 92 (2248), 303–18; *Automation, Education and Human Values*, W. W. Brickman and S. Lehrer (Eds.); *Technological Change and Human Dignity*, M. H. Goldberg (Ed.) (University Park, Pa.: The Center for Continuing Liberal Education, 1966). See also *Needles, Burrs, and Bibliographies*, Study Resources: Technological Change, Human Values, and the Humanities, *ibid.*, 1969.

implied in Lyndon Johnson's Message to Congress, January 17, 1965: "The role of the university must extend far beyond the ordinary extension-type operation. Its research findings and talents must be made available to the community. Faculty must be called upon for consulting activities. Pilot projects, seminars, conferences, television programs, and task forces drawing on many departments of the university—all should be brought into play." As we moved into what Frank Bowles described as an epoch of phenomenal democratization of higher education in the United States, this development was highly lauded. Yet it rendered our master dilemma more acute. Higher education was not prepared. In his message to Congress, Johnson took cognizance of the gap: "This is a demanding assignment for the universities and many are not now ready for it."

The problem is now even more acute, and it does not seem likely that in the next several years federal funds will do much to loosen the bind. There have been promises; nevertheless, there are doubts that significant proportions of these funds will go directly into equalizing opportunities in higher education for adults. There are even more serious doubts about sizable funds going into the customarily slighted sector of higher education—namely, liberal learning for adults. In the face of all these pressures—direct and indirect —it is not easy to resist the tendency to dissolve into ineffectual do-goodism. If we are unable to resist this tendency, if we try to become all things to all men, then we will have betrayed our trust. Yet we can prevent this betrayal by resisting demands to set up basic education programs for the masses of socioeconomically deprived or requests to take part in such programs (except on our own, as individuals). In this policy of restraint and selectivity, we seem to be running against the tide; we seem to resist direct mass-service policies emanating from political leaders and from our own academic administration; we seem to be antisocial, to run counter to the momentum of traditional American idealism, to be callous to many demands from the community and from student activists on campus, vociferously, even violently, pushing these demands.

In fact, this policy of restraint, selectivity, and concentration yields increase rather than diminution of appropriate services to the culturally disadvantaged. This point is illustrated by another CCLE project—one directly related to a disadvantaged group, the blind. In addition to academic representatives of disciplines in arts and sciences, participants were professionals in working with the blind. Although involved not with the disadvantaged themselves but with those who play responsible leadership roles, far greater ultimate benefits to the blind were provided for—both in our country and, through the published Proceedings, abroad.[4]

In coping with the problem of equalizing opportunity for adult liberal learning, we are fast reaching the crisis stage. To weather this crisis successfully, we must at times seem to move counter to various massive pressures and demands. For the greater good, we must resist many of the urgent calls that come to us, advocating that we plunge into all sorts of unevaluated activities in all sorts of ways. This resistance is the paradox in our stand that while we are against mass education, we are for education of the masses.

SENSITIVITY PROGRAMS

One of the most urgent pressures upon administrators responsible for adult education today—a pressure to which many respond —is for encounter groups, formalized in the Human Potential movement. Anyone surveying the area of continuing liberal studies cannot help noting, in the middle of the scene and outward toward the periphery, the streams labeled sensitivity training. Under this one appealing label, we have a mixed bag. On the one hand, through their multimedia outlets, there is the emphasis on sensitivity by such publicists as George Leonard, senior Editor of *Look*, vice-president of Esalen, and author of *Education and Ecstasy*. This sort of emphasis has been closely connected with the whole rebirth of romantic, nature sentimentalism. It consists in a rejection of the life of reason and common sense in favor of the life of sheer sensation and sheer emotions. It is an extreme reaction to an opposite extreme: the abuse of reason when it is forced into service with so many dehumanizing agencies, instrumentalities, and processes in a technetronic age. Characteristically, it invites us to blow our minds and to

---

[4] See M. H. Goldberg (Ed.), *Blindness Research, The Expanding Frontiers: A Liberal Studies Perspective* (University Park, Pa.: Pennsylvania State University Press, 1969).

regain the claimed pristine innocence, spontaneity, and joy of childhood.

Yet, as Max Birnbaum soundly points out,[5] the Esalen
enthusiasts, the advocates of the Synanon sensitivity games, the
apostles of liberal learning as ecstasy have tardily made the sensitivity scene. They arrive about two decades after Leland Bradford
first pulled the opening curtain on what was to become the nerve
center of his movement—the National Training Laboratory at
Bethel, Maine. In this movement, actually, a great amount of rationalism is involved. In almost every phase of the program, systematic analysis, implication, extrapolations are rationally developed.
Indeed, at the heart of the operation is the paradox that reason is
used to expose the nonrational forces that make up the underlying
behavior dynamics of the group. The assumption is that, by coming
to understand these dynamics, through actual stress experiences
and self-exposure, one is then better able, rationally, to handle his
own future personal growth and his relationships with others and
in groups or as administrator (manager, bureaucrat, boss) to handle
organizational problems and challenges. Thus, in their concern with
bringing to the surface the extrarational features of human behavior,
the Esalen and the Bethel sensitivity programs share a common de-
nominator.

Yet there are also some very important uncommon denom-
inators. The end goal, the telic model, of the first type of sensitivity
emphasis is the primitive wholeness of the Rousseauvian nature boy
set free from bondage to usefulness and the practical life. The end
goal of the second type is the well-formed wholeness of better functioning teacher, manager, administrator, bureaucrat—achieved by
improving his skill in manipulating others to achieve the practical
ends he wants. The one professes to be concerned, personally, with
psychic prophylaxis, therapy, or strength-through-joy outside the
world of usefulness. Some say this end goal will be a new religion.[6]

[5] M. Birnbaum, "Sense about Sensitivity Training," *Saturday Review*, November 15, 1969, pp. 82–83, 96–98. For a number of useful
comments, see *ibid.*, December 20, 1969, pp. 50, 71.

[6] The CBS News Report of June 29, 1970, featured an interview
with the leaders of the Unity religious group at Unity, Missouri. One of
these leaders told of Esalen-type sensitivity programs, which his church

The other professes to be concerned, primarily, with more efficient functioning in the plant, the office, the school, the institution, the organization, the forum, the marketplace. At times, of course, the two tendencies may intersect. The sensitivity-ecstasy program may be sold as one that sends the participant—refreshed, invigorated, and made newly whole—back into the utilitarian world where he functions all the more effectively for his strength-through-joy extra-curriculum experiences.

So may books reporting such programs be sold. In an advertisement for such a book,[7] we are told, below a picture of the beaming authoress, that this "charming, blue-eyed, clean-cut, all-American girl reporter from the middle west shed her inhibitions (and once or twice her clothes) to bring back alive the first, complete eyewitness account of the human potential movement." She was "sent by *Life* to witness the Esalen phenomenon. She ended covering (and uncovering) a wide sampling of encounter groups from Synanon to religious retreats, from T groups run by the National Training Laboratories Institute to Bioenergetic groups and a nude weekend in a 'womb pool.' " The book is recommended "for those of us who are desperately curious about instant intimacy but too shy to find out for ourselves."

It is, therefore, not surprising that in approaching university administrators potential clienteles for continuing liberal learning programs show considerable ambiguity or even confusion in the requests they make for sensitivity components. What may be excusable in the client, however, is not excusable in the university administrator. He should be clearly aware of the two major tendencies— at times toward unity, at other times toward direct conflict—in so-called sensitivity programs, and he should be able intelligently to

sponsors for both youngsters and adults. He went on to say that this sort of sensitivity emphasis might some day be a new religion (Chief CBS reporter Roger Mudd).

    [7] J. Howard, *Please Touch: A Guided Tour of the Human Potential Movement* (New York: McGraw-Hill, 1970), *New York Times Book Review*, June 14, 1970, p. 14. On the *Tonight* television program (October 14, 1970), Howard acknowledged that the "human potential movement" held something useful for the participant—increased self-knowledge and self-confidence —but she likewise observed that sometimes the exercises could be ridiculous, that for some it was merely an opportunity to play God for a week-end, and that there was "a lot of garbage in it."

guide his potential clienteles in their search. He should know well the potentials for personal, professional, and social wholeness in each of these tendencies or in their combination.

In part the uncritical mixing of these two modes of sensitivity education has led to much of the current shying away from the whole sensitivity kick. Because of this confusion, program projectors or promoters often indulge in double-talk. Conflicting or false expectations are set up in the prospective clients; then comes frustration and resentment during the program and disappointment at the end. Often the confusion signaled by the initial double-talk asserts itself destructively in the program itself.

It is tempting to try to pin on to various Rightist reactionaries[8] the rising negativism toward sensitivity programs. This scapegoatism is convenient but often erroneous. Such negativism is often expressed, rather, by responsible, open-minded professionals in human relations and continuing education. Their negative responses are prompted by concern about the adverse effects of the sorts of melange and confusions previously described.

When he seeks, objectively, to appraise the worth and relevance of a proposed sensitivity program, the university administrator should not be intimidated by such name calling as neanderthal, puritan, victorian, square, reactionary. He should note that recently such programs have been dropped altogether from university extension programs and from the in-service training programs of major corporations—and not because of reactionary prejudice or narrow ethico-ideological reasons.[9] Birnbaum reports that there are "many

---

[8] See Birnbaum, *ibid.,* p. 82.

[9] In her "Sensitivity Training and the Humanities Teacher," M. Rutherford seems to be unaware of this counterturn. ("New Symbols in Old Spaces," The 1969 NCTE Humanities Conference Highlights, pp. 12–13.) On the basis of their studies, D. Olch and D. L. Snow "challenge the common assumption that sensitivity groups are composed of well-adjusted people who will function even more successfully through group involvement." (*Behavior Today,* 1970, *1* (14), 4.) All the more need, then, for responsible post-training program follow-up! A session at the 1970 annual convention of the American Psychological Association and the Association of Humanistic Psychology discussed "the value systems and legitimacy of sensitivity training." It is significant that in an effort at responsible self-policing and professional advancement, sensitivity and human potentials people are getting together in a national organization. As such an organization gains strength and authoritative power, it will no doubt exhibit, from the point of view of the

tales, some maliciously embellished but many all too true, of school systems and communities where bad situations have been made worse by the unintelligent application of inappropriate forms of sensitivity training."

The university administrator should heed Birnbaum's observation that, far from making for personal and social wholeness, encounter groups or confrontation sessions between blacks and whites in the same school or community may lead to problems. Birnbaum acknowledges that in the past such sessions have sometimes had "useful shock value in revealing quickly the crucial problems that are polarizing the races today" and that they may lead to follow-up plans for action and changes. He notes, however, that unfortunately too often difficulty arises as a result of "routine application of what are basically gimmicks to an involved and highly charged area."[10]

Birnbaum observes further that "even at its most effective, the encounter session is a shocking and bruising experience." Indeed, where the participants are co-workers, the revelations of intimate personal information may be "so highly charged that it makes continuing work relationships very difficult, if not impossible." The same holds for nonverbal exercises. Birnbaum cites a recent case at a conference of foundation executives: "The initially surprised and then outraged participants displayed an enormous amount of openness—all of it hostile—toward both the trainer and the conference sponsors." He points out that both types of sensitivity training—the nonverbal experience and the confrontation session—are "particularly susceptible today to exploitation by the enthusiastic amateur or the enterprising entrepreneurs."

There is another sort of danger, too, in these sensitivity programs; it applies to both the sensitivity-ecstasy tendency and the sensitivity-utility tendency. Either may become the agency or the intermediate stage for coercive control. In fact, some people maintain that the whole sensitivity movement has been boosted by those seeking, however benevolently, to impose drastic and pervasive change in the interest of authoritarian control—mind control, consumer control, sociopolitical control. As Birnbaum declares: "The

client and that of the nonaffiliated practitioner, both the beneficial and the negative features of a guild.

[10] Birnbaum, *ibid.*, p. 96.

devilish reductivity of human-relations training stems from the fact that it can reduce individual resistance to change more effectively than any other known means."

All in all, it behooves university administrators and faculty to bear in mind Birnbaum's warning: "The most serious threat to sensitivity training comes first from its enthusiastic but frequently unsophisticated supporters and second from a host of newly hatched trainers, long on enthusiasm or entrepreneurial expertise but short on professional experience, skill, and wisdom." It should be added that they are also short on the enduring sense of responsibility for each trainee, beyond the sessions. This deficiency will exist until there is unqualified assurance that the trainee has adjusted fully in the home situation as well as in the group session.

The sensationalism and radical irrationalism of the sensitivity ecstatics are aptly described in Voltaire's statement to Rousseau when Rousseau invited him to accept his own nature-sentimentalism and to return to "the natural conditions as seen in savages and animals": "I have received, Sir, your new book against the human species, and I thank you for it. . . . No one has been so witty as you in turning us into brutes; to read your book makes one long to go on all fours. As, however, it is now some sixty years since I gave up the practice, I feel that it is unfortunately impossible for me to resume it."[11]

Certainly, so far as liberal learning is concerned, the human potential movement raises serious doubts as to its contributions—present or future—to the advancement of the participants toward personal wholeness and human dignity. It would be ironic if a movement dedicated to the furthering of human potential should contribute to personal and societal dehumanization.

PLANNING AND DYNAMICS

The discussion of unity, continuity, and centrality in liberal learning for adults has stressed the immediate problems that face university faculty and administrators and the dilemmas that arise out of current conditions for the university officers who make the policies governing the programs of continuing education. But this discussion has covered only one aspect of the subject. Once we

[11] Quoted in *Thought and Expression*, G. C. Clancy (Ed.) (New York: Harcourt, 1928).

practice constructive selectivity, concentration, and adaptive repli-
cation, our next step is to plan positively for wholeness in continuing
liberal studies. This positive approach is related in turn to the need
for institutional wholeness and consequently for collaborative coherence among the parts. Among other things the results of such an
approach are professional parity for faculty in continuing liberal
studies and academic parity for programs in continuing liberal
studies; for without parity the chance for wholeness is remote.

A crucial problem ahead is the education of the growing
number of mature adults in the United States who want and need
additional formal study and who will demand that colleges and
universities meet this need. To meet this problem, the college or
university administration must be committed to a radical reorientation of policy, program, and, above all, budget and personnel. From
the academic point of view, a radical reorientation is necessary also,
so that the competent or, hopefully, gifted teacher-scholar who
chooses to make his career in continuing liberal education of the adult
will be appropriately esteemed and rewarded. He will be seen as
rendering a professional service as meritorious as that of his colleagues putting their efforts into the conventionally esteemed sectors
of teaching and scholarship.

From the combined administrative-teaching point of view,
such a radical reorientation calls for raises, promotions, and fringe
benefits, which will assure the competent scholar-teacher of adults
parity in career development and parity with the scholar-teacher of
the highly regarded sectors. This reorientation does not mean a guar-
anteed favorable career—regardless of intrinsic merit—just by virtue
of willingness to give time to the education of adults. It does not
mean giving such an individual special protection or special bonuses.
Such special treatment would be detrimental to both the quality of
the education provided and the winning of esteem with academic
colleagues in the longer established sectors. Rather, the problem and
the challenge are to furnish optimum conditions at this enormously
difficult educational frontier and to include opportunities for bringing into graduate courses and programs, numerous young men and
women of promise as teacher-scholars in the adult sectors of American higher education. These opportunities are all the more important
since, so far as appropriately trained and committed teachers are

concerned, the fast-expanding areas of university education for adults are in sore need of both trained scholar-teachers and new recruits. In the solution of the problems of recruitment and retention, we must strengthen our competitive advantage in the academic marketplace. We must stress both the more tangible incentives for enlisting and remaining in this sector and the less tangible incentives, including those of recognition and esteem by academic peers and by administration.

In "The Expectations of Society for Higher Education,"[12] Frank H. Bowles highlighted the dilemma which makes it so difficult to win at least parity of status, esteem, and support for the humanizing components of the adult sector of American higher education. In its most general terms, Bowles presented this dilemma when he observed that Americans think they can at the same time grow intellectually (which implies rather severe academic criteria of professional accomplishment and acceptability) and socially (which, as Bowles elaborated, implies a rather low and broad-gauge criterion of scholarly accomplishment and acceptability). Further, he predicted that, as part of the egalitarian thrust toward democratization of education, new colleges would be established at the rate of one a day and that in such colleges we would witness a strong shift from cultural subjects to broad-gauge vocational subjects serving the needs of broad masses of people. At the same time, however, Bowles declared that never had the elitist academic disciplines, the graduate schools, the professional scholars and their guilds enjoyed such great national esteem; never had their power and their prestige been greater.

Despite current constrictions the situation today is still pretty much as Bowles described it. Those in higher education who are charged with liberally educating the adult are thus confronted with a dilemma that is to be resolved, if at all, with the greatest difficulty. To meet the increasingly heavy charge placed upon them for the democratization of higher education of the adult, they must often put their main efforts into devising programs at variance with the

[12] F. H. Bowles, "The Dual Purpose of Higher Education," *Current Issues in Higher Education*, G. K. Smith (Ed.) (Washington, D.C.: American Association for Higher Education, 1966), pp. 17–23. (Hereafter cited as Bowles, "The Dual Purpose.")

conventional criteria that make for scholarly prestige in academia. At the same time, the conventional scholarly criteria for acceptance, status, and prestige have recently achieved fresh authority and restrictive power and make it all the more difficult for the teacher-scholar, working with adults in our colleges and universities, to gain the parity of recognition and rewards helpful for collaborative unity and coherence among the various constituents of these institutions.

Hence, at all levels of academic leadership, we need radical conversions for those in the adult sector of liberal education. We need various authoritative groups—from boards of trustees, presidents and deans, to department heads—who will display parity of recognition, reward, and esteem. We need such full-hearted appreciation and backing from those colleagues who prefer to remain in the high-esteem sectors. Unless we get this backing, we are limited to institutional unbalance and disunity—to lack of wholeness—and we may have to see the higher education of adults taken over, increasingly, by agencies outside the colleges and universities. Such an outcome would mean that higher education had seriously defaulted in its responsibilities to the adult[13] and hence to its imperative for wholeness of liberal learning.

At least two compromise proposals seem worth consideration. The first is that new colleges for adults be established—either within a given university or as autonomous institutions. These colleges would then have the scope to realize their own new and distinctive wholeness. The second is that in their efforts for continuing liberal education the colleges and universities define their distinctive role as that of fostering high-level consultations and colloquies between leading scholars and leading men of affairs (industrial executives, government officials, and so on). This sort of program appeals to those scholars who, already in well-established sectors, feel the need of such extramural exchange both for the advancement of their own studies and researches and for the increase of their own scholarly stature.

The dilemma of those seeking to reduce the gap in higher education between responsibilities and realistic expectations for collaborative unity and wholeness applies not to the training but to the

[13] See footnote 2.

liberalizing programs for adults. In great part the reason is that the fiscal gap between responsibilities and realizable expectations will be closed—or at least significantly narrowed—sooner along the lines of training than along the lines of liberalizing programs.

Sensitive to the voice of the people upon whom their institutions ultimately depend for support and with an eye on income, administrators are more likely to favor the development of those programs in adult education which, minimally, give assurance of paying for themselves and which, maximally, will provide a fiscal overplus. This overplus in turn may then be plowed back into expansion of more adult education of the same profitable sort, or it may be drawn off to other university operations or developments which are better favored but which are in serious need of funds.

The training rather than the liberalizing programs respond to the highly vocal expressed needs of the people, and are most likely at least to pay for themselves. Yet there is at least one type of liberal learning program that meets a widespread and widely voiced popular need and hence is good for both public relations and fiscal well-being of the institution. This program is the less intellectually demanding sort of recreational or cultural exchange stereotyped by the phrase "arts and crafts." This sort of program certainly has a place in the higher education of the adult, but the longer such programs are identified, stereotypically, with veneer culture, diversional hobbies, and the artsy-craftsy, the longer it will take for programs in liberal learning for adults to win, even in the more progressive sectors of the academic world, the parity of status, esteem, and reward so desirable for collaborative unity and institutional wholeness. To fulfill its function, the liberal learning program—whether it deals with matters cognitive or emotive; esthetic, ethical, or social; syllogistic or symbolic—must have sufficient intellectual heft, which is usually lacking in the arts-and-crafts program. So long as liberal learning programs in higher education for adults suffer from this lack, their practitioners will not gain acceptance at high-prestige levels, and the route toward the sorely needed institutional wholeness will be hindered.

Here, then, is another dilemma that keeps imposing distance between the already grave and rapidly growing responsibilities of liberal learning for the adult and the expectations we may realistically entertain for their fulfillment. For these liberal learning functions, we need, among other things, generous funds for training, recruitment, and retention of faculty, for research and development of innovative programs to meet unprecedented teaching-learning problems. We need funds for programs to educate our potential clienteles to their own real needs in genuine liberal learning in and for personal and social maturation—as distinct from the superficial wants to which, regrettably, so much of our adult education has all too readily catered. Yet, from the immediate main trends of proposals, projects, and grants, the training programs of higher education for adults are more likely to get the greatest fiscal support from tuition payments and corporate sources and from private and public sources.

Moreover, within the liberal learning component of higher education for adults, this financial support is most likely to go to those aspects which are least likely to command the respect and hence the professional support of the well-established sectors of American higher education. These liberal learning programs need the willing support of their participating instructors to push proposed programs through academic committees to official acceptance. To sense the acuteness of this problem, talk with someone whose task it is to promote programs in higher education for adults. He will tell you that the easiest programs to sell are those of immediate vocational-professional utility; the hardest, those of cultural interest, especially when the latter try to go beyond the surface programs of current events and light appreciation or entertainment.

To solve this problem, there is a commendable way, at least as an interim measure. This means is the amalgam, which involves the combination of a humanistic component with a training component to yield a composite program in liberal learning. This idea is in line with Francis Keppel's reiterated stress on a single stream for vocational and general education[14] and with Bowles' observation that he does not see why general and vocational education cannot be combined.[15]

Minimally, this sort of program can provide a bonus of

[14] Brickman and Lehrer, *Automation, Education and Human Values*, p. 350.

[15] Bowles, "The Dual Purpose," p. 19.

liberal learning for a program otherwise useful for the participant when he is on the job or when, as a lay leader, he is rendering direct community service. Maximally, this sort of program can provide an educational experience in which the vocational-professional and the liberalizing components are so interpenetrated that they yield a new mode of adult education in and for maturity. This result has its own distinctive form and integrity, and it makes its own distinctive contribution.

The Danes have provided a classic model of this sort of amalgam. They start their distinctive adult education programs with the man at his machine. From vocational-technical study of this machine and its product, and the operator's functions with the machine, they move to increasingly generalized and liberalizing considerations. These take the participant through instruments and processes of procurement, production, and distribution to principles and theories of economics; to social theory and philosophy; to philosophic concepts. In such an amalgam, it becomes impossible to mark where the vocational ends and the liberalizing begins. Moreover, this type of program has the virtue of starting where the student is, of connecting with him at his points of immediate concern, of moving, inductively, outward to the more inclusive and upward to the more general.

This amalgamating may be done even within the programs described as artsy-craftsy. (Of course, this latter term is unfairly applied to those programs which are of intellectual and esthetic stature at least equal to that in academic courses conventionally assigned college credit.) Even with people doing the most elementary arts-and-crafts work, a leader of experience, insight, and academic discipline can provide, through the amalgam, creditable liberal learning experience of appropriate academic worth. He can start with these people where they are and gradually lead them to liberalizing considerations of more and more comprehensive principles. For example, he can lead them to suggestive implications in the contemplation of esthetic, social, and ethical forms. He can lead them to John Henry Newman's concept that liberal education is formative—that it shapes the intellectual character and hence the whole ethos of the individual who is experiencing it. He can lead them to such teachings as that of the Talmudic sage: "He who teaches tradition to his fellow man is regarded as though he had formed and made him and brought him into the world." Moreover, by adhering to a single line—in this instance, the central line of liberal learning, that of man as form maker—he keeps his program from becoming a mere practice of miscellaneous odds and ends. He provides that essential of liberal learning—creative discipline and rigor.

Here is a fortuitous turn. We start by using the amalgam as a device for solving a practical problem in the financing of liberal education for adults. According to this tactic, we continue to get the well-paying programs in higher education for adults (those of immediate vocational-professional use) to help carry, financially, the liberalizing program that is likely to run at a financial loss when it tries to make a go of it on its own. Yet, as we work out such an amalgam, we provide something more than a tactical maneuver or expedient. We discover a vehicle that combines the virtues of both the immediately useful and the ultimately—that is, personally and culturally—valuable, to yield a combination far stronger than either of these alone and humanely holistic.

This composite is worth the respect of even severe academic critics. To explore the full range of such combinations and to produce an adequate number for use nationally, we need funds in response to proposals different from those called for by the concepts of research that have been in vogue—that is, those called for by empiric, statistical, and behavioristic research. The goals for experimental amalgam programs in liberal learning are exploratory and stimulative (emulative) models, and the outcomes of such projects—having to do with human process values, intrinsically impalpable—do not lend themselves to quantification. Just how difficult such evaluation may be is seen in Alvin Toffler's "The Art of Measuring the Arts," which at times seems grandiose and grotesque satire in the style of Jonathan Swift's *A Modest Proposal* and which comes close to pushing its fist through the empiric, measurable wall when it finally advances the concept of "surrogates of quality."[16]

We should realize, to be sure, that before long there will be vastly expanded needs, in higher education for adults, of holistic

[16] A. Toffler, "The Art of Measuring the Arts," *Journal of Aesthetic Education*, 1970, *4* (1), 69–72.

liberal learning programs that are not to have the special advantage of riding piggyback on training programs. Through cybernetics, early retirement, lack of access to even first money-paying jobs, disabilities, and the like, larger and larger blocks of open time will be made available to more and more adults, who will have to seek personal satisfaction through activities and occupations yielding little or no reward in terms of the market economy. In short, the seriousness of the concern for the great gap between responsibilities and realistic expectations on the part of higher education, and on behalf of liberal learning for the adult, is proportionate to the strength of the threat implied in the term often used about continuing liberal studies—*rehumanization*—that is, the threat of *dehumanization*. This threat is the reverse side of the bright coin of the overwhelming industrial, scientific, and technological progress.

LIFELONG LIBERAL LEARNING

> *If you give a man a fish,*
> *he will have a single meal.*
> *If you teach him how to fish,*
> *he will eat all his life.*
>
> *Kuan-tzu*

The idea of continuous education as a way of life and of continuing liberal education as a major component of such life antedates, by decades, the current wave of concern provoked by the impact of advanced and drastically advancing technological change.[17]

In the Western world such education as a way of life goes back at least to Socrates and ancient Athens, and to this day the Socratic dialogue remains a major means of continuing liberal learning. Moving to the East, we find continuous education going back in Judaic life to the systematic adult study of Scripture and rabbinic commentaries. Farther to the East, such continuous education may be traced to the full regimen established for the good life of the individual in ancient India. The *Vedas* and the *Upanishads*

---

[17] See C. H. Grattan, *In Quest of Knowledge: A Historical Perspective on Adult Education* (New York: Association Press, 1955); and J. F. C. Harrison, *A History of the Working Men's College: 1854–1954* (London: Routledge & Kegan Paul, 1954).

may well be regarded as the expression of continuous education as a way of life. What of the idea of continuous education as a way of life envisioned by leaders of the labor movement in England—what of the Ruskins, the Maurices, and their Workingman's Institutes and eventually their Labor Colleges? And in the United States, what of the International Ladies Garment Workers Union (ILGWU) educational programs?

Just as Sputnik served as a catalyst for an already widespread concern in the United States to strengthen the quality—particularly the intellectual rigor—of American education,[18] so the recent, spectacular accomplishments and demonstrated potentials of the cybernetic and technetronic revolution, have simply given special point to the idea of continuous education as a way of life. Indeed, the current discussions of the impact of cybernetic change on education bring to a new light the educational ideal long inherent in American democracy: education *for* an informed electorate and *of* an informed electorate. Such education needs to be kept up-to-date and, hence, continuous. Yet this ideal of continuous education as a way of civic life is not merely the idea of continuous education for citizenship and public responsibility, nor is it merely this idea plus education for fast-changing job situations and career opportunities. It is also continuous education of the citizen as a person and by way of self-responsibility and self-realization through growth toward or in wholeness. It is continuous holistic education.

The historic dimensions and the lack of novelty in the present stir of concern about lifelong continuous education by no means belittles the magnitude and complexity of the challenge to developers of continuous education programs—now and in the coming years— of vastly accelerated technological and social change. The need for creative adaptation to changes that are happening so fast and are so powerful and pervasive yields, in effect, change in quality, not just in quantity. Donald N. Michael's statement that the new blocks of open time will come to those least prepared to use such time meaningfully indicates the effect of these changes on the individual and society. Yet people on the executive and professional levels will

---

[18] See M. H. Goldberg and N. D. Kurland, "The Abler Student," *Higher Education: Some New Developments* (New York: McGraw-Hill, 1965).

have far less open time than now and hence far less opportunity for full enjoyment of the benefits of continuous education as a way of life and for wholeness of living because the supply of qualified people will be decreasing in comparison to the increasing need.

There are at least three major modes of continuous education for life in a technetronic age. The first is education for fast-changing job opportunities and careers; second, for public responsibility, citizenship, and voluntary communal service; and, third, for personal self-realization and enrichment. For those systematically committed to the encouragement of continuous education as a way of life in and for the technetronic age, several guidelines are suggested here.

We are faced at the outset with the ethical problem of attempting to do all we can to encourage such continuous education without exercising coercion, however well intentioned. Otherwise, in trying to achieve a laudable objective, we would be violating basic values of the very way of life we are seeking to encourage—namely, the person's sense of his own individuality, autonomy, integrity, and dignity. We become the sort of character William Hazlitt treated more than a hundred years ago in his typology of Napoleon—the liberal authoritarian. It is significant that the fiercely liberal and democratic Hazlitt, like the Radical Left today, tended to approve of this sort of totalitarianism. This approval reveals how powerful is the attraction—even among altruistic idealists—of the use of benevolent coercion toward admittedly desirable ends.

Furthermore, we must guard against the tendency to underrate the potential, for life-long liberal learning, of the unschooled, the unlettered, adult. Continuing education must consist of more than relatively simple and superficial diversional programs, even though the latter are legitimate, especially in a period of enhanced leisure. Among the so-called unlettered, there is far more potential for the more bookish and more subtly artistic sort of liberal learning than is often realized. We must similarly guard against the tendency to underrate both the amount of reading and the skill at oral verbalization of men labeled as nonverbal. To illustrate, twenty men of supervisory level at an aircraft plant participated in an experimental ten-session seminar. The theme was technological change, personal wholeness, and the dignity of man. The semantic sensitivity that these participants displayed in their discussion of *dignity* gave the lie to notions often heard concerning such men.

These guidelines are a warning to avoid the treacheries of stereotypic thinking and hence of stereotypic educational prescriptions about those to be inducted into or confirmed in continuous education for life. In conceptualizing and envisioning such education for a technetronic age, we must resist the temptation toward over-simplification that resorts to satiric caricature, and broad type characterization. We must picture, as individuals, those to be advanced along the paths of continuous education, a view which is all the more important in a time when macrostatistics are the fashion and everywhere loom so large. We must resist the temptation to treat men in the lump.

We must adopt a two-faceted simultaneous attack upon the problems of encouraging continuous education for life. In encouraging such education we must guard against two types of provincialism that results in a failure to see the part in relation to the whole. One type of such shortsightedness is a vision of continuous education as limited to the adult years. The other type is a similarly segmented but opposite view—that is, the view of education as terminating with basic formal education—either upon high school graduation or college commencement. Here one assumes that this basic formal education, by a sort of delayed-action capsule for future educational dissolvement, takes care of the education of the individual once and for all. Both of these notions are provincial; they are unrealistic and against the very master principle that should characterize continuous education as a way of life—that of developmental continuity. In this respect, continuous education may allow for epiphanic jumps but not total breaks; it is cumulative and incremental.

In advancing the ideal of continuous liberal learning, we must rethink and revise our curricula in accordance with a model of vital, dynamic educative process. Through this process the later stages are deliberately anticipated and prepared for in the earlier phases. From the beginning, the later stages are held vividly in mind as providing the motivating end goal for the entire process. Moreover, as distinguished from Aristotle's entelechy, which pictures predetermined development along fixed lines, this telos is kept generalized, flexible, and open, so as to avoid a cramping, particularized determinism which freezes the future in advance.

In certain of his remarks prepared for the Second Annual Conference on the Cybercultural Revolution, Jaswant Krishnayya perhaps had this idea in mind. One of the advantages he saw in a country such as India, when it seeks to adopt the new computer technology, is that this technological newcomer from the West is assimilated into a culture which has a long-established and meaningful—that is, purposeful—pattern for life.

We must recognize the need of realism and practicality. At present we have vast numbers of adults who are neither adequately educated nor in the process of becoming adequately educated. We have urgent personal and family problems, urgent social and political issues upon which our present adult generation has to make up its mind, express its convictions, and act. Both circumstances certainly call for adult education programs that immediately help more and more adults exercise their personal and civic responsibilities in an informed, intelligent way and thus elicit their full potential. Similarly, the adults joining the already vast army of the unemployed through retirement or for other reasons call for immediate adaptive or innovative programs in liberal learning. In addition we must develop a statesmanlike and imaginative long-range rationale for continuous liberal education which seeks holistically to provide, from childhood on through the later phases of adulthood, for the full educational continuum of the individual's development.

A corollary of such a view of continuous liberal learning is that, as early as possible, it must become and continue to be flexibly, courageously, and increasingly competent in systematic and cumulative search and discovery. The student should become a self-powered continuous learner through new personal discovery, dialectically and synergistically combined with previous personal discoveries and with the present assurance and stimulation of a group of fellow learners. Moreover, this learning should be overlapping—that is, during a given phase of one's education, he should already be consciously and systematically preparing for later stages.

This imbricative principle applies particularly to vocational training for times in which, because of the speed-up in the rate of change, an individual may have as many as ten job changes and five basic career changes in his working life. These vocational-professional changes involve one's outlook, way of life, even operational and far-range values. Witness the abrupt changes in living patterns and attitudes now forced on the thousands suddenly jobless by the mass layoffs in the technetronic industries—on the West Coast, along the "Golden Crescent" Route 128 of Metropolitan Boston, and in so many other areas. So newsworthy have the implications of these changes become that the Sunday supplements, the mass-circulation magazines, as well as radio and television have made this phenomenon the subject of numerous interviews, reports, and articles.

Responses similar to those provoked by the immediate impact of abrupt change on vocation are also occurring with respect to the other aspects of the layed-off individual's life; these responses are sociopsychic and psychoethical in nature. While crash programs for adjustment are being set up, it would be far better if, in the earlier phases of one's education, anticipatory programs for a future of abrupt changes are provided. The content of such programs should be characterized by an overlap of liberal studies and vocational-professional training—as in the "universities without walls" and the programs for "external degrees."

Included in such imbricative liberal learning should be ample provision for the future needs of the individual faced either voluntarily or involuntarily with the prospect of more and more free time. Before the advent of this potential leisure such individuals will need to become accustomed to motivations and rewards other than those of the marketplace and the market economy. As the unemployed technologists are discovering, they will need to become motivated by the prospect of joy in achievement through competence or excellence, which David C. McClelland places so high on the list of our "achieving society"[19] but which so many are accustomed to think of only in terms of dollar-sign rewards.

Yet liberal learning provides joy beyond the realization of competence, achievement, and mastery; it provides the humanizing joy that comes through fulfillment of what is primal, spontaneous, exuberant, and prodigal within the individual—that is, through fulfillment of man's natural bent toward form shaping.

[19] D. C. McClelland, *The Achieving Society* (Princeton N.J.: Van Nostrand, 1961).

By stressing this impulse in the dynamic for continuous liberal learning, we locate within the individual both primary motivation and primary reward. In placing this dynamic within the individual in terms of the telic fulfillment of his own nature, we thus push toward the educative periphery the more obvious, mechanistic goad-and-carrot motivations and rewards from outside. In so doing, we go far toward freeing the individual from the motivations and rewards suggested by the phrase "keeping up with the Jones's" or from the desires to achieve public acclaim or to flaunt one's achievements. Above all, we go far toward freeing the individual from bondage to the dollar sign and the accolade of the market economy as the chief driving forces for his efforts in liberal learning.

Furthermore, we drastically reduce the need for such seriously recommended pseudorealities as the sidewalk computer-psychiatrist, the "programmed sociality," the "cybersociality" of the personal "friend-o-mat" computer (the great gift of technology to the lonely heart). Conversely, in locating the dynamic for lifelong liberal learning within the individual and in terms of the fulfillment of his form-making impulse, we enfranchise him for the internally prompted shaping of his self and for the joyous rewards won through the realization of his full human dignity, his full humanity, through the achievement and expression of his creative wholeness.

Yet, in locating the primary motivation to wholeness within the individual, we must not be misconstrued as advocating a narrowly egocentric, individualistic course in life. Rather, if for no other reason than the joy of his self-realization and self-fulfillment, the individual must include, in the expression of his form-making impulses, creative participation in that shaping of the communal whole which Aaron Levenstein[20] has so strongly stressed.

Something of this sort should be the projective model of developmental wholeness for those charged with the responsibility of developing continuous liberal learning as a way of life in a technetronic age of multiple jobs and careers and of increased leisure for hundreds of thousands. If we fail to meet this challenge, then mere busyness and sheer distraction will result in what Staffan B. Linder has called "the harried leisure class." Linder asserts that contrary to

[20] See A. Levenstein, *Why People Work: Changing Incentives in a Troubled World* (New York: Collier, 1964).

expectations, economic growth and affluence have not resulted in an abundance of free time. They have, in fact, produced a time scarcity. To substantiate his claim, he traces the ramifications in our economy between increasing goods and decreasing time and appeals not only to "economists and social scientists but to all 'trapped' in the complexities of modern living."[21] Those in continuing liberal learning should serve as enfranchising agents from this entrapment.[22]

[21] S. B. Linder, *The Harried Leisure Class* (New York: Columbia University Press, 1970).

[22] For treatment of the current publicizing of the "External Degree" and "The University Without Walls," see M. Golderg, *Liberal Studies Degree Curricula Especially for Adults* (University Park, Pa.: Center for Continuing Liberal Education, 1971).

❧ SEVEN ☙

The Conservative
Agency

A responsibility of liberal learning is to serve as creative custodian, conservator, and transmitter of those human values appropriate to a free man, setting him free so as to realize his personal wholeness and human dignity. In the conservative (traditional) and the progressive (experimental, radical) institutions of higher education, liberal learning must differentially fulfill this responsibility.

When we recall the older word *liberal* as paired with *arts*, we can appreciate the close connection between dignity and liberal learning. I do not mean here what Leo Strauss has so ardently celebrated, the dignity of learning in itself, but rather this learning as a means toward the sense of personal wholeness and human dignity. Historically, liberal arts have been studies appropriate to a free man for the purpose of educating him in and for responsible freedom. We can reinforce this appreciation by recalling the derivative meaning—popular in the last several decades—of the term *liberal*. The meaning is suggested in the new coinage, "the liberating arts." As envisaged by John Dewey, who launched the term *liberating arts*, these arts, to use Erich Fromm's distinction, liberated the person from various inhibitions and entrapments—liberated him for self-fulfillment. As Abraham Maslow has suggested, the arts liberate the student for self-actualization. We might aptly say that the liberating arts and sciences are the pursuits that enable the individual to realize his full worth—which is after all just what *dignity* means in the Latin.

We have an indication that dignity—together with the other values, especially freedom, which surround it—is central to our whole cultural enterprise and hence to liberal learning. This indication is from an unexpected source, B. F. Skinner, the authoritative figure so strongly linked with mechanistic behavioristic determinism and hence with the alleged devaluation of the individual. In his "Utopia as an Experimental Culture," Skinner reiterates his stand that a "scientific analysis of human behavior and of genetic and cultural evolution cannot make individual freedom the goal of its cultural design. The individual is not origin or source. He does not initiate anything." "Nevertheless," he continues, "a species has no existence apart from its members or a culture apart from the people who practice it." Hence, if by *man* we mean a member of the human species with its unique genetic endowment, its human nature, then man is still the measure of all things. In a footnote, Skinner adds that he has now in preparation a more detailed analysis, from this point of view, of "freedom and dignity."[1]

If the liberating arts are to perform their twofold liberating function, they must provide the successive student generations with numerous opportunities to test—at least vicariously—the limits of paradoxic accommodation of the heritage to their personal needs. These needs are perennial; yet at a given time youths experience them largely through the given circumstances of their own lives, in their now world. As Thomas Jefferson put it, for each generation the time is now. They transform the often dehydrated nutriments of the heritage into attractive food for their psychic economy. In turn, if educators are to fulfill their functions as creative custodians

---

[1] B. F. Skinner, *Contingencies of Reinforcement: A Theoretical Analysis* (New York: Appleton-Century-Crofts, 1969), pp. 48–49. J. R. Platt, *Perception and Change: Projects for Survival* (Ann Arbor, Mich.: University of Michigan Press, 1970): "Humanism and Science—in that order—are the wellsprings of these important and vigorous essays by the noted biophysicist John R. Platt. Ranging from a discussion of mystical experiences to a timetable for the achievement of peace, a livable environment, and true community, the essays focus preeminently on the dignity and creativity of man." (Publisher's notice, *Commentary*, 1970, *50* (5), 110.)

of the heritage, the professors of liberal learning must help the students with this transformation. Much as some students would like to think otherwise, with few and notable exceptions, they cannot accomplish the task alone. To turn it over entirely to the students may seem a liberality in the professor and a flattery of the student. Actually, such an idea is unrealistic and may reveal, rather, intellectual laziness, sentimentality, or irresponsibility. If this translation, transmission, and transmutation do not occur in liberal learning, then a great potential remains dormant. In India, a person may have sacred cows all around him and yet starve. Likewise in the midst of plenty, one may die from psychic and cultural deprivation and malnutrition, as in poverty one may perish from physical deprivation and malnutrition.

Creative custodianship is central to liberal learning. For the ultratraditional institution, this process demands the breaking up and hosing away of the conventions that induce rigidity; it means flexing muscles long unused and opening up the circulatory system of the institutional body to fresh blood.

A conservative institution of higher learning such as the church-related college errs severely if it rests on dignity and its related ethical values, and self-righteously says, "Well, *we* are all right! We have our traditional values, formulas, and doctrines related to dignity and dignity-related ethical values or spiritual values. We need only to reiterate them, teach them, indoctrinate. They will carry, by their intrinsic and eternal truth."

Responding to a call for demonstrating the relevance of liberal learning, a professor of philosophy patted a thick volume of readings in masterpieces of Western civilization and said, "It's all here. The answers were all worked out centuries ago." With such rich stores of perennial truths and values from the past, why fuss about relevance in terms of the present and future? Let us consider an analogy: The gold hoard of Fort Knox is useless unless it is made current through a complex set of banking procedures. Insuring its present use in the economy has to be an ongoing process. A similar ongoing process must be realized by conservatives who deny any need for special efforts to make the heritage relevant—that is, vital and vivid—for their students.

We should not neglect the heritage but rather determine the

sort of attention given it and, for the major purposes of liberal learning, direct this attention toward the here and now. In fulfilling the
responsibility of liberal learning to relevance, we should not rely
simply on the liberal studies themselves. We need to take a cue from
activistic clergymen[2]—such as those of the Detroit Industrial Mission
and the Boston Industrial Mission—who study their theology to do
now, in the technetronic complexes and the city slums, and from
those such as Reverand Richard Ottoway and The Church and
Industry Institute, who bring their theology into the executive suite.
Through the 1950s, in the conferences, institutes, and seminars of
the Humanities Center for Liberal Education in an Industrial
Society, we have precedents and numerous successful working models
for such liberal learning in action—liberal learning in the arena, the
forum, the plant, the marketplace.

The simplistic exploitation of a few significant similarities
between what is given in the heritage and what gives today is just
a gesture—and a rather inadequate one at that—toward creative
adaptation of the heritage. Witness the statement of a professor of
English, regarded by his dean as a boat rocker: "Why all this fuss
about technological change? People are bored with it. My mother-
in-law didn't even bother to watch the moon landing. In short, we
need to teach the traditional resources—literary, artistic, cultural;
classical, Renaissance, and seventeenth century literature. Such resources never bore; they are always exciting. If we must exert some
deliberate effort to bring the past into the present, let us take our
cue from our own contemporary far-out writers, dramatists, expo-
nents of the absurd, the destroyers of illusion, those who strip experience to its gutsy essentials. As Pinter does in his plays, let us stress
personal relations, including violence and sex—all sorts of sex. Let
us stress personal interrelations—one-to-one and of the moment."

"But," came the question, "how do you square your stress
on the adequacy of the enduring values in our traditional humanistic
heritage with your frenetic faith in the antitraditional countervalues
of Pinter's message?" "Oh, there are connections," the professor
replied. "In Homer, you get episodes treating the same sorts of

        [2] See M. B. Bloy, Jr., *The Crisis of Cultural Change.* See also his
"The Gracefulness of Technology," *The Church Review,* 1964, 22, 204.

relationships—including sex and violence—that you get in Pinter or in *Hair*. When you teach the older works, you just select out these intersections and stress them."

This idea is quite an inadequate way of mediating the heritage and the present-future: it violates historic justness; it practices intellectual barbarism; it hacks off limbs from a full body and treats them as if they were the whole. We must do better if we are really going to do a creative job of testing the limits of accommodation of the old values to the new circumstances and challenges of our countercultures. We must decide where to keep them as is, where to modify them, where to abandon them, where to replace them.

A case in point is the modification of the conventional work ethic to allow for a supplementary or complementary replacement— a leisure ethic—that fosters personal wholeness and human dignity. In the strenuous and creative mediation here stressed there is a paradox; logically, we seem to be impaling ourselves on irreconcilables, but psychologically, practically, this act can be done. One sees it accomplished by such New Englanders as Ralph Waldo Emerson and Henry David Thoreau—both very American, very Yankee in their interest in the experimental, the new; yet both of these rugged individuals revealed strong strains of conservatism. Hence, George Keller's observation: "The most intelligent position to adopt in the present is that of a radical conservatism." Elaborating, Keller observes: "One must be radical to keep up with, and on top of, the increasingly rapid rate of change in modern society." He then adds: "But one should be, underneath, ferocious about conserving those forms, values, and manners, fought for over the centuries, that have made civilization tolerable, pacific, humane, and just." In his "New, Newer, Newest," John Simon recognizes the progressively mediative contributions that conservatism may make. Disclaiming any attempt to argue that the conservatives in art are better than the radicals, he insists that "until they, too, are heard from, the serious danger exists that our arts will become ever more frantic, psychotic, solipsistic, and above all divorced from any relevance to humanity."[3]

Here we have a lesson to learn from the students who have said, "Stop the academic merry-go-round, we want to get off." We

[3] *The New York Times*, September 29, 1969.

have a lesson to learn even from those who have been presenting us with plastic explosives within their pretty bouquets. There is something at once both heartbreaking and heartening in these very extremisms, in the antics and agonies of these counterculturists. Henry Steele Commager remarks that what "the students are really concerned about is not, in fact, the university." They are concerned, he insists, rather with society, government, the economy, even the moral order. Even though he fails to tell the whole story, Commager here makes a legitimate point.[4] Thus, we must not ignore the other side—as presented, for instance, in a report by David E. Rosenbaum:

Some students, when pinned down, will reluctantly admit that they derive enormous satisfaction from the camaraderie of a demonstration or a building take-over. They provide the emotional outlet that an earlier generation of students found in fraternities, beer parties, panty raids, and water fights. A Berkeley coed, who says she is a radical, acknowledged: "I hate to admit it but there is a good deal of the goldfish swallowing syndrome within the student movement. Sure, we believe in causes. But, fact is, it's pretty groovy to get a bunch of kids together, all committed to the same thing."[5]

Dissidents may churn things up, overturn what is set, smash images[6] simply for kicks—because it's groovy, because it's a gas. Nevertheless, they have likewise succeeded in forcing up from the depths, in dragging out of obscurity, in putting the spotlight on the perennial hidden agenda for the individual or the group aspiring to realize its dignity. If wholeness and dignity are to be achieved at all, these ethical or social issues have to be successfully resolved.

What are these never-outmoded, never outdated agenda? They are found in such questions as: Who is the good man? Why do there seem to be so few of them? What is the good society? Why do we not have a good society? What do we need to do to achieve

---

[4] "Universities Can and Must Be Saved from Destruction," *Philadelphia Inquirer,* September 7, 1969. See also S. L. Halleck, "Twelve Hypotheses of Student Unrest," *Twenty-Five Years,* G. K. Smith (Ed.) (San Francisco: Jossey-Bass, 1970).

[5] D. E. Rosenbaum, *The New York Times,* September 13, 1969, p. 80. In the fall of 1970, the panty-raid was revived at Cornell.

[6] See P. Goodman, "The New Reformation," *The New York Times Magazine,* September 14, 1969.

a good society? Why can't we achieve it right away? Why are we told to wait? Are we not justified in taking, by instant violence, what we cannot seem to gain by the slow processes of dialogue or debate—that is, by discourse of reason? Why isn't participative democracy necessarily democratic? Why is the politics of confrontation just another name for a species of fallacious reasoning—the *argumentum ad hominem*—another term for name-calling, for brickbats —verbal or physical—for that primitive process of a word and a blow?

Who is right, the dissidents want to know: the purveyors of the new hedonism, of the fun and technology syndrome[7] (as Max Marshall has put it)? or the ethic suggested by Paul-Emile Léger, who resigned from the Bishopric of Montreal to work among the lepers in Africa and who recently said: "The lepers taught me a terrible lesson. Their joy was richer than all our abundance. I felt that our gifts [including sulfone drugs] could succor them, but that we would be fortunate if they allowed us to have but one morsel of their evangelical serenity and joy."[8] Some of the student protesters are saying, in part, that liberal learning should accept a major responsibility for this sort of ethical concern. A disproportionately large number of them are in the liberal arts and sciences. Their ideas are radical in the sense that they are not content with slogans, with the solutions coming from believers in such slogans as this one for Sherwin Williams paints: "Save the surface and you save all." They are radical in the sense that they want to get to the root.

These students are telling us that if the liberal arts, within academia, will not accept a major responsibility for this sort of radical ethical concern, the youth will seek it elsewhere. The quest for liberal learning will then pass, as Richard Arrowsmith puts it, "to the gurus of the mass media, the chauvinistic charlatans and sages, the whole immense range of secular and religious street-corner

[7] In accounting for the current attractiveness of the technology-fun syndrome, we have to differentiate. For the *kybernatai* (the controllers) it is a way of release from facing the hard issues of socioethical responsibility for what they do and a pleasurable escape from the amoral and antimoral technicism in which they are customarily immersed. For the consumer of technological products and the beneficiary of technological processes and services, the stress of fun helps assure their being placid, plastic, pliable conformists and predictable consumers—hence highly susceptible to control.

[8] *Look*, July 29, 1969, p. 38.

fakirs and saints."[9] Arrowsmith doubtlessly does not mean to imply
that the halls of liberal learning are altogether free of the pseudo-
enlightened nonacademics he has bitterly named. Not finding within
the liberal arts, as formally constituted and presented, vigorous,
frank, fearless, and competent probing of the perennial ethical issues
in their now contexts, many of the questioning students, as the
street group in Lawrence, Kansas, are being forced into the streets
and out of the academic orbit of liberal learning. The student who
does not find this primary ethical concern actually pursued in the
liberal arts frequently takes the alternative. He responds by unintelligent, willful, arbitrary, bull-horn proclamations and brutalities
in the name of these very values. He ignores responsibility, that
compensatory value without which freedom becomes meaningless.
As Arrowsmith further states: "The rebel's attempt at heroism . . .
becomes merely anarchism; he loses the skills of heroism while
attempting to assert them." Nevertheless, such students have thus
brought out into the open the defaulting, in many quarters, of
liberal arts—defaulting to central and unremitting concern as primary business with ideals, ethical issues, commitments, and impera-
tives.

We will have criticism. If not good, then bad; if not competent, responsible, insightful, then the opposite. The same may be
said for ethical concerns: we will always have ethically implicative
decisions and commitments with ethical implications. But will these
decisions be good or bad, mature or immature, responsible or ir-
responsible, for or against? Sheer sensationalism, extravagant indi-
vidualism or idiosyncrasy, iconoclasm, radical scepticism, nihilism,
anarchism, counterculturism—each has ethical impacts and implications. Each means ethical decision—at least ethically-fraught
decision. These isms may be uninformed, premature, simplistic—
even unintelligent, ill-advised, hysterical, desperate, arrogant. Their
advocates may betray that contempt for the past and that frenzy
for instant solutions which, according to S. I. Hayakawa and others,
show the massive influence, on our television-reared generations, of
the instant-solution formulas in television commercials. In his
address at the opening exercises of the two hundred twenty-fourth

            [9] R. Arrowsmith, "The Future of Teaching," *The Public Interest*,
1967, (6), 54.

year of Princeton University, Robert F. Goheen put his finger precisely on this point. He stressed that relevance "is a relative term;
that every branch of learning has relevance of a sort"; and that the
"real questions are what degree of relevance, on what time scale,
and to what purpose?" He then urged the students to "study all
the complexities of major human problems" and to avoid "quick,
wholly buttoned-up solutions."[10]

Nevertheless, even the instant activism of these quick, wholly
buttoned-up solutions is a rudimentary ethicism. It involves choice,
decision, and commitment as to what makes for the good life and
how one stands with regard to others. On the whole, we may say
that youth are ethically concerned and involved. In the fundamental
sense that Voltaire stressed, they are pervasively ethical; true, they
assiduously cultivate their own improvisations, and are not concerned with attempted adherence to conventional etiquette, manners, or superficial customs. They are ethical, rather, in their deep,
serious, persistent pushing of the basic questions about the good
man, the good life, the good society and in seeking answers that are
not just conclusions arrived at but commitments to life styles and
action. They are transforming the conventional, prudential pragmatism so characteristic of the middle-class American into a passionate and extravagant pragmatism which gives a new twist to the
old adage, "By their fruits, ye shall know them."

Yet, both on the level of conception and conviction and on
the level of action-directed decision making, the conservative institutions of liberal learning all too often have sadly defaulted in
recognizing, in these various aberrant forms and unprecedented
eccentric formats or antiforms and antiformats, the perennial ethical
drives. In the agenda of responsibilities for relevance, a crucial
question arises: Will the conservative institutions shy away from
these admittedly flamboyant signals for direct, explicit, and sustained
ethical concern? There has been the fashion of disinterestedness and

[10] Quoted in N. Glazer, *Remembering the Answers: Essays on the
American Student Revolt* (New York: Basic Books, 1970). Citation from
publisher's notice, in *New York Review*, October 22, 1970, inside cover page;
and D. N. Michael, *The Unprepared Society*, "Some Challenges for Education," pp. 106–25. S. Kelman, the Harvard senior who is the author of *Push
Comes to Shove: The Escalation of Student Protest*, has reviewed the Glazer
volume in *Book World, The Washington Post*, 1970, 4 (42), 4.

freedom from socioethical concerns in the sciences and among many of the humanist emulators of the conventional scientific style. Then there have been the purists of the esthetic strain,[11] seen most often and most clearly in the studious humanities and the practicing humanities (as John Burchard has referred to them). According to this fashion in the humanities, the poem, the novel, the musical composition, the painting are to be regarded as creative in an autonomous realm of esthetic values. These works have values of pure contemplation or sheer excitement owing no homage or tribute to any other world than their own, owing nothing to the world of action, nothing to the demands of ethics—personal or social. They are free of all values other than the esthetic. Those who have taken this stance teach poetry and art that are free of all contamination with the world of actuality. Professors of this sort would go to all sorts of extremes to avoid showing, except by way of contextual eludication for esthetic purposes, the slightest concern with ethical matters, issues, responsibilities, or actions.

Yet, as well illustrated at Columbia, Harvard, and San Francisco State, the art-for-art's sake professor has often been a sociopolitical activist. Keeping his art and his social relations in separate, logic-tight compartments, he is able to practice simultaneously as esthetic contemplative and as sociopolitical activist. He does not necessarily try to keep his activism out of his life within academia. Max Eastman illustrated this tendency. On the one hand, he wrote of *Marx, Lenin, and Scientific Revolution;* on the other hand, in the *Literary Mind: Its Place in an Age of Science,* he advocated his own version of poetry as pure esthetic experience, which he called a chronicling of moments of heightened consciousness. This dichotomy has enabled poets and critics of the extreme Right—some of them at least protofascists[12]—to join with poets and critics of the extreme Left, as demonstrated in the *Partisan Review.* Nowadays, one may see the same dichotomy among some of the

---

[11] See H. S. Broudy, "The Artist and the Future," *Journal of Aesthetic Education,* 1970, *4* (1), 12–22 and especially 15–16.

[12] See J. Harrison, *The Reactionaries: A Study of the Anti-Democratic Intelligentsia,* (New York: Schocken, 1967); and D. Donahue, "Literary Fascism," review of *The Reactionaries,* in *Commentary,* 1967, *44* (2), 86 ff.

academic radicals and the Marcusean ideologists of relevance. There is, however, a frequent variant. Escape from the contemplative-activistic dilemma is achieved by a ruthless destruction of the disinterested, contemplative life. What often results is a fragmented, rather than a unified, intellectual self.

One widespread mode of avoiding a head-on collision between esthetic purism and ethicosocial activism has been transmuting socioethical conceptualization, feeling, and action into matters of technique and sensibility. Esthetically sensitive professors with socioethical concerns have no monopoly on this sort of psychic euphemism. The literature of executive development is full of such euphemism as is the literature of management, human relations, and interpersonal relations. Journalists have frequently resorted to it. The key word in this evasion of direct ethical confrontation is *style*. Thus, we no longer speak of shaping our character or our personality but rather of playing roles and adopting life styles.[13] At least three sections of the Sunday *Washington Post* indicate this preoccupation: "Style: Woman/Leisure/Community"; "Style: The Arts/ Travel/Show"; and, finally, "Living Style: Home/Food/Gardens." Life itself—both personal and collective—thus becomes a matter of style.

Elizabeth M. Drews frequently uses the term *style*. For her, values and style are closely interrelated—with the ethical values seemingly subsumed under the heading of style. Similarly Russell R. Dynes, professor of sociology at Ohio State University, presents this idea in the title of a conference paper: "The Emergence of Violence as a Life Style." These two instances illustrate how conveniently the term *style*, with all its esthetic connotations, may easily provide a means of euphemistic detour around ethical cruxes as such. To make certain that the use of the term does not enable us to sidestep the specific ethical confrontations, we need to keep reminding ourselves of Buffon's statement that style is the man himself.

In the phrasing of the semantically adroit esthetic-radical

---

[13] Drews, *Policy Implications,* p. 140. *Life style* derives from Alfred Adler, who used the term in connection with a concept similar to that of our telic model. For Adler, the telic model was implicit, and the life style was an attempt to implement this model in one's life, see also A. S. Nash, "Prologue," *The Choice Before the Humanities* (Durham, N.C.: Regional Educational Laboratory for the Carolinas and Virginia, n.d.), p. x.

professor, name calling, hurling of obscenities, gestures, threats, and acts of violence all suffer a transformation into something new and strange—into aspects of style in the counterculture and politics of confrontation. Often, such radical apologists spray a mist of semantic deodorant upon the ugly brutalities, making them thus pleasant to their own exquisite sensibilities and to the squares whom they wish to charm into acquiescence and, hopefully, supportive action. They become experts in assessing the precise degrees of negative sensibility appropriate to different types and modes of iconoclastic and demolitional violence perpetrated by the alienated and disaffected, and the precise degrees of positive sensibility to be bestowed upon the badly misunderstood student activist, who at heart is their darling. Thus, through estheticism, they seek to anesthetize the apathetic and the hostile. Not right or wrong but productive and counterproductive become their touchstone terms.

Whatever the mode of ethical attrition and attenuation in liberal learning, professors of liberal learning have become astonishingly vulnerable to confused, unprincipled, sentimental, and above all irrational dissolution under the pressures of campus agitations and militant badgering and bullying. Their own appropriate powers of ethical intellect and imagination, of criticism and decision, have been lost through early abortion or atrophied through disuse. Under fire during a crisis, they have only sensations and feelings to fall back upon; they exhibit anxieties and fears about these young hoodlums or display sentimentality toward these youngsters who they have decided are such good kids after all.

Among the liberal artists and scientists, there are, however, signs that forthright expression of ethical concern has once more become intellectually reputable. This ethical concern includes that activistic socioethicism asserted by the radical professors and the dissenting academy, as expressed in the politics of confrontation. It is expressed through such means as the *American Scholar* symposium on morality.[14] Chaired by Daniel Bell—hardly to be dismissed as a

---

[14] *American Scholar*, 1965, *34* (3), 347–69. C. H. Holmes' *Aldous Huxley and the Way to Reality* (Bloomington, Ind.: the Indiana University Press, 1970), citation from *New York Review of Books*, October 22, 1970, p. 50; B. Suhl, *Jean Paul Sartre: The Philosopher as a Literary Critic* (New York: Columbia University Press, 1970), citation from *New York Review*,

rear-view driver, a belated puritan or victorian, a prisoner of the so-called protestant ethic—and numbering, among its participants, such humanistic biologists as René Dubos, this gathering, as well as subsequent commentaries, provided more than a few straws to show the way the wind was blowing. The symposium was characterized by an agonizing struggle to break free from conventional formulas and phrasings, from the clichés and banalities of established wisdom, from religious shibboleths, from prudential wisdom and those litanies of honorifics which are often a substitute for general ethical scrutiny of the heritage and for assessments of the present or probings of the future. Furthermore, the symposium maintained a determination to follow the Socratic model: to pursue the argument wherever it might lead. This effort meant frankly admitting to painful doubts and resisting the impulse for retreat from embarrassing cruxes and collapsed structures to strongholds of dogmatism. At the other extreme, it meant resisting the hypnotic alternative to yield to flux.

The publicity of Charles M. Holmes' *Aldous Huxley and the Way to Reality* appeals to the rising neoethical concern: ". . . Huxley's discovery of mescaline and the visionary experience it induced in him was but a step in a lifelong search for an ideal and a discipline that would have ethical relevance for the modern world. . . . He deals with ultimate reality, good and evil, suffering and death, the good society, friendship, sex and love." Likewise, the description of Benjamin Suhl's *Jean Paul Sartre: The Philosopher as Literary Critic* is also geared to such a concern: "What has in fact emerged—closely linked to Sartre's esthetics—is a radically new point of departure for an existentialist ethics." Both writers deal with literary figures. Both highlight an explicit ethical concern.

Again, in the alarums and excursions between George Kennan and his student-faculty detractors from varying degrees of the Left, although worlds apart in the particular ethics or counterethics that they professed, both parties agreed that the basic issues were moral ones, and both showed ethical concern of similar primacy, pervasiveness, and tenacity.

The same public debate between Kennan and his disparagers brought to the fore the need to conquer another obstacle if liberal

---

ibid., p. 43. See also E. Neumann, *Depth Psychology and a New Ethic*, E. Rolfe (Trans.) (New York: Putnam's, 1969).

learning is to fulfill its responsibility toward relevance. To some extent, that controversy provided dramatic support for those who, taking their cue from Madison Avenue, proclaimed or denounced the so-called generation gap.

Since, beneath the cliché and the banality of the term *generation gap*, there is psychosocial reality that closely bears on our theme, it is well to identify the nature of that reality. "There bubbles in each of us," says Irwin Miller, the Indiana industrialist, nationally noted churchman, and Yale trustee, "the ancient hostility between the old and the young. It is necessary to confess this straightway." With Miller, as with the cultural anthropologists and the Freudians, we must recognize this perennial warfare of the generations: youth's drive to slay their personal and cultural fathers; youth's own residual and generic fears of being slain, as in primitive tribes, by its own elders; youth's sensing of the implicit dangers of liquidation—now in a metaphoric rather than a literal sense—by the elders of the present Establishment. We must also recognize that with the radical transformations and innovations of the technetronic and biogenetic revolutions, with the corresponding sociocultural changes or unprecedented pressures toward such change, the youth of today have experiences that their elders never had. As Margaret Mead has put it: "Until recently our elders could say, 'I have been young and you have never been old.' Today, the young can reply, 'You have never been young in the world I am young in.' "[15] Moreover, ironically, the same headlong changes that enable the young to make this claim tend to make the older man "stand at a greater distance from his own childhood and adolescence," with a consequent impairment of the "immediacy of the remembered experiences," and hence a further handicapping of his efforts to empathize with those who are young now.[16]

Even if we recognize all these problems, it is nevertheless sad to have more and more declarations of the widening gap; and there is pathos in the circumstance that a military incursion into Cambodia and the slaying of four students at Kent and two at Jackson are necessary to bring us—although temporarily and precariously—

[15] M. Mead, *Culture and Commitment,* pp. 74 ff.
[16] Kennan, *Memoirs,* p. 3.

within talking distance of one another and to induce some slight movement toward communing and community.

The adverse pressures exerted by the contemporary cult of youth should also be acknowledged. These result in a superlative stress on those admirable characteristics and capabilities—physical and other—which the young naturally possess but for which those over thirty have to work so hard yet often so unsuccessfully and hence so ludicrously or pathetically. We see this vogue of the youthful in the boast of the large corporation: "We are a young company! We may be long established but our executives are young, and our motto is an open career to young talent." We see this vogue too in the duplicate outfits for father and son and for mother and daughter (in Winston-Salem, North Carolina, there is a large department store named Mother and Daughter), with the stress on youthfulness as the common motif. We see it in the television commercial which demonstrates that, thanks to the beneficent effects of the advertised detergent, one cannot tell the difference between the mother's hands and those of her teen-age daughter or in the commercial which shows mother and daughter as they bound up the path from a swim to a refreshing, energy-building breakfast of the cereal being promoted. Both females are indistinguishably girlish—suffused in the glow of youth—slim, energetic, vibrant. A clinic in the Bahamas, just minutes by plane from Miami, provides youth-restoring treatments with Geronital H3, a formula containing procaine, discovered by Ana Aslan, a seventy-three-year-old Rumanian. We see the power of this cult of youth, too, in the use of KH3 pills (containing Geronital H3) which jet setters smuggle in from Europe and pass on trays at cocktail parties to their friends. I too have felt the full impact of this incessant accent on youth. Seated in the barber's chair, I suddenly saw in the mirror a transformed image of myself. The barber, who, I now realize, had been wearing it himself, had slapped a hairpiece on my balding head: "Just two hundred dollars, and it makes you look twenty years younger." I felt like protesting: "But who says I want to look younger?" A dangerous question that might lead to being torn to pieces by the cultists of youth. Exacting, harsh penalties fall on those who resist or those who find it very hard to keep up or to turn the morphological, physiological, and psychic clock back. This sort of enveloping threat by youth contributes heavily to the general impression of the widened and widening gap, publicly proclaimed so often, between those over thirty and those under thirty.

In the general acceptance of the idea of this alleged gulf between the generations, there is enormous personal and cultural waste of psychoethical resources and psychoethical energy. It is sad to see such energy slipping downhill into the cultural voids. It is sad, similarly, to see the still valid, still applicable stores of personal experience so blithely, angrily, or hysterically jettisoned. It is sad because the hard lessons those who are well over thirty have learned, which could be useful to youth, are being wasted. Both through years of direct coping with experience and through studies, we have gleaned some kernels of insight and have panned out some hardwon nuggets of ethical wisdom. These insights could be useful to youth if only the channels of transmission could be reopened. Conversely, to this joint enterprise of making liberal learning fulfill its responsibility to relevance, youth could bring so much: unbounded energy, fresh views, freedom from excessive complications, freedom especially from inhibition of intellectual complexities. They could be a wholesome corrective to ideas which, in those well over thirty, may fall unhealthily between thought and action. Youth could provide checks against our falling victim to Hamlet-like paralysis of the will through excessive considering, hesitating, weighing, and balancing, teetering between *to be* and *not to be*. We may recall, in this connection, Cardinal Richelieu's ringing annunciation: "In the bright lexicon of youth, there is no such word as fail." On the other hand, there is that humility—likewise needed for sagacious living—which comes from years of responsible effort. If only youth would be willing to accept the responsibility that goes with the freedom they so strongly demand. One function of this responsibility on their part is to meet the professor—that is, the nonradical professor—at least halfway. It is time to renew with youth the great dialogue initiated by Socrates, for which the Platonic dialogue and the Socratic method still provide the irreplaceable and ever-fresh model.[17]

[17] See R. Redfield, *The Educational Experience* (Pasadena, Calif.: Fund for Adult Education, April 1955), especially Lecture 2, "Conversation," pp. 24–40, which contains a wide-ranging and illuminating treatment of the liberally educative functions of "The Dialogue"; and J. Wilkinson, "The

Out of the depths of the tragic spring of 1970, we hear voices seeking to renew that humanizing dialogue in which heart speaks unto heart. In class, a student, as if an agent of inquisition, peremptorily demands of his professor: "Where do you stand on Cambodia?" "Your question is impudent and irrelevant," the professor replies. "But," protests a coed, "you mustn't dismiss it that way. You just don't understand how intensely we feel about Cambodia and about our four fellow students murdered at Kent."

"You are right—in part. No matter how hard I try, I can't get out of my own skin, I can't extricate myself altogether from the experiences I have lived through: two world wars, the Great Depression, the Nazi and Fascist totalitarianisms of the Right, the Stalinist totalitarianisms of the Left, McCarthy's reign of terror, the fighting in Korea. Nor, try as I may, can I put myself into your psyche. But, believe me, I do try; and I think that by analog and parallels—by imaginative vicarious experiences—I come closer to how you feel and why than you give me credit for. I ask that you try to do the same for me. For me to understand and sympathize with you, you must try to understand me. I don't wear my heart on my sleeve, but in these troubled days I'll try to tell you how I feel. And I ask you to listen, to give me my day in court. Listen and read—read such books as Studs Terkel's *Hard Times,* Hermann Rauschning's *Revolution of Nihilism.* This will help."

"Tell us, then, about Fascism, Nazism. You lived through it. Are we in danger of it again, today?"

Thus, from the students comes an invitation to make it two-way—this yearning, erratic movement toward real dialogue. But before the professor can explain, another student jumps in: "That's just it. You've been through it. You've had your chance to cope, to

Civilization of the Dialogue," Center for the Study of Democratic Institutions, Santa Barbara, Calif., 1968, *2* (1). Both works rescue the term *dialogue* from its current triteness, flatness, and looseness of meaning. They restore the dialogue to centrality in the art of civilization, which is the more generalized form of liberal learning. W. Stein, *Criticism as Dialogue* (New York: Cambridge University Press, 1970), ". . . believes that literary judgments must ultimately be consistent with the faith by which one lives. In this book he suggests what the radical Christian humanist attitude should be in dialogue with the liberal humanist or the Marxist about critical values and the issues raised by important literature." [Publisher's notice, *New York Review of Books,* 1970, *15* (9), 7.]

run your risks, to take it. You mustn't deny us. We have a right to
our own exposure to danger, to violence, and to our own struggles
against what we feel is bad and what we want as good."

"You insist upon this awful right?"

"Yes."

"Then all I can do is watch with tragic qualm, with pity
and terror. Terror at the thought of the dangers you court and the
disaster that may fall. Pity at the price, the sacrificial immolation of
so many golden lads and girls. Is the personal experience worth the
awful price?"

Thus, we hear the stirrings of renewed dialogue. This dialogue fumbles and falters, yet it goes on, as do the incapacitated
when they try to relearn the use of their limbs. At New York University a group of students offer to share lunches and talk with the
hard-hat construction workers who just a few days before had been
beating up the peaceniks. The barriers are skyscraper high, but they
get lowered. And after the first round both sides agree: they want
more. At Tennessee State University, two thousand students assem-
ble before the home of the president. They are angry and they
threaten. He says, "Tell me what you want; I'll listen." Item by
item they relate a long list of grievances—some grave, some trivial,
but all intensely felt and pugnaciously put. He then replies, "I've
heard you out. Now hear me." Item by item, the president takes up
their demands. Some, he says, are justified, and he can and will act
upon them. Others—as, for example, the distribution of The Pill
through the University Health Center—he cannot go along with,
and he patiently explains why. The anger has subsided, the pug-
nacity drawn off. The students are listening. They are thinking it
through—with their president, who has leveled with them.

Here is communication, exchange, the beginning at least of
dialogue, of community if not of communion. Yet, this communication is not what the extremists mean. They thrust at the administrator a big list of unnegotiable demands. After he has indicated that
he cannot or will not favorably act on some of them, they declare
that he is not receptive and proceed to abuse verbally and to burn
buildings. For receptivity, mutuality is necessary, the minimum
mutuality being forbearance in hearing the other fellow out. Such
a receptive mutual exchange occurred before the president's house

at Tennessee State University. For the conservative institution of higher education, there are signs of hope as such responses occur on more and more campuses.

According to Seymour Lipset and Earl Raab, on the American campus, the *intra-* rather than the *inter-*generation gap, now and in the near future, will be most evident. If so, then current efforts at renewed dialogue between the generations—or at least between corresponding sectors of each generation—through liberal learning should be less difficult than has been asserted in recent years.[18]

---

[18] "The Non-Generation Gap," *Commentary*, 1970, *50* (2), 35.

◎ EIGHT ◎

The Progressive Agency

We have previously mentioned that educational processes unduly influenced by conservative agencies of liberal learning are likely to suffer rigidity. Liberal learning influenced completely by progressive agencies has its dangers too. Educational processes unduly influenced in this direction are likely to deprive students of the chance to strengthen, for maturity, habits that cannot be developed in an environment where the student decides on his own what he is to study, where and when and how. The student's idiosyncrasies, his moods and wants, often fluctuate widely,[1] and as a result in the permissive environment the student is likely to be deprived of those disciplinary skills, intellectual habits, and styles which, for maturation in liberal learning, are crucial counterpoises to the permissive environment and educative processes that characterize the progressivist or ultraprogressivist institution.

This position does not imply that a revived or recrudescent authoritarianism is necessary; nor is discipline for discipline's sake or restrictions for the sake of restriction. What it does urge is that, for true inner liberation and for true maturation through liberal

[1] See T. Borton, *Reach, Touch, and Teach: Student Concerns and Process Education* (New York: McGraw-Hill, 1970): "Proposes an emphasis on personal feelings in educational processes and argues that education should be seen as a means of personal growth."

128

learning, constraints are just as important as the sheer expressive flow and the expansive drives. The constraints are necessary to contain constructively the outward thrusts of self-expression. The latter, at their extreme, become vast explosions of uninhibited energy, as Hippolyté Adolphe Taine said of William Shakespeare—perhaps with more vividness than justness. In stage makeup we need both the light and the dark lines, often to create a single effect. In tennis we need the net to play the game. As in making a poem, "pulling" a pot, or painting a picture, we need creative constraints for effectiveness in liberal learning.

In the nontraditional or antitraditional agencies of liberal learning, there is likely to be an overstress on the expansive impulses and an understress on the deliberate cultivation and creative discipline of the forming impulses. We now even have the "open classroom"[2] and "universities without walls." If recognition is given to the forming impulse, it is left largely to the individual's mood at the moment. It becomes a matter of hit-or-miss happenings. Thus, the need for systematic constraints should be strongly stressed for the progressive or radical agency of liberal learning to fulfill its responsibility to relevance. These constraints should be creative; they should not inhibit or destroy self-expression and self-realization but rather continue the process of shaping and sensing one's dignity, one's personal and general wholeness.

In the creative interplay and counterplay between the expressive thrusts and the constraints we get the dynamic patterning— the Gestalt formations and projections at the heart of liberal learning. This dynamic patterning was demonstrated by La Argentina, called "Queen of the Castanets," who combined classical ballet with Spanish folk dances. Once having established her basic pattern, she kept straining as far as possible from it yet without altogether breaking it down; she maintained dynamic equilibrium, however precarious. This patterning is also shown in jazz as the musician establishes a basic rhythmic and melodic pattern and then keeps working at variations and departures to see how far he can go in

---

[2] H. R. Kohl, *The Open Classroom: A Practical Guide to a New Way of Teaching* (New York: Random House, 1970). *New York Review of Books* (October 22, 1970, p. 52) announces that there are in print over 100,000 copies of this book "that is revolutionizing American teaching."

fighting the pattern without causing the constraining tension to snap and the form to fall apart. Again, however precarious, this pattern is a matter of dynamic equilibrium. *Perilous Balance,* the title of a book on Jonathan Swift, aptly points up this affair of thrusts and constraints. The word *perilous* suggests a balance that is anything but staid or dull; it involves unremitting risk. At each moment the dancer, the player, the artist, the poet puts it on the line. In his desire for achieving mastery through creative resolution of the deliberately sought tensions between sheer expression and counter-vailing constraints, he takes his chances with and against the constraints.

This dynamic equilibrium applies to cognitive matters—whether rational or esthetic—and to ethical matters, involving personality and character. Whether rightly or wrongly attributed to Benjamin Spock, the concept "Spockism" is the alleged outcome—at the school and college level—of the student's prior lack of creative constraints essential to his inner growth. Perhaps this idea of contest and conflict is what Ingmar Bergman meant when, after giving a rather negative picture of the dour Swedish Lutheran home atmosphere in which he was brought up, he acknowledged that at least his parents gave him something to fight against.

There is, then, the idea of dynamic thrust and counterthrust, contest and conflict, tension perhaps at the moment unpleasant or disliked yet productive which ultimately contributes to the shaped personality, the character with wholeness. We tend to forget this idea when we espouse the totally unstructured class or course. This so-called course is merely a string of improvisations—happenings without beginning or end—leading from nowhere to nowhere. It may be full of sound and fury. Yet it celebrates formlessness and signifies nothing. For the iconoclast or the nihilist, this nothingness is just the point.

Thus, for strengthened design in liberal learning, neither progressivists stressing change nor conservatives stressing the status quo is the answer. We need Erasmians: creative mediators between fixity and change. Denying neither, ignoring neither, they realize that the emergence of the mature self—the achievement of genuine self-identity, of personal wholeness and human dignity—lies in the paradoxic and creative reconciliation of both.

In his distinction between civilization and culture, René Dubos provides illustrations of this creative mediation between fixity and change:

I shall use "civilization" when referring to the values that can be shared and are increasingly shared by most people, irrespective of origin, race, or religion. In contrast, I shall use "cultures" to designate the body of values, ideas, and beliefs characteristic of a particular group. Science, the technologies derived from it, and certain ethical concepts are meaningful to most of mankind and might serve as the basis for universal civilization . . . Cultural values differ from group to group, change with time, and imply the diversity in mankind. As I shall repeatedly emphasize, universality and diversity are two complementary aspects of man's nature.[3]

One may wish clarification of the specifics that Dubos cites as his universal values shared by mankind. One may wish to ask if science, in itself or in the technologies derived from it, is to be designated a universal value or if it is to be regarded as universally related to such values, raising issues and problems about them. Nevertheless, the principle I assert illustrates the necessary habit of mind. Instead of adopting a polarized either–or attitude, one way or the opposite, this principle seeks in a both–and way creatively to mediate the paradoxic claims of the enduring and the transitory.

The strong cultural forces working in the world-at-large and those invading the educational process strive to dislodge the individual from the durable patterns from which he forms his sense of self and self-worth—his sense of personal dignity. Neither fixity nor change in itself is necessarily detrimental to the individual's or to the group's search for self-actualization, dignity, and wholeness. Total fixity spells certain death. Except with regard to strongly traditional agencies of liberal learning, this fact nowadays hardly needs stress.

However, the opposite—a total yielding to change—can likewise be detrimental, whether the yielding is to the external, environmental change with all its turbulence and violence or to the internal stream of change, the personal stream of consciousness—for example,

[3] Dubos, *So Human an Animal*, p. 41.

the psychedelic trip or the trip powered by "Speed." The First Commandment in the Revolutionary Decalogue of the heroine in *I Am Curious (Yellow)* is that thou shalt hold none but a temporary philosophy. Stress on the uninhibited expression of the ego is, in the last analysis, a commitment to all-transient flux.

At the 1969 NCTE conference on humanities teaching, a participant proudly announced: "I have one hundred twenty-five students. No two are doing the same thing." The announcement was enthusiastically received. The stress on individual variations setting up an aggregation of one hundred twenty-five mutually repellent particles was favorable. Yet the other conference participants did not seem aware that this announcement was causally related to a classroom situation that another teacher reported: "My kids are *groovy*—just groovy—some through drugs, some through imitations of Eastern mystics and gurus. Some . . . are just edgy, jumpy." This report gives the impression of hair-triggered readiness for explosion. At an experimental college dedicated to maximum permissiveness, administrative officers report a similar impression. Their students are described as being groovy, and the administrative officers say they just don't know what will happen next or which way the students will go. Furthermore, they admit that they don't know which direction they themselves prefer.

At a conservative liberal arts college, one of the young professors is delighted, for he has turned the kids on. He has succeeded in releasing them from all conventional, all rational restraints, from the fixities that, in his view, cripple the self in adulthood. He has sent them back to the presocialized, preconventionalized, prerational, polymorphous fluidity of infanthood. In this uninhibited, unselfconscious spontaneity, he has had them crawling around on all fours, talking baby talk. He has got them unbuttoned, inarticulate, unstructured. He has had them laughing hysterically at these recollections from babyhood in the halcyon days before they were toilet trained. He has facilitated this return to infanthood by participating with them, crawling around on all fours, making baby sounds. He has not only got with *it* but got with *them*.

Politeness and joy in his enthusiasm restrain one from throwing a damper on this professor's enthusiasm. Actually, however, one cannot help wondering whether this act does not confuse means and ends. From the point of view of the responsibility of liberal learning toward personal wholeness and human dignity, is not this means of turning on just a start, a possible start, that might seriously and sadly abort? Turning the kids on, turning them loose, is just the beginning; the crucial phases are still ahead. What do we do with them after we have turned them on, after we have set them loose— whether backward or forward—in the stream of change? This question becomes all the more pertinent—perhaps even poignant—if an adult should desire to be carried back to his childhood, back to the primal, prenatal warmth and security of the womb,[4] rather than forward toward the continuous enrichment of maturity.

When we have the students turned back, do we leave them there? When we have thus released them from fixities and opened them up to flux, what then? Do we just leave them open to all the electronic or physicopsychic pulsations of worldwide ferment that crowd in on all sides, from all directions. Do we leave them, like jellyfish blobs, floating on or immersed in a highly charged ether? Or do we expose them to every oscillation from within—fluctuations of whim, mood, desire, urge, or drive? From the point of view of one's psychic economy, does this turning back not lead to the limbo of dissatisfaction or hysteria, to the phantasmagoria of the acid trip, or to the arctic chill of psychic withdrawal?

At this national conference on humanities teaching, for example, we had serious discussions on the drug high as one type of educative experience open to the student. This experience was described as "living high through chemistry," as providing a "short and easy up" and climactic meeting with one's self—although a disjointed version of the self. En route, one experiences loss of a sense of limits, looseness of association, and fluidity of constructs. The psychology professor who clinically describes this model for ecstasy provides the needed countertruth. Granted, he says, that we should open up the students to sensationalism (some would call it *sensatism*); yet we must get them to realize its limitations. We can't cop out to sensationalism. We can't leave them at the level of

---

[4] According to J. Howard, some of the programs in the "human potential movement" go this professor one better. They have an exercise in which the women lie, as in labor, on coverings spread on the grass, and in the role of infants during birth, the men emerge as from the womb.

the Gloria, the great Aha. We, the professors, are to let them turn us on, but we are not to let them hang us up. We are to turn them on; but we are not to hang them up. We are not to let them suffer the fragmented-self caricature of self-actualization. We must accept and assert cognitive knowledge and understanding. We must link the sensational and the intellectual-cognitive in the dynamic interplay that makes for integration, that is, for wholeness.

When, ostensibly in the interests of liberating education, we encourage students to turn on and let go, we may sound so sympathetic, so liberated. In truth, we merely get them to exchange one yoke for another. We commit them to serving the shifting currents of consciousness and the oscillations of their moods and yearnings. We do so even when they do not thereby become enslaved to the pseudoemancipation of drugs. We may likewise sell students into another bondage—authoritarian control from outside. There is a historic parallel with what happened to German youth under Adolf Hitler, as Bruno Bettelheim, of the University of Chicago, has observed. He has sensed in our youth today a restlessness, a rebelliousness parallel to that of German youth just before Hitler took over.[5] Caught in violent change, rendered extraordinarily pliable by the forces of change, the German youth became easy marks for Hitler's totalitarian caricature of the humanizing social structure. If we do not develop appropriate competencies in imposing creative constraints upon flux, then we expose ourselves and our students to arbitrary outside controls—to authoritarian coercion. We negate our avowed objectives. We fail to help our students achieve a proud and joyful sense of freedom, responsibility, dignity, and wholeness.

This matter brings us close to the central aspect of liberal learning and the demands for relevance: the issue of constraints. In a given two-hour discussion at the NCTE humanities conference at least three times the group came up to this issue and backed away from it. It proved impossible for these teachers to face the real issue: not the issue between absolute freedom and authoritarian control but rather the issue between arbitrary coercion and the exercise

---

[5] Stated by Bettelheim in his testimony before a Congressional committee on student unrest. Confirmed through a letter to me (December 7, 1970). For comments on related matters, see W. Braden, *The Age of Aquarius: Technology and the Cultural Revolution* (Chicago: Quadrangle, 1970), pp. 93–94.

of control in such ways as are compatible with the dignity of the individual and with the educational aim of nurturing growth toward that self-identity and self-realization which are integral to the maturation and maintenance of one's sense of personal wholeness and human dignity.

Consider the slogan which, on the front cover of the October 1970 issue of *American Education,* accompanies the picture of a teen-age girl—long hair and shirt-tails flowing—caught, like the discus thrower, in a kinetic moment: "Talent runs free. . . ." Those teachers who professed to be committed to total freedom for the student repeatedly admitted certain stubborn realities. They recognized that, in both philosophical and operational terms, we have no absolute freedom anywhere and at any time. They admitted that in the last analysis the instructor cannot evade an ultimate responsibility for what happens in those phases of the education of his students during which they are entrusted to him.

These teachers likewise admitted that in practice they did not let the students do whatever they pleased and whenever they pleased. They tried to get the students to do what they—the teachers—considered desirable, which was sometimes little more than what the teachers regarded as convenient, prudent, or politic. This admission came with chagrin, as though they had defaulted. They thus revealed that they were letting themselves get hung up on the dilemma of absolute freedom versus any kind of control. Had they realized that in making their admission they almost succeeded in posing a paradoxic issue—how to get freedom and control to work creatively in tandem and to nurture that personal wholeness and human dignity which is the major responsibility to relevance of liberal learning—they would have had peace of mind on the soundness of their thinking. K. U. Smith and M. F. Smith might well have been cited to illustrate the role of creative constraints in human exertions: that constraints are not necessarily restrictive, repressive, life-diminishing.

While in his bodily motions the individual makes multidimensional responses, there is differentiation among these. There are the manipulative or articulative movements for the fine adjustments; there are the larger postural and transport movements. Both are necessary to the successful act. The finer, most skilled movements cannot be made without the support of the larger-movement components, which "maintain orientation and attention and establish the overall response pattern within which the skill is executed." Nor is this response pattern limited to overt psychomotor skills. It is "no less true of the implicit responses [such] as thinking." It applies to the "organization of highly complicated human skills, including symbolic skills."[6]

Joseph Tussman's *Experiment at Berkeley* illustrates the paradoxical nature of the creative constraints we are urging. Both the grounding of the program on the progressivist ideas of Alexander Meiklejohn and the very term *experiment* suggest change, innovation, novelty, freedom of expression. Yet the actual working out of the program suggests constraints since the program has a "completely required faculty-determined curriculum and structure," which, as one reviewer puts it, is "utterly alien to the spirit of 'student-initiated' programs." Yet at least for three years the program was operated "in complete freedom," and "much of the opposition based on misunderstanding disappeared."[7] The apparently extreme presumptiveness of this procedure is not here held up for emulation. The relevance here lies in the apparent attempt to effect a creative resolution of free expression versus constraint and thus to achieve a creative mediation.

Exercised tactfully, empathetically, justly, compassionately, and wisely, constraints are not merely useful, they are essential to purposive, self-actualizing, life-enhancing ends that are intimately bound up with the sense of personal wholeness and human dignity. At the Humanities Conference, what finally needed to be brought out was that competence in the imaginative, responsible, and constructive exercise of such constraints is a positive function of the process of enfranchisement for wholeness, which in its responsibility to relevance should be one of the cardinal aims of liberal learning.

For liberal learning in both the progressive and the traditional institutions of higher education, we urge creative mediation, which includes creative conservatism. There are signs that such

[6] K. U. Smith and M. F. Smith, *Cybernetic Principles of Learning and Design* (New York: Holt, 1956), pp. 50–51.

[7] J. Tussman, *Experiment at Berkeley* (New York: Oxford University Press, 1969). Reviewed in *Improving College and University Teaching*, 1970, *18* (1), 77.

conservatism is gaining renewed vigor and public attention. One sees the signs in those often cited as apologists for the now-ecstatics and for the anarchistic utopians. The signs of nascent, future-oriented neoconservatism are fast increasing—a conservatism that is resilient, dynamic. This neoconservatism is cutting across and penetrating below the extreme stereotypes, ideologies, and anti-ideologies of current polarizations and fanaticisms—both of the ultra-Left and of the ultra-Right. It taps reservoirs of sociocultural energy generated by the past and drawn into service on behalf of the perennial values—such as freedom, autonomy, and authenticity—that give life to the sense of personal wholeness and human dignity and that make so powerfully for the dignity of man.

I do not refer here particularly to that use of the past demonstrated in the sudden vogue attraction to such long-neglected Romantic visionaries as William Blake. Nor do I intend to espouse the primitive tribe as the model for the society of the present or the future or to adopt primitive shamanism as a revalidated, relevant, and viable telic model of the admirable man. I do not here point to Theodore Roszak's celebration of this sort of neomagical, neomystical epistemology, esthetic, ethic, and politic—this counterrational, comprehensive conception of the world, which pictures a sensate-emotive-mystical New Jerusalem "so vast, so marvelous that the inordinate claims of technical expertise must of necessity withdraw to a subordinate and marginal status in the lives of men."[8] Nor do I espouse Roszak's apocalyptic annunciation (echoing that of Thomas Carlyle when the latter was initiated into the Romantic movement by Madame de Staël's L'Allemagne) that "the primary project of our counterculture is to proclaim a new heaven and a new earth." I do not point to the Rousseauism of our George Leonards and Noam Chomskys or to the Wordsworthian nature primitivism and the sentimentalism of Paul Goodman.

I have in mind, indeed, the Goodman whom Roszak cites as a fertile contributor to the counterculture and whose New Reformation Roszak characterizes as "certainly the most discriminate dis-

---

[8] See T. Roszak, The Making of a Counter Culture: Reflections on the Technocratic Society and Its Youthful Opposition (Garden City, N.Y.: Doubleday, 1969). (Hereafter cited as Roszak, The Making of a Counter Culture.)

cussion of our youth culture yet to appear."[9] But my image is not
of Goodman the radical; it is of Goodman the conservative. Goodman doubly emphasizes his affinities with conservatism and his own
regard for it in the subtitle to his *New Reformation* and in the title
of one of his recent articles: "Notes of a Neolithic Conservative."[10]
The paradox of old and new in the term *neolithic* is likewise suggested in the title of Roszak's review of *The New Reformation:* "A
Radical Defense of Culture." *Culture* is used here to suggest the
experimental and traditional humanism of such men of letters as
Matthew Arnold who revered William Wordsworth and yet most
severely condemned him for his rejection of intellect.

In this paradoxical character of Goodman's conservatism—
as in that of Samuel Taylor Coleridge, John Milton, and Desiderius
Erasmus, the rebels and traditionists that he cites as his models—we
have compound illustration of the sort of creative mediation that
is the proper subject and method of liberal learning. This mediation
is achieved through unceasing and strenuous dialectic by which the
mighty opposites of drastic change and persistent duration, under
high pressure and temperature, may be bonded into a unified and
effective cultural matrix with forward thrust. Drawing heavily on
the past, a most subtle critic of positivistic rationalism, new sciences,
new technologies, new industrialism, and utilitarianism (that is,
philosophical radicalism), Coleridge wrought an entire literary and
esthetic revolution, the full effects of which we begin to appreciate
only now. He championed and demonstrated the role of imagination
and symbolic reason, functioning toward integration, synthesis, and
wholeness. Milton, rebel against the University Establishment, the
Ecclesiastical Establishment, the Political Establishment—champion
of the right to divorce and of the freedom of the press and the
autonomy of the individual—was nevertheless, to the end, a lover
of tradition—the grandeur that was Greece and the glory that was
Rome, as well as the Hebraic-rabbinic heritage. Erasmus, likewise
severe critic of the Ecclesiastical Establishment, rebel against the

[9] *Book World* (*Washington Post*), May 17, 1970, pp. 6–7; and
Roszak, *The Making of a Counter Culture*, pp. 178–204, 299.
[10] P. Goodman, *The New Reformation, Notes of a Neolithic Conservative* (New York: Random House, 1970); and "Notes of a Neolithic
Conservative," *New York Review of Books,* March 26, 1970, pp. 35–39.

University Establishment, advocated the revived classical humanities
for a new, life-giving mode of education with love not fear as the
master motivation. Yet in these views there was not destruction, not
root-and-branch extirpation as with Martin Luther, but integral
re-formation and re-creation, not destroying the past but conserving
it for purposes of creative transcendence toward comprehensive
unity.

     Goodman refers to himself as having a "conservative, maybe
timid disposition"; yet he trusts that "the present regime in America
will get a lot more roughing up than it has." Citing George Washington as a good example, he also mentions John Acton as one who
understood conservatism when he praised the character that is
"conservative in disposition but resolute in the disruptive action
that has to be performed." He calls himself an anarchist; but he
describes himself as a conservative anarchist: "I want to derange
as little as possible the powers that be; I am eager to sign off as soon
as conditions are tolerable. . . ." As a man of letters, he sees himself
finally as "most like Coleridge," whom he calls "the most philosophical of the conservatives writing in English: 'To have citizens we
must be sure we have produced men'—or conserved them."

     Goodman understands that "all positive value and meaning
is in present action, coping with present conditions," and that an
individual "behaves as the whole he has become." He nevertheless
gets "a kind of insight from seeing how a habit or institution has
developed to its present form and the remedying of certain lapses
in the present through taking into account some simplicities of the
past." He concedes that "the simpler state before things went wrong
is hopelessly archaic as a present response, but it has vitality and may
suggest a new program." He calls this idea the therapeutic use of
history—the therapeutic use of that which is conserved from out
of the past. A further use of the past—a telic-model use—is to "re-
mind of man's various ways of being great," and Goodman calls
this idea the "humanistic use of history"—a humanistic and telic
conservatism.

     In still another respect, Goodman shows himself to be, even
in his radicalism, a creative conservative. One of the most serious
shortcomings of so many of the social revolutionaries today is that,
as Rauschning said of Hitler's movement, theirs is a revolution of

nihilism. They may be effective as iconoclasts and destroyers, yet they are often terrifyingly deficient in what they have to offer by way of telic-image replacement. Here lies the difference between their ideologies and Goodman's. He explains: to "avoid arousing metaphysical anxiety, . . . I am rather scrupulous about not attacking unless I can think up an alternative or two." He adds: "Usually, indeed, I do not have critical feelings unless I first imagine something different."[11]

We previously called for an Erasmian temper of creative mediation in liberal learning. In his laudatory review of Goodman's *The New Reformation,* Roszak's stress on the author's Erasmian stance—as he calls it—is all the more significant to our present purposes. Roszak seeks to bring to bear upon his subject the Erasmian habit of seeking for the creative mean won by strenuous contestation between extremes. Just as Erasmus sought to keep from violent extremes the "impetuous moral outrage of the sixteenth century Protestants," so Goodman wishes to do the same for the young reformers of the present, who are "assuming many an ugly and foolish aspect of late." Their intolerance for real evils comes over into an indiscriminate rejection not only of science and technology but of intellect and culture generally. Referring to these young apostles of the counterculture, Roszak concludes his review thus: "Let us hope they will muster the goodwill to see how real is their critic's concern for the health of their soul, the strength of their cause." The task of liberal learning, in its role as creative conservationist of the heritage and as agency of creative mediation between the heritage and the creativity of the present, is to show this same sort of concern for the health of the students—for their wholeness. Elsewhere, Roszak spells out more specifically what such a concern implies. In his discussion of the collection of papers he has edited in *The Dissenting Academy,* he declares "that the proper and central business of the academy is the public examination of man's life with respect to its moral quality." He further affirms that "from first to last, the spirit of Socrates broods on the 'dissenting academy' which this volume comprises."[12] In this affirmation with its tribute to the

---

[11] Goodman, "Notes of a Neolithic Conservative," *ibid.,* p. 35.
[12] T. Roszak (Ed.), *The Dissenting Academy* (New York: Random House, 1968), p. viii.

perennial vitality and relevance of the spirit of Socrates, Roszak testifies not only to a residual conservatism even among the radical dissenters but, more specifically, to that strong vein of positive and critical, yet imaginative and ethicized, rationality which Socrates so persistently and variously urged and exemplified. This sort of rationality helps distinguish the paradoxic mediative and creative conservatism I now urge for both the progressive and the conservative institution of liberal learning.

Paul Goodman is not alone in showing this revived interest in creative conservatives of the past such as Matthew Arnold. This interest is also evident in a *New York Times Book Review* feature of its "Speaking of Books" series. The article is entitled "Matthew Arnold's Times, Our Times." It is not, as might at first be expected, written by a specialist with a vested interest in a revival of Victorian literary figures. It is by Richard Schickel, critic for *Life* and author of *The Disney Version* and a biography of D. W. Griffith.

Schickel cites the quotations from Arnold so generously scattered through John Fowles' best seller *The French Lieutenant's Woman* and "cannily selected to demonstrate the modernity of most Victorian thought." He then reports his impressions upon reading Arnold's *Culture and Anarchy,* so aptly titled for the present times also: It reveals how "really remarkably like our own was the epoch, a century ago," about which Arnold wrote; how the middle class then was "so blinded by its belief in technology as to be nearly inhuman"; how Arnold's "doing what he likes" is very close to the present catch phrase "doing your own thing," with the same personally and socially destructive implications.

Schickel further points to Arnold's distinction between the "everyday self," which is "always separate, personal, at war," and the "best self"—the telic self. He also points to Arnold's stress on the crucial role of the "man of culture" (or in our terms, the "man of liberal learning") who, having devoted himself to the activities of art, scholarship, and the written word, has likewise developed "the capacity to consistently be one's best self" and who therefore "could act as a balancing power between the forces of tyranny and the forces of anarchy." Transcending the classes, this man of liberal learning would resist the pressures to "become involved in transitory activism," for he would remember Goethe's dictum, "To act is easy, to think is hard." He would be devoted to esthetic cultivation; yet he would engage in "an endeavor to come at reason by means of reading, observing, and thinking." Hence, by learning to think more clearly, the men of affairs and action might "come at last to act less confusedly."

Schickel acknowledges that this potential view seems a bit too delicate "to oppose the mechanized, bureaucratized, media-manipulated spirit of our age, which so quickly, so unthinkingly, so temptingly beckons to the artist and the intellectual." Yet, he finds persistent relevance in Arnold's constant insistence that "the major issue is always civilization, and one can scarcely adopt incivility and unreason to its defense." Paying tribute to Arnold's "awesome sense of duty"—expressed as an educator, through years of hard work as well as through words—and acknowledging his flaws, Schickel nevertheless recommends *Culture and Anarchy* as "a model of disciplined social criticism," which "still teaches us much directly" and which "teaches even more by example."[13]

[13] R. Schickel, "Speaking of Books: Matthew Arnold's Times, Our Times," *New York Times Book Review,* October 11, 1970, pp. 2, 48. Compare J. Jerome, *Culture Out of Anarchy: The Reconstruction of American Higher Learning* (New York: Herder and Herder, 1970).

❧ NINE ❧

Formative Nature
of Man

Chapter Eight has shown that particular needs for constructive constraints exist in liberal learning which accepts its proper duties to
relevance. Such constraints may serve as creative counterpoises and
compensatory correctives to the negative aspects of sheer expression-
ism, with its explosiveness. The need for such constraints is deepened
by the fast-increasing pressures of change. Within many colleges
and the world at large, change—ignoring, inundating, or dissolving
traditional channels of constraint—is becoming the order, or disorder, of the day. Since the days of ancient Greek philosophers, what
has been designated as the flux is fast becoming the master principle.

Chief among the powerful changes that encompass the
students are those induced positively by our technetronic age and
negatively by resistance or counterthrust. One of the features of this
age is the tendency of technological change—if we may indulge in
an anachronism—to take the bit into its own teeth and to develop
along lines and toward ends not intended by its initiators. Lewis
Mumford pointed to this autarchic drive when he observed that
"the extravagant heights of Le Corbusier's skyscrapers had no reason for existence apart from the fact that they had become techno-

143

logical possibilities."[1] The same compulsion is seen in the American scientists and technologists who echoed John F. Kennedy when he stated that we must go to the moon for the simple reason that we can do it.[2]

Another feature of this age is that the rate of speedup of technological change is not arithmetic but geometric, in great part because change can now be induced by systematic invention. In the Author's Note to the 1969 reissue of *The Biological Time Bomb*, Gordon Taylor observed that, since he finished the manuscript of the book toward the end of 1967, important advances had occurred in several of the fields he had examined, which he had hardly expected to take place before the book was in print. He then asked: "If this is what twelve months of biological research has notched up, what will the next twelve months bring?" "The next ten years," he added, "may reveal as much as the past fifty."[3] Headed by Nobel Prize winner H. Gobind Khorana, scientists at the University of Wisconsin announced that they created a man-made gene which duplicates one occurring in a yeast cell. The Associated Press story described this accomplishment as a "profound step toward correction of inherited diseases, perhaps genetic 'engineering' of improved humans and animals, and perhaps ultimately artificial creation of life itself."[4] Here is just one item to corroborate Taylor's anticipation of the exponential rate of speedup in the one realm of biological research and application.

A third characteristic of the technetronic age is the totalistic impetus of technological change. While Victor Ferkiss and others consider that Jacques Ellul had stretched his use of the term *technique* too far, Ellul's definition is illustrative: "In our technological society, *technique* is the totality of methods rationally arrived at and

---

[1] L. Mumford, *The Urban Prospect* (New York: Harcourt, 1968), p. 135.

[2] In citing this instance, Dubos points out that Kennedy in turn was echoing G. Mallory's statement that Mount Everest *had* to be climbed simply because it was there (*So Human an Animal*, p. 16).

[3] G. R. Taylor, *The Biological Time Bomb* (New York: Signet, 1969), pp. ix–xi. See M. Ways, "Gearing U.S. Policy to the World's Great Trends," *Fortune*, May 1, 1969, p. 65: "During the last five years, while attention was focused on Vietnam, change has accelerated everywhere, calling for a restatement of goals and a restyling of operations."

[4] *Pennsylvania Mirror*, 1970, 2 (147), 1.

having absolute efficacy (for a given stage of development) in every field of human activity. . . . Technique is not an isolated fact in society (as the term *technology* would lead us to believe) but is related to every factor in the life of modern man."[5] The impacts of sheer technological change are thus seen as surging in upon social and educational agencies and processes and upon the individual's personal life.

A fourth characteristic of this technetronic age is that the changes induced by technological developments are not just in degree but add up to change in kind and hence yield unprecedented outcomes. As Ellul said of *technique*: "Its characteristics are new; the technique of the present has no common measure with that of the past."[6] When Peter Drucker wrote a book giving, as he said, guidelines to our changing society, he entitled it *The Age of Discontinuity*.[7] In so doing, he emphasized this attribute of discrete and abrupt changes yielding the unprecedented. *Fortune* put out a special issue in January 1969, now available in book form. Its title declares *American Youth: Its Outlook Is Changing the World.* By its very emergence and mushrooming growth, *The Chronicle of Higher Education* signals and stimulates the fast-rising tides of change that surge around, into, and out of the American colleges and universities. Another educational journal, with generous foundation funding, is *Change in Higher Education.* Writing, on October 15, 1968, to "persons interested in change and innovation in higher education," Samuel Baskin invited contributions to a column entitled "Innovators' Workshop," which would provide an Ann Landers for innovators. Imagine getting a grant, nowadays, for a publication entitled *Fixity in Higher Education* and with the motto "Hold fast to that which is good!" With a psychedelic cover *American Education* keeps blaring away at the need for change—drastic change, ubiquitous change in American education—from nursery school to geriatric center. "There is a computer in your future," declares this publication. It spells radical change, and the old-

[5] Ellul, *The Technological Society*, p. xxv.
[6] *Ibid.*
[7] P. F. Drucker, *The Age of Discontinuity* (New York: Harper, 1968). As applied to higher education, see also M. G. Scully, "A New Breed of Faculty Is Seen Producing 'Marked Discontinuities' on Campuses," *The Chronicle of Higher Education*, 1970, 5 (3), 1.

fashioned human-type professor had better get with it. If he does, he may still have some left-over teaching tasks. If he does not, he will be tossed on the pedagogic scrap heap.

Don Fabun, editor of the *Kaiser Aluminum News,* has devoted one issue to "The Children of Change." A whole collection of articles from the *Kaiser Aluminum News,* with the theme of drastic and pervasive change, has been published as a textbook—*The Dynamics of Change*—for large humanities programs in colleges and universities.[8] The dust jacket assures us that the questions raised in this book "have nothing to do with science fiction; they have to do with a reasoned and reasonable extension of accelerating trends in our society." The answers to these questions will "profoundly affect every aspect of the world as we know it," and the volume as a whole "suggests that the world will be almost totally different in character and texture from the world we live in today."

Commenting on this collection, *The Green Bay Gazette* has observed: "Fabun's view of the future is both frightening and challenging: frightening because the world of tomorrow seems to question man's whole way of doing things and challenging for the same reason." Concerning *The Dynamics of Change,* the *Huntsville Times* has reported: "The overall effect is to leave one slightly dizzy and in awe of our times." Taking his cue from the use of the term *culture shock* in a Peace Corps report, Alvin Toffler has referred to this dizziness in the face of accelerating technological change as future shock, and he has described it as the disorientation that we experience when the future hits us before we are prepared for it.[9]

[8] D. Fabun, *The Dynamics of Change* (Englewood Cliffs, N.J.: Prentice-Hall, 1967).

[9] A. Toffler, "The Future as a Way of Life," *Horizon,* 1965, 7 (3), 108. Since then Toffler has contributed an article entitled "Future Shock" to *Playboy,* February 1970, and in the same year a book by the same title (New York: Random House, 1970). Shortly after its publication, he presented his future-shock ideas on the NBC television program *Today* as well as on other talk programs. *Future Shock* appeared for the first time on the *New York Times Book Review* list of best sellers, in the issue for October 5, 1970. According to J. Beatty, Jr., by the spring of 1970, "future shock" had entered the language and was being used by doctors, psychiatrists, admen, publishers, and film critics (*Saturday Review,* 1970, *53* (20), 16). In his review of W. Braden's *The Age of Aquarius* (Chicago: Quadrangle Books, 1970), A. Toffler's *Future Shock,* Z. Brzesinski's *Between Two Ages,* and N. Calder's *Social Control of the Uses of Science* (New York: Simon and Schuster, 1970), E. E. Morison, author of *Men, Machines, and Modern*

Richard E. Farson, director of the Western Behavioral Sciences Institute, declares: "Each change produces a variety of fresh changes, each of which in turn produces more change, in a sort of expanding spiral; and the acceleration of change is so fast that soon there will be no coasting period, no resting time, no breathers. Change itself will be a way of life." In this statement, he is echoing Margaret Mead, who has frequently stressed that we are to educate our youngsters for a society in which change is the thing and which is geared in unpredictable directions toward an unprecedented culture.[10] Most important, parents should "adapt to this world of constant and often drastic change" and thus "discover how to bring up children to live in this unknown world, how to bring them up without absolutes." According to Dr. Mead, "the greatest gift we can give our children is to teach them to nest in the gale."[11]

Although this compulsive fixation on change has no discernible goal but instead exalts change as an end rather than as a means, a certain strain in American culture finds it agreeable. We may note clearly how Stephen Vincent Benet's unfinished *Western Star* aptly voices this strain when he asserts that while we do not know where we are going, we are on our way. He describes us as whistling as we go without really knowing or caring where. These words have their contemporary echoes in the now trite "The times they are a-changing" and in the ironic "The world is going nowhere, but the supersonic transport will get us there all the faster." Jerry Rubin declares: "I support everything which puts people into motion,

---

Times (Cambridge, Mass.: MIT Press, 1968) observes: "These are hardheaded men who have put aside Jacques Ellul's melancholy conviction that technology would do us in, have dismissed Marcuse's assumption of technological dictatorship, and have passed beyond Teilhard de Chardin's beclouded Omega Point" (*The New York Times Book Review*, July 20, 1970, p. 20). The review carries the caption: "What to do today before tomorrow gets you" (p. 3).

[10] For more elaborate treatment of this double stress on drastically changing education in and for an age of maelstrom change, see M. H. Goldberg, "The Structure and Problems of Human Values," *Symposium II*, pp. 69–98. See also *Automation, Education and Human Values, passim,* but especially M. Mead's contribution and M. H. Goldberg's introductory and concluding chapters.

[11] Cited by J. Sakol, "Margaret Mead: Remarkable Woman," *McCall's,* June 1970, p. 129.

which creates disruption and controversy, which creates chaos and rebirth."[12] The rebirth, moreover, is left to the vagaries of spontaneous generation and is to manifest itself from moment to moment; it is a matter of chancy change.

One of the omnipresent signs of change and reinforcement of the heightened awareness of change is evidenced in the term *throwaway*. We have throwaway cans, throwaway dishes and utensils, throwaway dresses, throwaway diapers, and even "throwaway children."[13] The self-destructing, anticultural or countercultural art happening is a throwaway as is the unstructured course. Each in the end self-destructs. Each heightens the impression that all is flux. In the title of his novel *Things Fall Apart,* borrowed by Chinua Achebe from William Butler Yeats' "The Second Coming," we have a concentrated statement of the sense of flux and dissolution so widespread in our times.[14]

One finds this same overwhelming accent among the prophets popular with the children of change: Herbert Marcuse, Timothy Leary, George B. Leonard, Marshall McLuhan—to mention a few. Featuring an article by McLuhan, *Harper's* magazine calls him "the Canadian comet." Perhaps a more descriptive name is the "Pied Piper of the technetronic flux." When his distinguished fellow English scholar Douglas Bush tried to sum up his impressions of McLuhan, he revived that Aristophanic dictum long before it was adopted by Walter Lippmann as epigraph for *The Good Society:* "Whirl is king, having driven out Zeus." It is no coincidence that Quentin Fiore, McLuhan's coauthor for *War and Peace in the Global Village* and R. Buckminster Fuller's coauthor for *I Seem To Be a Verb,*[15] is likewise designer of Jerry Rubin's *Do It.* In *Education and Ecstasy,* George B. Leonard revives the sensate emotionalism of Rousseau and describes how American schooling may take a leap toward joy and emotions so that all children become geniuses.

---

[12] Rubin, *Do It,* p. 247.
[13] See L. A. Richette, *The Throwaway Children* (New York: Dell, 1969). These are the "young victims of sex, drugs, violence, prostitution, and crime."
[14] C. Achebe, *Things Fall Apart* (New York: Fawcett, 1970).
[15] M. McLuhan and Q. Fiore, *War and Peace in the Global Village* (New York: Bantam, 1968); R. B. Fuller, J. Angel, and Q. Fiore, *I Seem to Be a Verb: Environment and Man's Future—By the Visionary Genius of Our Time* (New York: Bantam, 1970).

The book places major stress on the moment. Each moment of learning is a moment of ecstasy. Education is a matter of accumulating many such moments of learning. The children play learning games with computers that have a sense of humor and beauty. For them, technology thus becomes a turn-on for practicing psychic mobility.[16]

In its description of the ideal girl, *Glamour* magazine pays tribute to this contemporary passion for the momentary. She is the Breakaway Girl. "Intelligent, intense"; a heroine of our "inventing society," she is described as "inventing today." She is that "new generation girl risking the new experience." The Breakaway Girl "travels to be part of the world, not to escape it." She is "past discussing sex"; she is "concerned with sexuality." She has "made nudity acceptable fashion, naked beauty the new glamour." She has totally rejected the drab past. "Multiplied by millions," "massive in numbers, infinite in influence," the Breakaway Girl "equals the young force of change."[17] She is described as having "restructured just about everything." She seems, rather, to have unstructured all.

In reports of the murders of Sharon Tate and the guests in her Bel Air mansion in 1969, we have suggestions of what this restructuring of just about everything may come to in practice. Steven V. Roberts' *New York Times* feature on this massacre reports the principals as being "a part of the sexual revolution" depicted, for example, in John Updike's *Couples;* as "loving fast cars and motorcycles"; as "dramatizing a particular kind of hedonism: 'Eat, drink, and be merry, for tomorrow your agent may not return your call'; as being "mod, hip, swingy, trendy."

The characterization of Gibby Folger, one of the victims, is particularly pertinent. Heiress to a fortune made in wholesale coffee, Gibby, we are told, attended the Catalina School for Girls, had a "sumptuous debut," and "emerged from Radcliffe as a bright, well-educated, and aimless young woman."[18] In view of the need for

[16] G. B. Leonard, *Education and Ecstasy,* (New York: Delacorte, 1969), pp. 145, 153, 190 ff. See "Visiting Day," *Look,* October 1, 1968 pp. 40–41.

[17] *Glamour,* May 1969.

[18] See S. V. Roberts, "Polanskis Were at Center of a Rootless Way of Life," *New York Times,* August 31, 1969; and "Tate Principals Are Called Rootless," *St. Louis Post-Dispatch,* September 14, 1970. As has gruesomely been evidenced at the Manson trials, this rootless way of life of the

constructive constraints in one's development, it is worth noting that
one of Gibby's friends, speaking of the influence upon her of "an
uprooted Polish emigré" (another one of the victims of the slaughter), said: "He changed her outlook. She realized she didn't have
to conform to that damn Protestant ethic." The implication is that
since the sorts of prohibitions stressed in certain forms of the so-
called Protestant ethic are intrinsically bad or outmoded, all notions
of ethical patterning and shaping are likewise bad and outmoded
and must be rejected.

Vannevar Bush has written a book called *Science Is Not
Enough*.[19] We may adopt a parallel caption for our immediate
theme. In all this stress on change, we find indications that change
alone is not enough—that patternings are also needed, and patterning suggests something that stays in the midst of the change. We
may ask, with François Villon, "Where are the snows of yesteryear?"
Yet even the snowflake that melts in the stream and, as Robert
Burns put it, is "gone forever" has at least a momentary pattern that
resists change. Even a virus of fleeting life is a pattern.

Norman Mailer is commonly associated with uninhibited expression and outright explosiveness. Yet a critical study of him is
entitled *The Structured Vision of Norman Mailer*. Ezra Pound is
often associated with fragmentary poetic insights and critical impressions that shoot off in many directions and pierce like pieces of
shrapnel. Yet a study, "The Barb of Time," seeks to demonstrate
The Unity of Ezra Pound's Cantos.[20]

Often sharp and imaginative observation is necessary to discern the signs of pattern or the impulses toward pattern. The study
of cubism affords an instance. According to John Berger, in recreat-

---

alleged victims was more than matched by the moment-to-moment, mood-
to-mood improvisations of the "family" to whom the murders have been
attributed and of Manson himself. See also L. Schiller, *The Killing of
Sharon Tate* with "the exclusive story of the crime" by Susan Atkins (New
York: Signet, 1970); and "Life with Father," *Time*, February 15, 1971, p.
23. Manson called himself "a man of a thousand faces." During the nearly
nine months of his trial, his appearance "varied as drastically as his moods."
(Associated Press, *Pennsylvania Mirror*, March 8, 1971, p. 12.)

[19] V. Bush, *Science Is Not Enough* (New York: William Morrow,
1967).

[20] B. Leeds, *The Structured Vision of Norman Mailer* (New York:
New York University Press, 1969). D. D. Pearlman, *The Unity of Ezra
Pound's Cantos* (New York: Oxford University Press, 1969).

ing the syntax of art so that it could accommodate modern experience, cubism did not repudiate responsibility for pattern. In his paintings, the cubist "broke the surface of the coherent image into facets whose relationships could not be perceived instantly as a gestalt but only in relationship to each other in time."[21] In his poem "Nude Descending a Staircase," X. J. Kennedy illustrates this idea of Berger's painting. Kennedy claimed that the famous painting thus titled was merely the inciting stimulus for his poem.[22] But the relationship is closer than that. The poem verbally realizes the very sort of patterning that Berger ascribes to the painting. We can get this relationship in the concluding stanza. Through most of the poem, we have images of parts in motion. Even in the last stanza, we get this same notion of things in flux. But then a different tendency asserts itself. The analytical details in motion are pulled together into a preliminary whole when the poet describes the nude as wearing her slow descent like a long cape. However, when the poet declares that she collects her motions into shape, this description is prelude to the final unification of the details into a dynamic, comprehensive form. Marcel Duchamp's comment about his painting "Nude Descending a Staircase" provides another illustration of how variously and powerfully the love of wholeness asserts itself in man. The picture is simply a part of the original: "I lacerated part of myself in cutting off part of 'Nude Descending a Staircase.' " This statement testifies to the strength of that impulse which expresses itself in the deep love of wholeness and of what Plato called "the pursuit of the whole."

Art exhibitions that seek to celebrate flux by providing for the self-destruction or for the destruction by other agents of the very artifacts being shown nevertheless show at work man's basic will to form. Consider, for example, the program of multimedia psychedelic art experiences that the students at Pratt Institute staged. This program was widely publicized as one of happenings, and to the eye of the ingenuous beholder or the true believer these art experiences may have seemed to be many fleeting improvisations. However, the whole program was most meticulously planned, down to the finest

[21] Cited by C. Lehmann-Haupt, *New York Times*, September 15, 1969, reviewing J. Berger's *The Movement of Cubism and Other Essays* (New York: Pantheon, 1969).

[22] X. J. Kennedy, *Nude Descending a Staircase* (Garden City, N.Y.: Doubleday, 1961).

detail. It was carefully designed and structured. It was presented from an elaborately worked-out scenario. From its initial unfolding to the final self-destruction, it testified paradoxically to the basic form-making impulse in man. Immersing itself in the destructive element, it did so through a new idiom, seeming to give the lie ironically to the traditional doctrines of art as the preeminent vehicle for the expression of man as a maker of forms. In fact, it accomplished the opposite.

In the television series *Civilisation* and in his book of the same title, Kenneth Clark has vividly illustrated the positive correlation among the strength of civilization, the dominance of bold, purposeful planning, and the "cosmicizing" of their space. Clark cites the carvings on the prows of the Viking ships, which depict serpentine twistings and writhings and are thus the objective correlatives of the restless, unstable, unsettled—even atomistic—cultural milieu of the Vikings. Conversely, pointing to the isolated Christian outposts of Iona, in Wales, on the edge of Europe, Clark cites the Ionans' resort to art as a spell against the precariousness of their cultural situation. He exhibits their marvelously wrought ornaments, sword handles, scabbards, and the like—in their complex and intricate unity and wholeness—as so many triumphs, on behalf of civilization, against the flux.[23]

The successful poem, song, or painting is a particular instance of a human capacity that is antecedent to these particulars, which subsumes them and many others besides. Goethe—to whom Ludwig von Bertalanffy dedicated his *General Systems*—gave primacy in man to his formative nature. He thereby exposed something even more comprehensive and fundamental than the capacity that Ernst Cassirer and Susanne Langer, among others, have cited as a distinguishing feature for man: his symbol-making power. Starting generically with man's formative nature, we then find the symbol-making power more specifically falling into place as a most distinctive manifestation.

In a basic way the crucial function of form-making is recognized and employed in psychotherapy. A sign of extreme withdrawal is the abandonment of any efforts at patterning. Conversely, thera-

---

[23] See K. Clark, *Civilisation* (New York: Harper, 1970).

pists watch for even the most rudimentary and tentative efforts at shaping. They watch for such things as attempts at patterning through personal grooming, taking little sticks and putting them side by side, or taking a piece of string and knotting it at more or less regular intervals. They regard these actions as indications of the patient's incipient efforts to reassert his personhood, and they seize upon these indications as opening the way to further, complex patterning on the long road to normalcy—that is, to full humanity. In our everyday experiences, we can observe numerous instances of man's formative nature at work. When a child makes mud pies or when he and his father make a sand castle, they are testifying to the primacy in man of his formative nature. When we stack a cord of wood, organize a neighborhood improvement league, design a business firm or government agency, or transform a crowd into a community or a group into a commune, we display this formative nature. But, above all, we do so when we try to shape our own character, when we try to form our own wholeness.

For Goethe, as with the ancient Stoics, man's striving toward his wholeness was simply the expression of his participation in that wholeness nature reveals "in her every part." Recent evidence for this pervasive wholeness is found in cloning. The whole organism can be reproduced not just from germ cells but from cells in other parts of the organism; hence, each cell has encoded on it the whole genetic pattern.[24]

In no teleological, mystical, or even old-fashioned vitalistic sense and resisting contemporary pressures toward survival-utility reductivism, the Swiss biologist Adolf Portmann has affirmed, as an ultimate fact of the organic world, the universality of the surface patterns of form, color, movement. He cites species such as the sea snail, which has no eyes. For some species the visible pattern has a useful purpose, such as courting, hence reproduction, hence survival of the species. Yet for the sea snail, as for other species lacking sight, the visible pattern, which serves no useful function, "is nevertheless constant, intricate, and universal, even as it is in the

[24] See "Cell's Quality Shown," *Pennsylvania Mirror*, Oct. 20, 1970. J. B. Gurdon and R. Laskey of Oxford University "have demonstrated experimentally that a single adult specialized cell, such as a skin cell, actually contains all the genetic information needed to produce a complete creature with skin, bones, organs and everything else."

high forms of life. . . . It is a basic character of living things."
There are suggestions that the symmetrical patterns of this organic
phenomenon are, in turn, related fundamentally to functions that
actualize what may be encoded on cerebral templates or models.
Using the amplified light waves of the laser and the analytical aid
of the digital computer, scientists have shown that controlled brain
disturbances yield corresponding disturbances in the normal symmetrical pattern of the spider's web.[25]

In their word *poet,* which means maker or shaper, the ancient Greeks gave specificity to the primacy in man of his formative
nature. Similarly, when the Elizabethans talked of art in playwriting,
they did not mean technique or mere craftsmanship; they meant,
to borrow from Fuller, the artist's skill in comprehensive design.

In his autobiographical writing, John Milton, a musician as
well as poet, stressed the importance of education in the *architec-
tonice,* which freely translated means the intellectual, rhetorical, and
poetic art of dynamic structuring. Such art is a matter not of set
forms but of forms in process of becoming, striving to fulfill the
law of their own being. It was not by chance that of the classical
heroes Milton was most attracted to Orpheus, for the myth of
Orpheus celebrates this Apolline demigod's architectonic power.
Through the patterns of musical harmony he created, Orpheus is
said to have caused towns to rise in corresponding symmetrical form.
These towns were thus shaped by templates of harmonies.

Milton described pandemonium, the rebel angels' great
council hall in hell, as emerging "like an exhalation" to musical
accompaniment, as by a counterarchitectonic. By virtue of the constructive power of his music, Orpheus was also claimed to have
tamed the chaos of animal passions into peaceful harmony. Thus,
according to the Orphic myth, to bring order out of chaos—whether
civic chaos or bestial passions—was the master art of civilizing.
This master art is the more general form toward which the more
specific liberal learning tends. Both the general and the specific

[25] A. Portmann and M. Grene, "Beyond Darwinism," *Commentary,*
1965, *40* (5), 31–41 (the present citations are from Grene's exposition of
Portmann's doctrines); and Science Service story, *New York Times,* April 8,
1964. The researches on the Spider were carried on by C. F. Reed and P. N.
Witt of the State University of New York, Upstate Medical Center, Syracuse.

forms—civilization and liberal learning—are in turn expressions of man's formative nature.

Hence, a central function of liberal learning is to help the student gain rich and varied experiences in diverse modes of fulfilling his formative nature. Liberal learning performs this function through the expressive disciplines of the practicing arts and through the cognitive disciplines—the natural sciences, mathematics, and philosophy at one end of the disciplinary continuum; the social sciences at the other end; and the intermediary disciplines, notably poetry and other creative literature, in the middle.

Since the 1950s we have put renewed emphasis upon the cognitive aspects of the processes of liberal learning as a matter of form-making. This emphasis is evident within a given discipline or field and involves comprehensive interdisciplinary integration and unification toward wholeness. The movement toward education through fundamental structuring is represented by such figures as Jerome Bruner. In 1963, Donald K. Smith stressed five points indicating the trend: each intellectual discipline worthy of the name rests on some underlying conception and methodological structuring; the knowledge generated by the discipline is most effectively learned as it becomes linked to an understanding of this underlying structure; such understanding presumably facilitates the transfer of knowledge; one "of the pressing tasks of our age is that of uncovering the conceptual and methodological structure on which our numerous disciplines rest"; conceivably, these might turn out to be "relatively few."[26] Stresses on interdisciplinary form-making, as evidenced by the literature on the taxonomy of knowledge (see Benjamin Bloom and Giorgio Tagliacozzo), are a few indications of the scope of form-making and experiencing in liberal learning.

At the Center for the Study of Democratic Institutions, Ileane Marcelescu, the Roumanian philosopher and geneticist, summarized the interdisciplinary, multinational dialogue on European structuralism as an "emerging, highly controversial new method of looking at things past, present, and future." He noted further that the "universality of structure also imposes a limitation on understanding structuralism. . . . Whatever you utter, look at, or do has,

[26] *Alumni News*, University of Minnesota, April 1963, pp. 8 ff.; see also D. Bell, *The Reforming of General Education*.

irrefutably, a structure. If, then, you go on defining structure as an organization of elements in which modification of the parts correspondingly affects the whole, the enterprise becomes undistinguishable from gestalt psychology or from the most common praxis of any scientist. Thus the specificity of structuralism gets lost, and with it goes its usefulness." From the point of view of liberal learning as designed heuristics, what Marcelescu regards as a limitation could become a welcome pedagogic opportunity and challenge. Meeting the student where he is, through practice and gestalt exertion, one may then lift him to education at the much higher levels of structuralist concerns—at the complex, sophisticated, and intellectually challenging levels. As for the expressed fear of structuralist desiccation, forewarned is forearmed. The limitation of an otherwise useful instrumentality for liberal learning should not mean its rejection.[27]

To the strongly ratiocinative modes should be added the dominantly psychoethical and socioethical, as well as the esthetic, as evidenced and experienced through the practicing humanities—namely, the fine arts. However, the stress should be on the total balanced and proportionate development of these several modes of form-making and experiencing in liberal learning.

Several circumstances seem to have conspired for the Humanities Endowment and the Arts Foundation to give primacy to the esthetic modes, as is apparent in the new humanities movement.[28] Significantly, the *Journal of Aesthetic Education* seems to

[27] "Made in France: A New Way of Looking at Things," *Center Report*, Center for the Study of Democratic Institutions, 19790, *3* (4), 20–21; D. A. Sears, "The Failure of the Humanities," *CEA Forum*, 1970, *1* (1), 13; J. Ehrmann (Ed.), *Structuralism* (Garden City, N.Y.: Doubleday, 1970). See also D. W. Gotshalk, *The Structure of Awareness: Toward a Situational Theory of Truth and Knowledge* (Urbana, Ill.: University of Illinois Press, 1969); and T. C. Oden, *The Structure of Awareness* (New York: Abingdon Press, 1969). In addition to the aforementioned Ehrmann book, *Paperbound Books in Print*, 1970, *15* (7), 1473, lists under the topic "Philosophy—General" the following books with *structure* or *structural* in the title: A. Grava (Ed.), *Structural Inquiry into the Symbolic Representation of Ideas;* N. Goodman, *Structure of Appearance;* A. Stigen, *Structure of Aristotle's Thought;* M. M. Ponty, *Structure of Behavior;* D. Riepe and J. Pustilnik, *Structure of Philosophy;* R. S. Hartman, *Structure of Values: Foundations of Scientific-Axiology.*

[28] G. Weinstein and M. Fantini, *Toward Humanistic Education: A Curriculum of Affect* (New York: Praeger, 1970): "Investigators for the Elementary School Teaching Project discovered that the 'secret' of involving

be the most ambitious and impressive "think journal" for the new interdisciplinary humanities programs in the schools and colleges. One senses this strong esthetic predilection of the new humanities movement at the annual conference on humanities teaching, sponsored by the National Council of Teachers of English, and also in *The Humanities Journal,* organ of the National Association for Humanities Education.

Not all who stress an esthetic approach to the new humanities programs place much emphasis upon systematic, intellectually self-conscious disciplines in form-making and experiencing. For some, the overwhelming emphasis is upon spontaneous self-expression. Another strong motif is the sociopolitical, with dominant emphasis on direct-action programs of social reform or revolution. This emphasis is seen in the manifesto of the New Art Association, which at its first national convention declared in part that the members are "against the myth of the neutrality of art" and that they object to "the study of art as an activity separated from human concerns." Denying that esthetic experiences flow only into further esthetic experiences, they "believe there is a firm tie between the artistic imagination and social imagination" and in the words of one spokesman they "must struggle to inject in our society a concept of use for the artist and his product"—the "writer's sensibility is required to maintain life in a better fashion." Among the topics on the conference agenda was teaching of undergraduate art and art history.[29]

In this movement we see a parallel with the estheticism of the New Critics and the activistic socioethicism of the Popular Frontists during the early thirties. Often those who stress idiosyncratic self-expression as their esthetic (with ignoring or destroying established structures as corollary) come together with those who stress social anarchism or nihilism in enthusiasm for the destructive element and the countdown to chaos.

All in all, form-making and experiencing are to be found mainly among those who have a more or less consciously and system-

---

any child in the learning process is to offer him a 'Curriculum of Affect'— based on his own concerns and responses to the world."

[29] G. Glueck, *New York Times,* November 1, 1970, p. 86.

atically developed esthetic rationales for the humanities programs.[30]
An extreme emphasis on the esthetic component in the form-making
phases of liberal learning is just as much to be deplored and resisted
as that upon the high-and-dry ratiocinative modes, which easily lead
to celibacy of the intellect. We thus return to our theme of creative
mediation for strenuous and progressive balance on behalf of personal and societal wholeness.

Man's formative nature, then, expresses itself through shap-
ings other than those of the practicing arts. Most important for
liberal learning and the achievement of personal and human dignity,
it does so to avoid the fragmented person and to realize personal
wholeness. The shaping of the whole person is a comprehensive
expression and fulfillment of man's formative nature. It is his
masterwork. The search for this wholeness connected with patterning is illustrated in an observation by Christabel, a character in
James Kennaway's novel *The Cost of Living Like This*. The observation has to do with the issue of the "ghost in the machine"—
that is, the issue of telic purposiveness: "If I were to describe my
heart, and I do not mean the physical organ, I would have none of
the difficulties which beset philosophers when they argue about the
ghost in the machine. My heart, I see now, is the design of my life
. . . the sense I have made of experiences invited and experiences
thrust upon me."[31]

On the bulletin board of a midwestern liberal arts college a
sign reads: Celebrate your existence even though it is fragmented.
Man's formative nature says, rather: Celebrate your existence by
pulling the fragments together around a durable template of wholeness, by gathering together, as Isis did, the scattered limbs of Osiris,
and by reconstituting them as a vital whole. Students feel the primal
impulse toward personal wholeness within themselves and social
wholeness for the group. As Jonathan Swift and other satirists have
so often done, they reveal this impulse by registering their sense of
its lack, achieving, through irony, a catharsis—a purgation of protest and yearning. Before the Harvard uprising, the student editors

[30] See H. S. Broudy, "The Artist and the Future," *The Journal of
Aesthetic Education*, 1970, 4(1), 12–22, especially pp. 15–16.
[31] J. Kennaway, *The Cost of Living Like This* (New York:
Atheneum, 1969), p. 135.

of the Harvard *Lampoon* put out a *Life* parody issue with the permission of the publishers of *Life*. Prophetic of local events, the front cover carried the ominous caption: End of the World. The cover picture shows an oversized egg on which is depicted a vari-colored map of the world. This depiction is reminiscent of a painted Easter egg and all its associations with joy, fertility, life, growth, hope, wholeness. However, the egg and hence the map are fractured, and through the jagged break the yolk is spilling out. Ludicrous yet grim, it is Humpty Dumpty all over again but magnified to cosmic proportions. The magnification is symbolic of the way the students feel about the fractured wholeness.

Students would not be content with the sort of surface whole-ness that Frank Borman pictured (as *Life* quoted him and as the May 1969 issue of *American Education* requoted on its cover with a picture of the earth viewed from outer space): "We are one hunk of ground, water, air, clouds, floating around in space. From out there, it really is one world." This one world would seem to be an echo of the forties and of the phrase that was a favorite of Wendell Willkie. Yet there is a crucial difference. Willkie's use of the phrase *one world* was a synecdoche. He had in mind the world being brought together through more than transportation and communi-cation networks.

Even so, the eagerness with which the Borman statement was grasped and widely broadcast is a tribute not only to the yearning for human solidarity but also to the need in man for a sense of wholeness. So, too, were the tremendously enthusiastic receptions of the astronauts in their triumphal visits abroad. These tributes should be recognized. The statement of the astronauts that what they achieved was not for themselves, the space administration, or the United States but for mankind may seem like propaganda. One cannot ignore that an American flag was placed on the moon. Yet, even if one tends to hear hypocrisy in the astronauts' declaration, one needs to recognize that, in fact, the achievement of the astro-nauts has contributed toward the realization of Willkie's vision of one world. This contribution is due in part to the universal need among men for heroes to worship (among many teen-age girls, the current replacement of the middle-aged model of male lover for the teen-aged model has been attributed to the hero worship of the astronauts, who from the teen-age perspective are middle aged). It is also due to the fresh surge of pride in human prowess. We assume vicariously the grand capacity and accomplishment which we witness in the hero. Thus, Borman's statement also expresses one of the central concerns of liberal learning—namely, wholeness.

A humanities teacher, discussing her son's college education, complained: "We sent our son to college. We told him we wanted him to be educated into a 'whole' man. And, it seemed, he wanted that, too." Then she added: "By the time he was a senior he had forgotten that this goal was why he had come to college." The particular agency of liberal learning to which he had been entrusted had apparently failed in two aspects of its responsibility to relevance: in its task to help him develop and experience his formative nature and in its task of helping him formulate and move toward the realization of his wholeness.

Hence, without being a gradgrind, sadist, or reactionary, one should regard education in and for sheer change as bad, for it is not merely such reactionary thinking that sees in it betrayal of the student and defaulting of liberal learning. Rather, whether conservative or progressive one should regard such education as defaulting in two respects: because it is at variance with basic humanizing impulses in man and hence with basic needs of the psyche and of society for personal and social health—for wholeness.

From scientific research come welcome reinforcements to faith in man's capacity to assert and embody his formative nature through creativity. We have, for example, the findings of René Dubos, distinguished microbiologist and experimental pathologist of Rockefeller University. In his article "Toward a Humanistic Biology" and in his book *So Human an Animal*,[32] Dubos generalizes about the behavior of organisms, and these generalizations have far-reaching importance for liberal learning and its responsibilities to relevance. In contrast to B. F. Skinner's claims, Dubos' generalizations are nondeterministic, nonmechanistic, nonbehavioristic. Here

---

[32] Dubos, "Humanistic Biology," pp. 179–98; and Dubos, *So Human an Animal*. See also C. H. Waddington, *The Ethical Animal* (London: Allen & Unwin, 1960); R. W. Westcott, *Divine Animal: An Exploration of Human Potentiality* (New York: Funk & Wagnalls, 1968).

is new scientific support for the insistence that, in the words of
William Henley, "I have a bit of fiat in my soul." Regrettably, the
dust jacket of *So Human an Animal* carries the misleading caption,
"How we are shaped by surroundings and events," which throws
the beat on the wrong foot—on the foot of environmental determinism, which Dubos does not affirm, rather than on that of self-
fiat, which he so strongly affirms and convincingly demonstrates.

Each person has primary power of initiation, hence power
of choice, and thus ethical responsibility. These capacities go far
toward contributing to one's potential for personal wholeness and
human dignity. Each person has the implicit will and potential
ability to assert himself upon the environment and, conversely, by
thus successfully and purposively asserting himself, to cause changes
in that environment which redound to his further internal gain. The
individual moves toward fulfillment of his formative nature and,
hence, toward maturation of his personal wholeness and social dignity through this complex process that starts from within and ultimately returns or brings returns to him.

According to Dubos, the justification in biological research
for this assertion of man's power of initiation and, hence, of his basic
ethical responsibility may be found in the behavior of organisms
from amoeba to man. None is just a passive responder to stimuli
but is also a reactor. Here the difference lies in the distinction between letting oneself be pushed around and asserting, "See here, I'm
not going to be pushed around." From one end of the behavior
spectrum, man appears as "an ordinary physiochemical machine,
complex, of course, but nevertheless reacting with environmental
forces according to the same laws that govern inanimate matter."
From the other end of the spectrum, however, "man is seen as a
creature that is rarely a passive component in the reacting system."
Indeed, "the most characteristic aspect of his behavior is the fact
that he responds actively and often creatively." He "does not react
passively to physical and social stimuli. . . . Whenever he functions, by choice or accident, he selects a particular niche, modifies
it, develops ways to avoid what he does not want to perceive, and
emphasizes that which he wishes to experience." Indeed, "man is the
more creative the better he is able to convert passive reactions into

creative responses."[33] These creative responses, expressive of man's formative nature, often exert themselves toward the actualization of patterns projected by the imagination.

Bertalanffy distinguishes between closed systems and open systems. A closed system functions only in predetermined ways. An open system, such as a living organism, presents a different picture: "Present-day biologic theories emphasize the 'spontaneity' of the organism's activity which is due to built-in energy." The organism is not a passive but a basically active system. "Internal activity rather than reaction to stimuli is fundamental. . . . Spontaneous activity is primary and stimulus-response is a regulatory mechanism superimposed upon it." Therefore, the organism is not a robot, but originally holistic behavior becomes progressively, yet never completely, mechanized.

In several ways, such statements release man from bondage to behavioristic and mechanistic determinisms and through granting this freedom contribute to the sense of personal wholeness and human dignity. They free him from incarceration within the robot model of automaton manipulation and from the deterministic tendencies within the homeostatic systems principle. This emphasis exclusively on the tendency of systems toward equilibrium provides a deterministic model for the psychoanalytical theory that health consists in the achievement of the only primary tendency in man—equilibrium through the discharge of tensions.

Hence, we have the reorientation in psychology to emphasis on "the creative side of human beings, aspects that are nonutilitarian and beyond homeostatic adaptation to external factors and the biological values of subsistence and survival." Here, too, lie such epistemological and ontological consequences as freedom from what Bernard Kaplan called the "dogma of immaculate perception"—that is, the idea that the "organism is a passive receiver of stimuli, sense data, information—whatever you call it—coming from outside objects." Then, in a rather mysterious way, this information is "reprojected into space to form perceptions which more or less truly mirror the external world." Man expresses his formative nature

[33] Dubos, "Humanistic Biology," p. 185; and Dubos, *So Human an Animal,* p. 49.

through form-making: "The principle of the active, psychophysical organism thus pertains not only to the motoric or 'output' part of behavior but also to 'input,' to cognitive processes. Perception is not a passive mirroring of a world outside like a color photograph; rather incoming information is, by a creative act, organized into a universe."[34] In responsibly asserting his fiat, the individual thus contributes a factor toward his sense of personal wholeness and human dignity. Since wholeness and dignity are the creative responsibility of liberal learning, part of the dynamics of liberal learning is to help the student recognize, strengthen, and assert this implicit sense of personal initiative.

Modern scientists demonstrate what the masters of yoga have known and exemplified for centuries: we can learn to control body functions once believed to be involuntary, to change the rhythm of brain waves, to sweat more, to salivate less, to control heartbeat. Both ancients and moderns thus testify to the individual's extraordinary potential for voluntarism.[35]

The functioning of man's formative nature is an expression of his breakthrough out of the iron ring of stimuli pushing in on him from the outside. It is an assertion of his creative might against shapelessness and chaos. It is suggested by that opening operation of pulling a pot, when, in his attempt to get the lump firmly centered, the potter fights the clay, and the clay, instead of just being passive, plastic, docile, fights back.

It would follow, also, that the Dubosian and the Bertalanffian stress on voluntarism plays an important part in man's formative

[34] Bertalanffy, *Organismic Psychology and Systems Theory*, pp. 50–53.

[35] M. Pines, *McCall's*, June 1970, p. 48; and M. Eliade, *Patanjali and Yoga*, Charles Lam Markham (Trans.) (New York: Funk & Wagnalls, 1969). See also D. R. Rorvik, "Brain Waves: The Wave of the Future." "Psychedelic drugs may soon give way to the electronic high, a new brain-wave mastery over mind and body" (*Look*, October 6, 1970, pp. 88, 90–94, 97). Rorvik reports that B. Brown—Chief for Experimental Physiology at the Veteran's Administration Hospital in Sepulveda, California, a psychopharmacologist and psychophysiologist with the development of five important drugs to her credit—"agrees wholeheartedly" with E. and A. Green of the Menninger Foundation, who in a paper authored with D. Walters conclude that "the most significant thing that may be facilitated through training in the voluntary control of internal states is the establishment of a Tranquility Base, not in outer space but in inner space, on or within the lunar being of man" (p. 97).

nature through patterning—through telic, projective model-making and image-making. This voluntarism shapes the appealing ideal image of man. The aspiring individual falls in love with such an image (this is the large meaning of the Platonic eros), and he shapes it enthusiastically toward realization, in love. Thus, to man, "a work of indeterminate form," endowed with a capacity to strive to be that which he will, Pico Della Mirandola declares: "Thou . . . art the molder and maker of thyself; thou mayest sculpt thyself into whatever shape thou dost prefer."[36] To which should be added that potent force named last in the following bulletin board appeal: "Whoever took the wood sculpture from Room 119, please put it back. A lot of time and effort and love went into it."

The term *form* is not used here in an exclusively or technically Platonic, Aristotelian, or Scholastic sense. Nor is it used in a narrowly mechanical sense, but rather, in its full range of general meaning, it includes the perceptive, emotional, imaginative, esthetic, ratiocinative, intellectual, ethical, social, and spiritual. Frost said that art strips life to its basic form. Similarly, in Nietzschean terms, form is the Apolline force: It exercises a benevolent constraint or coercion upon the spontaneous, expansive drives within liberal learning, disciplining these exuberant drives to their appropriate and responsible fulfillment.

Nowhere, perhaps, is this paradox of freedom and form more variously and engagingly resolved than in play. Why are the great archetypal activities of human society so permeated with play? Why is play regarded as so important, so necessary, or at least so useful a function? A frequent answer is that play is a response to the life instinct or the sexual instinct and that the latter "demands a union with others and with the world around us based not on anxiety and aggression but on narcissism and erotic exuberance."

---

[36] Mirandola, *On the Dignity of Man,* p. 5. See also B. O'Kelly (Ed.), *The Renaissance Image of Man and the World* (Columbus, Ohio: Ohio State University Press), 1966. See also *The Problems of Civilizations,* Report of the First Synopsis Conference of the S.I.E.C.C. (International Society for the Comparative Study of Civilizations), Salzburg, October 8–15, 1961, O. F. Anderle (Ed.) (The Hague, Netherlands: Mouton, 1964); and S. Radhakrishnan and P. T. Raju (Eds.), *The Concept of Man: A Study in Comparative Philosophy* (Lincoln, Nebr.: Johnsen, 1960), especially p. 39; R. Bourne, "Introduction," *Twentieth Century,* J. C. Colton (Ed.) (New York: Time-Life, 1968), pp. 5–6.

If this explanation is true, the exuberance is not at all unbridled. According to Johan Huizinga, it is a creative reaction to the necessity for order that so often seems otherwise to determine our lives and to impose itself upon the apparent randomness of so much about us. In Huizinga's opinion, play "creates order, *is* order: the impulse to create orderly form animates play in all its aspects. Into an imperfect world and into the confusion of life, it brings a temporary, a limited perfection"—that is, an intrinsic wholeness. The terms often associated with play suggest the successful mediation of the paradox of freedom and form. On the one hand, there are such terms as *contrast* and *variation;* on the other hand, *poise, balance, rhythm, harmony,* and most notably *tension.* Through the successful management of tension, the paradox is creatively maintained, and we experience the resulting order and rhythmic harmony as enchanting, captivating, beautiful, and joyous.[37]

In this context, then, form does not mean restrictive, life-denying inhibition. Rather, it means the disciplining yet guiding, nurturing, encouraging push of initiating motivation and impulse, and it also means the end purpose of the creative process toward which the creative effort is prompted or drawn for its telic fulfillment.[38]

[37] J. Huizinga, *Homo Ludens: A Study of the Play Element in Culture* (Boston, Mass.: Beacon, 1955), p. 8.
[38] See, also, T. C. Kuhn, *The Structure of Scientific Revolutions* (Chicago: University of Chicago Press, 1962); and C. H. Waddington, *Behind Appearance* (Cambridge, Mass.: M.I.T. Press, 1970).

Serving sciences . . . are all directed to the highest end of the mistress knowledge, by the Greeks called architectonike, *which stands . . . in the knowledge of a man's self, in the ethic and politic consideration, with the end of well-doing and not of well-knowing only, . . . the ending end of all knowledge being virtuous action.*
—*Sir Philip Sidney*, Defense of Poesy

❧ TEN ❧

Architectonic Mode

A major crux, implicit in the discussions of the preceding chapters, has been grotesquely twisting the American university. The problem is a result of two antagonistic forces—the technocratic and the apocalyptic. Both forces are at odds with the design in liberal learning that we have been elucidating: generously reasonable, respecting and including the extrarationlistic, humane, dynamic, organismic, telic, and holistic. Both are at odds with the architectonic mode in liberal learning. For these forces the architectonic mode may well serve as a means of creative accommodation and reconciliation, as a regenerative force. Let us consider the holistic, organismic design in liberal learning as used in the context of the architectonic mode.

166

Holistic is a term with many connotations. Colloquially, we have a holistic statement when, in a revived motion picture, Will Rogers says to his wife: "Without you I'd have been scattered all over the prairie. Somehow or other you always piece me together again." We also have a holistic statement when we say that we are at one with ourselves or when, referring to karate, we say that one has to put his whole body into the blow. Holistic may be applied to a feeling about experience, to a comprehensive feeling about life, to a heuristic motivation, to an intellectual style or way. Moreover, within each meaning, significant differentiations are made—for example, between holistic as related to the static and as related to the dynamic, between holistic as mechanistic and as organismic.

Organismic imaging has a long history in Western culture. Plato used it; scholars such as Morse Peckham made organicism a major distinguishing attribute of the Romantic movement in Europe and America in the late eighteenth and early nineteenth centuries. Social Darwinism helped make organicism a master image for society[1] (sometimes analogetic, sometimes literal, sometimes confused). As used in reference to holistics, this organicism gains psychosomatic as well as cultural meaning when it is thought of in connection with the development, since the early twenties, of the organicism school. As advanced by this school, the organismic doctrine emphasizes the organized structural pattern of living systems. It regards an organism as a complex system of relations with a characteristic form of ordering and change.

Lancelot Law Whyte has mentioned Alfred North Whitehead, d' Arcy Thompson, Charles M. Child, Kurt Goldstein, Ludwig von Bertalanffy, Joseph Niedham, and Joseph Woodger as among those who have contributed to this school. He might have added numerous others, such as Jan Christiaan Smuts, Lewis Mumford, José Ortega y Gasset, Wilhelm Dilthy, Erwin Schrödinger, Jean Piaget, Edmund Sinnott, Ray E. Torrey, Howard Lee Nostrand, and Kenneth Boulding. Organismic holism, moreover, has gained specificity from Walter B. Cannon's *The Wisdom of the Body*.[2]

[1] H. S. R. Elliot, *Herbert Spencer* (Freeport, N.Y.: Books for Libraries Press, 1917, reprinted 1970), pp. 128, 140–42.
[2] L. L. Whyte, *Internal Factors in Evolution* (New York: Braziller, 1965), p. 32ff. (cited in Burnshaw, *Seamless Web*, p. 41). For Schrödinger,

The division of counseling of at least one very large state university is offering group experiences for undergraduate and graduate students who wish to work on various personal concerns or improving relationships with other people (friends, dating partners, parents, and so on). The bulletin board announcements of this service carry the caption Get It Together. This caption helps explain why the human potential movement is often called holistic. Yet its holism touches the architectonic mode of liberal learning only in spots and in fact may much more often work at odds with it.

The present use of the term *holistic* is not far from that found in Allen Sievers' explanation of what, among economists, binds together such varied figures as John Kenneth Galbraith, Howard Hanson, William Ramsey Clark, and Hermann Alexander Keyserling. "They have one trait in common," says Sievers, "which makes them particularly suitable for this quest—their philosophical outlook." He elaborates: "We may call their common approach *holistic*: The essence of this outlook is to recognize the wholeness or *organic unity* of society and the combination of voluntaristic and deterministic forces which give it unity."[3]

In *Cure for Chaos,* Simon Ramo offers a borderline case between a mechanistic and an organismic holism. "In the systems approach," he states, "concentration is on the analysis and design of the whole, as distinct from the analysis and design of the components or parts." The systems approach, he further states, "depends upon use of a team of cooperating experts. . . . It starts by a definition of goals and ends with a description or a design of a harmonious, optimum ensemble of the required men and machines." Ramo stipulates that his cooperating team be made up of "experts in both the technological and the nontechnological aspects of the

see the combined volume *What Is Life? Mind and Matter* (Cambridge, Eng.: Cambridge University Press, 1967). W. B. Cannon, *The Wisdom of the Body* (New York: W. W. Norton, 1963). See also B. F. Wegener, *Organic Philosophy of Education* (Dubuque, Iowa: William C. Brown, 1957): "The philosophic orientation is 'organic' in the tradition from Plato and Aristotle to the contemporary thought of Alfred North Whitehead."

[3] A. M. Sievers, *Revolution, Evolution and the Economic Order* (Englewood Cliffs, N.J.: Prentice-Hall, 1962), p. 45. See too W. Buckley, *Sociology and Modern Systems Theory* (Englewood Cliffs, N.J.: Prentice-Hall, 1967); and *Source Readings in Integrative Studies. A Bibliography* (New Rochelle, N.Y.: Center for Integrative Education, 1971).

problem." He criticizes those who have "all too often the naive assumption that technological tools can be used for real-life problems of the humanized aspects of our civilization." He insists that "such views are based on unnecessarily limited definitions of the systems approach." This view " 'in large' includes emphatic reliance on consideration of the often controlling qualitative factors and on judgment and intuition and experiences that are not quantifiable."[4] This open-ended view at least allows for the possibility of absorbing a dominantly mechanistic holism into a more comprehensive organismic holism, which stresses that the whole includes much more than the sum of its measurable parts—more, even, than the sum of quantifiable interrelationships among these parts.

It is useful to introduce, at this point, the terms *technocrat* and *technocratic*. Some, among them Henry David, object to the use of these terms in relation to certain people and processes today. They insist upon limiting its use to that movement which had a brief but dramatic life in the depression of the early thirties and which engaged the lively attention—whether favorable or unfavorable—of people such as Dwight MacDonald. However, vogue is not the only factor attributing to the prevalent use of these terms today. They are prevalent not merely because writers about the counterculture—such as Theodore Roszak—have adopted them. As is clear from recent writings in France and from the literature of the New Left in this country, *technocrat*[5] provides a name for one species of the New Class that David Bazelon and others have been talking about: the combined bureaucrat-technologist-politician. *Technocratic* points to the cultural phenomena associated with the rise to power of the technocrat.

Daniel Bell's reference to the technocrats as "riders of technology and rationality" suggests that they are positively linked with the philosophy of this book. The technocratic mode stresses reason.

    [4] S. Ramo, *Cure for Chaos* (New York: David McKay, 1969), p. 11. See also Ramo, *Century of Mismatch* (New York: David McKay, 1970).
    [5] See W. H. G. Armytage, *The Rise of the Technocrats* (London: Routledge and Kegan Paul, and Toronto: University of Toronto Press, 1964); H. Elsner, Jr., *The Technocrats: Prophets of Automation* (Syracuse, N.Y.: Syracuse University Press, 1967); J. Meynaud, *Technocracy* (New York: The Free Press, 1969); S. A. Hetzler, *Technological Growth and Social Change: Achieving Modernization* (New York: Praeger, 1969). See also J. J. S. Schreiber, *The American Challenge* (New York: Atheneum, 1968).

So do I. The technocratic mode stresses interrelations, coordination, design-making. So do I. But there are crucial differences beneath the surface likenesses. The reason favored by the technocratic mode is linked with the objective consciousness that has been claimed—rightly or wrongly—to characterize the scientific spirit (sometimes called, pejoratively, *scientism* or *scientificism*). The reason we favor admits a subjective component which it regards not only as unavoidable—even if avoidance were sought—but as often quite desirable. The reason favored by the technocratic mode is the empiric, pragmatic, operational reason—what Percy Bysshe Shelley called the calculative principle. This reason is efficiently displayed in the Weberian "rationalizing" of a company, an agency, an organization, a social aggregate, an aggregate of educational agencies, an institution of higher education. The reason we talk about is far more inclusive than is the technocratic reason. We are concerned with the revival of a concept of reason viewed as functioning integratively with perception, feeling, and imagination, ethically powered by justice and compassion—that is, imaginative reason.

According to Aristotle, Plato was unable to distinguish between unity and uniformity.[6] Uniformity may be the outcome of the bureaucratic-technistic process of rationalizing an industry, a governmental agency, defense, a school system, or a university. One may be certain that the concept of rational efforts toward the accomplishment of uniformity (compare Hitler's ordering for political coordination by bringing in line and eliminating opposition) is quite at variance with the rational efforts which Stanley Rosen recommended in his *Nihilism*[7] or with the "rational efforts" Abraham

        [6] H. D. F. Lee (Trans.), *The Republic of Plato* (Baltimore, Md.: Penguin, 1967).
        [7] S. Rosen, *Nihilism* (New Haven, Conn.: Yale University Press, 1969). See W. Berkowitz (Ed.), *Let Us Reason Together: Dialogues on Vital Contemporary Issues* (New York: Crown, 1970); L. Rosten, *A Trumpet for Reason* (Garden City, N.Y.: Doubleday, 1970); R. Bendix, *Embattled Reason: Essays on Social Knowledge* (New York: Oxford University Press, 1970), includes treatment of the university's role in society; and T. Nagel, *The Possibility of Altruism* (New York: Oxford University Press, 1970), rejects the view that "motivation always begins with desire" and "argues for certain formal conditions on rational maturation which determines the general form of a moral theory and provides a rational basis for its control." In terms reminiscent of Whitehead's "reason suffused with imagination," W. Booth is described as reasserting in his *Don't Try to Reason with Me*

Maslow referred to when he wrote, "This volume springs from the belief, first, that the ultimate disease of our time is valuelessness; second, that this state is more crucially dangerous than ever before in history; and, finally, that something can be done about it by man's own rational efforts."[8]

The architectonic mode provides a concept of reason infused with imagination and conscience, as suggested in C. Wright Mills' study *The Sociological Imagination*.[9] As Mills viewed it, the sociological imagination involves a quickening moral sensibility (sometimes, he declared, a sociologist has to let himself become angry at injustice and cruelty), "a quality of mind that enables the individual to develop reason in order to achieve lucid summations of what is going on in the world and of what may be happening within himself." It "enables its professor to understand the larger historical need in terms of its meaning for the inner life and the external career of individuals; to grasp history and biography and the relations to the two within a society."

The order that we seek to embody is correspondingly a vital not a mechanized order. It is a magnanimously shaped order, the end goal being not operational efficiency for profits or power but rather efficacy for personal growth and self-actualization, within a context of social responsibility and social action. This goal is in marked contrast to the one-dimensional modular man produced, according to the Marcuseans, by the technocratic mode.

We have testimony to the grave deficiencies of the technocratic mode from the technocrats themselves—for instance, from the *Memoirs* of Albert Speer, designated as "Hitler's master technocrat." Describing his charismatic (to him) leader as the "most terrible simplifier in all history," who "so compellingly . . . systematized the future," Speer has declared that under Hitler the "nightmares shared by many people that some day the nations of the world may

---

(Chicago: University of Chicago Press, 1970) "the need for a passionate pursuit of what is reasonable, for an approach that will unite the truths of the heart with the truths of the head" (Publisher's Notice, *New York Review of Books*, 1970, *15* (9), 56).

[8] A. H. Maslow (Ed.), *New Knowledge in Human Values* (New York: Harper & Row, 1959), p. viii.

[9] C. W. Mills, *The Sociological Imagination* (New York: Oxford University Press, 1959), p. 5.

be dominated by technology was very nearly made a reality."
Warning that every "country in the world today faces the danger
of being terrorized by technology," he has gone on to say: "Therefore, the more technological the world becomes, the more essential
will be the demand for individual freedom and the self-awareness
of the individual human being as a counterpoise to technology."[10]
The architectonic mode in liberal learning, concerned as it is with
self-awareness, personal wholeness, and human dignity, should help
provide such counterpoise.

A historic prototype for the apocalyptic mode is found
among young Romantics at the time of the French Revolution and
among the dispossessed young intellectuals depicted in nineteenth-
century Russian novels. In America, Norman Brown's "Apocalypse:
The Place of Mystery in the Life of the Mind"[11] did much to give
the term its present vogue, so it is now part of the sports writer's journalese. Thus, Shelby Coffey III refers to the professional
wrestling ring as "an archetypal scene of America's very own pop-
morality play," and he describes the enormous difficulty Japanese
wrestling officials have in getting the viewers not to take the shows
too seriously. The officials have issued statements imploring "fans
to remember that professional grappling" is "really more of a klieg-
light performance than an earnest apocalypse."[12]

The generally religious, prophetic impulse within the apocalyptic mode is seen in both the title and the contents of an article
entitled "Bob Dylan and the Poetry of Salvation"; it is treated in
Harvey Cox's *The Feast of Fools,* especially the chapters entitled
"Fantasy and Religion" and "Mystics and Militants."[13] In a review

---

[10] P. Jacobson, "Hitler's Master Technocrat," review of A. Speer,
Inside The Reich: Memoirs, R. Winston and C. Winston (Trans.), (New
York: Macmillan, 1970), *Book World (Washington Post),* September 6,
1970, p. 2.

[11] *Harper's,* 1961, 222 (1332), 46–49. See also N. Brown, *Life Against
Death: The Psychoanalytical Meaning of History* (Middletown, Conn.:
Wesleyan University Press, 1959).

[12] S. Coffey, "And in This Corner, The Great American Morality
Play," *Potomac (Washington Post),* June 21, 1970, p. 11.

[13] S. Goldberg, *Saturday Review,* 1970, 53 (22), 43–46, 57; and
H. Cox, *The Feast of Fools, A Theological Essay on Festivity and Fantasy*
(Cambridge, Mass.: Harvard University Press, 1969), pp. 68–97, 101–20;
and compare T. Jones and H. Schmidt, *Celebration* (New York: Music
Theater International, 1969). Reviewing several books on campus unrest and

of Joe Glaherty's *Managing Mailer,* we are told that this "anti-technologue" decided to take his "apocalyptic vision to the people" by entering the Democratic primary for mayor.[14] The noun is featured, in huge, raised, capital letters, on the double-page bill-board montage that precedes the back cover of Jerry Rubin's *Do It: Scenarios for the Revolution: APOCALYPSE.* It suggests the Book of Revelation, the terrible day of judgment, the day of wrath and doom, and the glory of new birth, the ushering in of a New Jerusalem cleansed by baptism of fire and total demolition; purged of all cruelty, hatred, and violence; peopled by those who have survived the winnowing flail and lustral fire: perennially childish, uninhibited, and loving innocents, bathed in spontaneous primal goodness and universal love.

The new children of the apocalypse were heralded by the apocalyptics of American ultrafundamentalism and the extreme right, who spoke of the world as facing the last days, of the coming battle of Armageddon, of the horrors of doomsday, of the final judgment. They entertained an "apocalyptic premillennialism,"[15] the reverse image of which has become part of the eschatology of the apocalyptics of the New Left.

While it is the antithesis of the technocratic mode, which it regards as the Anti-Christ, the apocalyptic mode is not our way. Its adherents abhor the remoteness and coldness of sheer scientific social inquiry, stress the infinite richness of the finite moment, and profess a love of community. Except in degree, the architectonic finds no difficulty with these attitudes. Yet the professed social feeling of the apocalyptics quickly undergoes ironic phase reversal into the anarchism of mutually repellent particles. Their antiestablishment, anticonventional iconoclasm turns into nihilism, smashing all forms and dissolving the idea of the personal and social life as a matter of creative constraints and of durative design. Hence, their impact upon liberal learning does more than cause what Bell called "a rupture of moral temper." They seek to turn the Freudian

---

violence, S. McCracken entitled his article "Armageddons on the Campus" (*New York Times Book Review,* November 8, 1970), pp. 45–46.

[14] A. Cooper, *Saturday Review,* 1970, 53 (23), 36.

[15] E. Jorstad, *The Politics of Doomsday* (New York: Abingdon Press, 1970), pp. 20, 21.

formula upside down: Where ego is, there id will be! This post-modern sensibility seeks to abolish constraint by substituting raw experience for art, sensation for judgment, and undifferentiated elemental experiences for those formative discriminations which are essential to the architectonic mode of liberal learning.

This apocalyptic mode seeks to recapture the spirit of the immortal child in us for pure play, for the perverse, and for the purity of sheer sensate experience, with all that Susan Sontag has called its "indiscriminateness, without ideas, . . . beyond negation." In short, its prerequisite is that we blow our mind, zap our reason. If the technocratic mentality leads to current vogues of built-in obsolescence, the apocalyptic mode leads to on-the-spot consumption of the impromptu and to self-destructive happenings—just for kicks.

The notion of doomsday runs counter to the basic feeling that animates the architectonic mode. This feeling affirms the worth of the attempt to achieve more than moment-to-moment sensations or even momentary configurations of experience. It further affirms that the attempt to shape a durative pattern for one's life and character is not only functional to our humanity but also natural. The crucial issue thus depends on what to the apocalyptics is natural. With Rousseau, they claim to be rejecting what is artificial in the name of what is natural. The architectonic mode insists that the impulse toward durative patterning is both natural and conducive to self-actualization.

In his "Children of the Apocalypse," Peter Marin distinguishes between the apocalyptic mode and the architectonic mode. He describes the "frantic soup in which we swim" as a mixture of "innocent yearning and savagery, despair and exhilaration, the grasping for paradise lost, paradise *now,* the reaching for a sanity that becomes, in frustration, a new kind of madness." He then observes: "If this is not the kingdom of apocalypse, it is at least an apocalyptic condition of the soul."

The aspirational level Marin pictures has much positive bearing on the elucidation of the architectonic mode. The telic model that Marin holds up includes strength, sanity, and wholeness. These qualities he sees as "a function of *relation*," and relation, he thinks, is "a function of culture, part of its intricate web of approved

connecting and experience, a network of persons and moments
that simultaneously offer us release and bind us to the lives of
others."[16] To represent the wholeness he would have us realize,
Marin uses the network metaphor. The network has become a widespread symbolic replacement for the metaphor of the machine, which
Floyd Matson has treated as a dominant feature of the epoch ushered
in by the scientific discoveries and theories of the seventeenth century.

A measure of the importance of the recommended architectonic mode lies in certain implications to be drawn from Bell's
observation: "The tension between the technocratic and the apocalyptic modes will be expressed most sharply in the university." Bell
goes on to predict that "the confrontation between these two
modes . . . will be the most urgent cultural problem of the university of the future."[17] However, this confrontation will not be just
between two modes. We must not overlook the potential of a third
force. There is an imperative for such a third force to be applied to
the technocratic-apocalyptic vector. Aristotle's doctrine suggests
that politics is the architectonic moral science since it determines
the total shape of society. Suggestively, in a nondoctrinal sense, this
third force may be called the architectonic mode. This book attempts
both to articulate it and to bring out its relevance and effectiveness.[18]

Bell notes that, by intention, in *The Reforming of General
Education,* he has not concentrated on the changing concerns of the
student body and the character of their demands.[19] In the light of the
subsequent rebellion at Columbia University, in its most violent stage
while Bell was teaching a course in futuristics, this omission is indeed ironic and not without hints of tragic defaulting. This book, in
contrast, is written with the demands of the student dissidents very
much in mind. One of the major themes is that an important
reason for the upsurge of student discontent with the university lies

[16] *Saturday Review,* 1970, *53* (38), 71–72; and F. W. Matson, *The
Broken Image: Man, Science, and Society* (Garden City, N.Y.: Doubleday,
1964).
[17] D. Bell, *The Reforming of General Education,* p. 311. See also
pp. 307–10.
[18] For earlier treatment of this term, see M. H. Goldberg, "The
Impact of Technological Change on the Humanities," *Educational Record,*
1965, *46* (4), 393.
[19] Bell, *ibid.*

in the betrayal, by liberal learning, of its architectonic trust. Further, part of the thesis is that strenuous efforts at reconstituting an architectonic organon to replace the present technology-plus-fun syndrome should help to meet the demands of the students for reform of liberal learning. Through the regeneration of the architectonic mode as the dynamic of the humanistic spirit, this reform is one of the most relevant challenges confronting liberal learning today.

One of our responsibilities is to try to discern and encourage the remaining or renewed affirmatives within the iconoclasms and nihilisms that so often seem to characterize the doomsday attitude of the apocalyptics. In the fifties, James T. Farrell tried to demonstrate such affirmatives within the seeming negativism in his novels and in the work of other naturalistic writers. We need to do something similar for the cultists of the absurd and the current demolitional experts in literature, the arts, and education. We may take our cue from the official explanation for the Nobel prize in literature given to Samuel Beckett in 1969. Admitting that the "degradation of humanity is a recurrent theme in Beckett's writing," Karl Ragnor Gierow, secretary of the academy that made the award, added "and to this extent his philosophy, simply accentuated by elements of the grotesque and of tragic farce, can be said to be a negativism that knows no haven." But, using a photographic analogy, Gierow said that, when a negative is printed, it produces "a positive, a clarification, with the black proving to be the light of day." We may take our cue, also, from the observations of Charles Marowitz that the wholesomeness of Beckett's message is its remorselessness and that Beckett reaffirms "the holy solitude of the creative artist." Hence, as Gierow concluded, from "the realms of annihilation the writing of Beckett rises like a miserere from all mankind, its muffled minor key sounding liberation to the oppressed and comfort to those in need."[20]

The paucity and sentimental naiveté or the patent cynicism of the affirmational parts of the manifestos of the apocalyptics— hence, the pathetically deficient resources and sustained will for effec-

[20] J. M. Lee, *New York Times* News Service; and C. Marowitz, "A Poet Who Has Seen Hell," *New York Times*, November 2, 1969. The French Academy's favorable action on E. Ionesco's self-submitted candidacy for membership suggests that in his iconoclasms, too, as in T. S. Eliot's *Wasteland*, we may expose filaments of affirmation. (Reported in the *New York Times* News Service, *Pennsylvania Mirror*, January 29, 1970.)

tive telic model making and actualization—so often leaves initial sympathizers in the lurch. Rubin presented his newly concocted Yippie myth and model, and he piously stated: "People try to fulfill the myth; it brings out the best in them." But then he added: "The secret of the Yippie myth is that it's nonsense. Its basic informational statement is a blank piece of paper."[21] It's phony; but it works.

A thoughtful Vietnamese—journalist, novelist, former military officer—dramatically portrayed the essential hollowness of such instant myths and models, in contrast to organically developed, genuine telic models. He observed that until recent decades his people had a generic telic model of the good man, the good life, and the good society and that it had served well for generations. He went on to say that the impact of Western technology has shattered this telic model and the way of life it both envisaged and energized. He further declared that a new model to reconcile the old and the new and to produce a new and potent synthesis is now necessary. He pointed, in contrast, to the absence of even the first rough sketches for such a model in the literature of the new revolutionaries in the Western world, particularly in America. He therefore set out to give a course on this very matter at a Washington, D.C. college and recruited, as students, twenty of the toughest revolutionaries he could find. He acknowledged that he might get chewed up, or blown up, in the process but maintained that the risk was worth taking. The stakes were high—nothing less than the conversion of cynical nihilists into potent affirmers of worthy models that would take them beyond sentimental and anarchistic utopianism or grim iconoclasm and demolition. It would take them to the imaginatively rational and generously ethical building of their new society.

Neoromantic enthusiasts, thrilling to a new renaissance of wonder, now celebrate the biblical prophets as exemplars of primitive and prerational shamanism. The architectonic mode, in contrast to the genetic fallacy, the critical anachronism, the simplicism, and

---

[21] Rubin, *Do It,* p. 83. See also J. R. Walty, concerning J. A. Lukas' *The Barnyard Epithet and Other Obscenities: Notes on the Chicago Conspiracy Trial* (New York: Harper & Row, 1970): "Lukas knows . . . that Abbie Hoffman is not a real person, that he is instead a myth packaged and wed to television by Abbott H. Hoffman a psychologist from Worcester, Massachusetts . . ." ("The Trial of the Chicago Eight," *Book World,* (*Washington Post*), 1970, *4* (43), 1, 3).

the reductivism of these magic-intoxicated rhapsodists and without denying the nonrational component in the prophetic utterances, stresses the ethical and impassioned rationality which at their greatest the prophets powerfully exemplify. This realistic rationality, which they applied both to personal and to political morality, lifts them out of the orbit of the primitive magic and shamanism; it sublimates the trace of medicine man within them and enables them to achieve an ethical mutation in the humanizing of men. We are called to this reasoning of the understanding heart in the Isaiahan injunction: Come, let us reason together.

In citing the biblical prophets as examples of the ancient shamanism that he would have revived for our time, Roszak seems to overlook the factor of impassioned and courageous rationality in the prophets. This omission is all the more ironic since elsewhere Roszak shows his enthusiasm for a "significant injection of intellect and conscience into our society's problems" and since he regards the contributors to *The Dissenting Academy* as seeking to "formulate a concept of intellect that would make the professions and higher education as a whole relevant to the task of creating an active and enlightened citizenry."[22] Regrettably, when it comes to the tracts and polemics themselves, the dissenting academicians, in seeking to get rid of what Mary McCarthy called the paramilitary intellectuals, often succeed in discrediting intellect altogether—certainly the rational components of intellect.

For purposes of liberal learning, *architectonic* is an apt term for more important reasons than as a phonetic match for the terms *technocratic* and *apocalyptic*. There is its suggestive power, its historic sweep and reverberation. There is its archaic flavor of the beauty and glory of classical antiquity, of Renaissance magnificence, of the times of Milton and Newton, of the nineteenth-century architects of the modern mind and of technological apparatus, and of the fantastic technetronic structurings and projections of our times.

In the term *architectonic*, further, there is the suggestion of the dynamic, rather than, as in the word *architectural*, of the fixed. There is its root meaning of to build, to construct, which in turn

<hr/>

[22] T. Roszak (Ed.), *The Dissenting Academy* (New York: Pantheon, 1968), p. vii.

connotes purpose, telic intention, plans, designs, models, and translation of these into structures; hence, it suggests form-making and ultimately man's formative nature. Architectonic, moreover, implies the ancient wisdom of constructive crafts and the extension of the brain and the body through technical instrument. It further implies the esthetic sensitivities and powers of the fine arts, the symmetries and harmonies combining in a useful and esthetic integrity.

Because of its historic usage in scientific and philosophical studies, architectonic suggests cognitive, ratiocinative, even speculative form-making and striving toward wholeness. This idea is seen in the assertion that classification is the architectonic science, and in the nineteenth-century reference to theology as the primary architectonical science. It is seen in William Hamilton's definition of architectonics as that science or branch of metaphysics that "treats of those conditions of knowledge which lie in the nature of that which we think about" and that "treats of the method of building up our observations into a system." It is seen, likewise, in a nineteenth-century treatise on Immanuel Kant that speaks of the architectonic impulse of reason, which seeks to refer all science to one principle.

Yet, at the other end of the spectrum, architectonic suggests the opposite of the deliberate, self-conscious, critical, and analytically inductive processes of systematic intellection and the discursive intellect. It suggests the instinctual—the intuitively holistic—as expressed in the tangible, the concrete rather than in the immaterial, the abstract. From the early seventeenth century comes the exclamation: Bees "build their combes with such an architectonical prudence"; and from the eighteenth century: "With what different degrees of architectonic skill Providence has endowed birds!"

Nor, in this wide range of implications for architectonic, are the ethical and social—and, in the generic sense, the political—aspects overlooked. There is George Grote's reference to the architectonic functions ascribed to Pisistratus and Aristotle's favoring a poetic aphorism on the architectonic supremacy of justice, to which we might add Aristotle's own characterization of politics as the architectonic art.

These citations bring out a main feature of the idea of design in liberal learning—the function of deliberate direction and control toward an actualization of a telic form. Aristotle used the term along this line. Finally, as in the microcosm, so in the macrocosm: architectonic suggests the effective might of cosmic making and shaping. Hence, architectonic becomes almost a definition of the outcome of liberal learning, as has been said of ancient art: "the simple fitness . . . with which the manifold purposes and aspects of life were architectonically satisfied."[23]

If, as key symbol for liberal learning, which is so future oriented, the appropriateness of architectonic is questioned on the grounds of its archaism, one has only to point to the archaism of apocalyptic, a term which has been turned around completely so as to stand for radical now-ism and for even more radical futurism. Part of creative mediation and creative conservation takes advantage of the miraculous powers of linguistic and other symbolic regeneration, as we have done with the architectonic mode.

In his *The Undirected Society,* Geoffrey Vickers pervasively illustrates the architectonic mode. For him, structure is a key term and a key concept. He views it as dynamic rather than static, as process rather than product or object. He regards individuals and societies as "energy systems, maintaining themselves by preserving the precarious balance of the inner forces whereby they hang together and the equally precarious balance between themselves and their environment and thus carrying on an endless dialectic."

Vickers favorably cites those social psychologists who define society as a "structure of mutual expectations." He refers to value systems—both social and personal—as "architectures of expectation." He declares, "No great development of organic life was possible until the nervous system had become able to organize experience in time, to make projections of observed sequences, and to correct and refine these by experience." He then goes on to say, "Man's achievement of the powers represented by language and thought, including the power to hypostatize himself, has clearly opened a much wider field to the architecture of his expectations."

Vickers' elaboration of this "inner architecture" further suggests the architectonic mode, especially in connection with

[23] This treatment draws on the *New English Dictionary.*

holistics, the shaping of telic models, and the attempts to actualize them. He proceeds to postulate as a basic fact of the inner organization of men and societies a set of standards defining the relationships between themselves and the world around them which are to be "sought and shunned." This set of standards constitutes a "hierarchy of norms and limits, extending from the particular to the general, from the conscious to the unconscious, defining from day to day the objectives which they pursue and the contingencies which they try to escape." For Vickers, moreover, there is a factor of deliberate will in his personal and social architectonics. He makes this emphasis in his distinction among three types of adaptation. The first two apply to the subhuman: that seen in biological evolution, independent of learning and operating so slowly that the individual's nature may be taken as given, and that learning "by which the individual, in the course of its lifetime, finds out how to adapt its behavior to meet the needs inherent in its given nature." At the human level, there is a third form of adaptation, "rudimentary in other creatures but dominant in men and societies." This adaptation is a "process by which not merely new responses but new norms and limits are evolved and transmitted," for men "have a discretion in choosing not only how to be themselves but also what sort of selves to be." Indeed, "they can and do design their own aspirations—if not wholly consciously, yet in ways not wholly beyond conscious control." Hence, comprehensively, "we are increasingly the architects of our own nature."

The key to our well-being, moreover, lies in performing this architectonic function "more in the design of our aspirations than in the devising of means to satisfy them." In a word, the designs to be effected are not working models—not the particular design of the moment—but rather the design of our aspirations, telic design.

One sign of the architectonic mode in operation is the frequent appearance of the term *apprehension* in place of, or in addition to, *perception* or *comprehension*. This use of the term does not imply worry, anxiety, or foreboding but rather a total cognition. Not only are the sensory functions of perceiving and the workings of the calculative principle in comprehending involved, but the factors of intuition, imagination, envisionment, and other extrarational activities of the consciousness are also taken into account.

The Elizabethans used the term *apprehension* in this comprehensive, intuitive sense—for example, Hamlet's words, "in apprehension how like a god!" In the nineteenth century John Henry Newman used the term in the older, broader sense to designate a pervasive means and end of liberal learning. Vickers likewise uses *apprehension* in its comprehensive sense. Concerning the Canadian Round Table on Man and Society convened by the School of Social Work of the University of Toronto, he observes: "By focusing attention on particular situations and maintaining it for two years, the design of the conferences invited its members to apprehend the Canadian situation as an ongoing process, in which conditions relevant to well-being are continually being created, lost, sought, and renewed. . . . Such an apprehension required an understanding of the historical process and especially a sensitivity to the dimension of time. . . . These changes and the new forms needed to achieve them must be realized in action before they can be fully apprehended in thought; yet thought can speed their realization."[24]

The holism of Elizabeth Monroe Drews conveys much that is congenial to the architectonic mode for liberal learning. Yet in its cosmic mysticism, its at times sentimental stress on natural goodness and the perfectibility of man, and on students of the "creative intellectual style," within the "youthful phalanx of the counterculture," Drews's holism moves more closely toward the apocalyptic than toward the architectonic mode.[25] Charles A. Reich's instant best seller *The Greening of America*—antitechnocratic and quite apocalyptic—calls for at least one major provision congenial to the

---

[24] G. Vickers, *The Undirected Society, Essays on the Human Implication of Industrialization in Canada* (Toronto: University of Toronto Press, 1959), pp. 53, 54, 55, 56, 61, 161 respectively. John Augustus Roebling, the creator of Brooklyn Bridge, provides an example of the architectonic mode—in this instance, having explicit Hegelian affiliations, with probable Goethean echoes. See A. Trachtenberg, *Brooklyn Bridge, Fact and Symbol* (New York: Oxford University Press, 1965); H. Schuyler, *Roeblings: A Century of Engineers, Bridge Builders and Industrialists* (Princeton, N.J.: Princeton University Press, 1931); and D. B. Steinman, *Builders of the Bridge: The Story of John Roebling and His Son* (New York: Harcourt Brace Jovanovich, 1945). Steinman, who claimed to have been directly inspired by Roebling, was himself both noted bridge builder and poet, as well as generous patron of poetry and the humanities. (Based on notes of my talks with A. M. Sullivan, editor emeritus, *Dun's Review*.) See Steinman's *Songs of a Bridgebuilder* (Grand Rapids, Mich.: Eerdmans, 1960).

[25] See Drews, *Policy Implications*, pp. iii–iv.

architectonic mode:[26] "Most of the kids today are in a trough," he remarks. "All they know how to do is hitchhike and play guitars and lie on the beach and 'relate' to people." He then observes, "But we aren't all going to be able to sit in the trees and play harmonicas." He complains, "The new generation doesn't know how to work or how to create a structure of society that will work or that will reflect their own values." In short, the new generation does not know how to apply deliberate imagination and reason to shaping effective telic models by which to lift itself by its own bootstraps.[27]

[26] In his poem on Brooklyn Bridge, Hart Crane—who insisted that poetry must come to terms with technology and creatively assimilate it—both demonstrates and celebrates the architectonic mode. For a very useful compilation of holistic materials, see *Some Readings in Integrative Studies: A General Bibliography* (New Rochelle, New York: Center for Integrative Education, 1971). For suggestive treatment of *organicism,* see Jack Burnham, *Beyond Modern Sculpture: The Effects of Science and Technology on the Sculpture of this Century* (New York: Braziller, 1967), especially Chapter Two: "The Biotic Science of Modern Sculpture" and Chapter Three: "Formalism: The Weary Vocabulary."

[27] M. G. Scully, "New Consciousness Can Humanize Society, Yale Professor Says in Fast-Selling Book," *The Chronicle of Higher Education,* 1970, 5 (7), 6. Scully's accompanying feature (pp. 1, 6) is entitled: "Reich's 'Greening of America' Makes Him Prophet of Youth." The book is published by Random House, 1970.

Index